How to Be an Adult in Love

How to Be an Adult in Love

Letting Love in Safely
and Showing It Recklessly

DAVID RICHO

SHAMBHALA
Boulder
2014

Shambhala Publications, Inc.
2129 13th Street
Boulder, Colorado 80302
www.shambhala.com

14   13   12   11   10   9   8   7   6

Printed in the United States of America

Shambhala Publications makes every effort to print on acid-free,
recycled paper.

Shambhala Publications is distributed worldwide by
Penguin Random House, Inc., and its subsidiaries.

The Library of Congress catalogues the previous edition of this book as follows:
Richo, David, 1940–
How to be an adult in love: letting love in safely and
showing it recklessly / David Richo.—1st ed.
p.   cm.
Includes bibliographical references.
ISBN 978-1-61180-034-0 (hardcover)
ISBN 978-1-61180-081-4 (paperback)
1. Love. 2. Interpersonal relations. 3. Love—Religious aspects.
4. Interpersonal relations—Religious aspects. I. Title.
BF575.L8R528 2013
158.2—dc23
2012037028

To those who loved me no matter what.
You showed me how to love me and you and everyone.

May I show all the love I have
In any way I can
Here, now, and all the time,
To everything and everyone, including me,
Since love is what we are—and why.
Now nothing matters to me more
Or gives me greater joy.

Contents

Preface

WRITING IS PART OF MY SPIRITUAL PRACTICE. I find myself focusing intensely on the topic I am writing about. The practices I design become my work on myself.

When I decided to tackle the topic of how to be adult in the way we love, I faced my biggest writing challenge ever. I knew it would mean finding out how I show love, how I have been loved, and how I may not love enough.

Writing this book has indeed turned out to be a wonderfully revealing and releasing experience. A very specific synchronicity, a moment of meaningful coincidence, has occurred often. Out of the blue, I have recalled people who have loved and cared about me over the years. I have suddenly pictured myself with them and become aware of the many ways in which they showed how much they loved me. It has been as if my family and friends were returning to help me see what love is. Some of the people are long dead, but I feel that they still love me.

I now understand that all the people I have ever known have come into my life to teach me about love. I am coming to trust that every moment of affection I received has been carefully recorded in me, ready for playback. The love I received from others shows me how to love those who need it from me. This is how the people who loved me have helped write this book.

Specific memories also come through about how much people have had to put up with from me. What did they see in me that made them stick with me when I was so damned afraid to return their love? Maybe they saw something lovable in me that I need to see in myself. Their uninterrupted love also helps me trust that I must have shown more love than I give myself credit for.

Memories come back to me of the times in childhood when family members showed love to one another. Only this morning, in fact, I was recalling how I enjoyed spending Sundays when I was about eight or nine with my great-aunt and great-uncle. They had no children, and they doted on me as the son they never had. My company made them very happy. Then suddenly today, for the first time, I recognized that my mother knew all this, so her motivation for having me go to their house was her love for them. Now I wonder how many other times my mother had a loving motivation that I did not notice.

I never realized any of these things until I began writing this book. It is as if each unremembered moment of love, every unnoticed loving motivation, are revealing themselves to me one by one. Is all this happening so I can finally grasp that love is what is meant by amazing grace?

I feel gratitude to all the characters in my life story who have taught me how to love. I am sorry that I did not appreciate them fully. To paraphrase the first poem by Emily Dickinson that I learned by heart in high school, I "blame the scanty love I was content to show."

All I can do now is make up for my deficits by being more consciously loving here and now. This is definitely my present, though not always successful, practice—and a joyous one. It is a practice I don't ever intend to give up.

All this happened as I was writing what you are about to read. I am hoping that your reading this book reminds you of how much love you have received. That will prompt you to build your confidence in how much love you can give.

Love is so powerful that it makes everything ordinary.
—ANONYMOUS, *The Cloud of Unknowing*

Introduction

I scarcely know where to begin but love is always a safe place.
—EMILY DICKINSON

THIS LITTLE LIFE OF OURS rests between a longing to be loved and a calling to show love. These two stunning possibilities, so tender, so fugitive, are the subject of these pages.

I must admit, however, that this is mostly a book of guesses—as any book on love must be. My guess is that loving is what we are here for, that love is what every one of us deserves to receive and is here to give, that love alone makes this earth the heaven it was meant to be. The guess turns into a conundrum when we realize that so many of us prefer the signs that point to heaven over heaven itself. We yearn for and talk about the love we want. We lament the love we have been deprived of. Yet we sometimes fail to take the steps that can help it happen for us.

The puzzle becomes even more confounding when we sometimes prefer the hell of no love at all, which we bring on by our own unskillful choices or by our endurance of abuse or betrayal, especially from those who say they love us. This book proposes that love is real when we dare to become as loving as we can be toward ourselves and others and as careful as we can be not to confuse a history with someone or a connection that does not work for us with true love.

Biology shows us that the universe is a vast web of interdependence from the cellular to the planetary level. Nothing exists by itself. There is no being-in-itself only being-in-relation-to. So to be is to be connected. Thus, relatedness, or connection, is the essence of our and of all being. Reality is relatedness. John Muir must have grasped this mystical fact when he wrote, "When we try to pick out anything by itself, we find it hitched to everything else in the universe."*

Muir's comment applies both to nature, since ecology is about the interconnectedness of all things in the universe, and human psychology, which is also about connectedness. Our present behavior is connected to what happened to us in childhood. Indeed, our whole life is a tapestry of relationships. We are connected to our past, hitched to everyone we know and even to those we don't know.

For us humans, to be is to connect and to cease connecting is not to be. Life began because of a connection between our parents; we survived through an umbilical cord that connected us to our mother; we thrived thanks to connections with our caretakers. We are still here because of our ongoing connections to the natural world and the people in it. In fact, connectedness is the essence of emotional well-being. Healthy development proceeds most successfully and joyously when we have had a safe, secure, enduring experience of at least one person caring about us. Because of that original connectedness, we know ever after how to love and hold others as we were loved and held. We also know how to love and hold ourselves so that we can cope with whatever happens to us rather than being stymied by it.

Love is a specific kind of connection; it is a caring connection. The word *caring* is from the Latin for "dear." We care about someone who is dear to us. *Dear* also means costly; love requires a selflessness that is challenging and taxing at times.

When we care about someone, he or she really *matters* to us. Caring includes noticing, taking an interest in, and responding to the specific needs of others. It includes a genuine concern for what happens to someone and a hope for positive outcomes.

---

* John Muir, *My First Summer in the Sierra* (Boston: Houghton Mifflin, 1911).

Love happens between us and others when we welcome connection from them and make connections to them. To decide if an act is loving, we can ask, "Does it serve to connect us in a caring way?" We learned in grammar school to convert fractions by finding the lowest common denominator. Caring connection is our lowest—and finest—common denominator of love in this world of so many unconverted fractions.

Here is a central point of this book: Giving and receiving love can become our primary life focus. Focusing on this combination is a way to become fully human, to fulfill ourselves psychologically. If love comes our way, it is welcome and enriching. But in spiritual practice, our focus is on giving love rather than finding someone from whom to receive it. We feel fulfilled spiritually when we show all the love we have, no matter how others respond or act toward us. This is a radical alternative to showing love in order to receive it in return or showing it only to those who love us.

We will probably fail at this spiritual style of love almost every day. But as long as we maintain a pure intention to be as loving as we can be and keep putting honest effort into it, we are already on the path to spiritual awakening. Truly enlightened living is knowing that love is all we ever want and making it all we ever give.

Loving becomes easier when we open to it as our inner psychological and spiritual *code,* the equivalent of a genetic code. A code dictates how we fulfill ourselves as individuals and how we make our contribution to the world of others. It provides us with a blueprint. The code of love tells the whole story of what it means to be human and what the world we inhabit means by its very existence. Love is the point of it all. What we can be is the same as what love can be: endless in duration, infinite in extent. Yes, we humans have that much time in our story (as much as eternity), that much space in our hearts (as limitless as outer space).

The love in us arises from an innate goodness beyond causes, conditions, predicaments, or stories. It is inherently and ineradicably within us, whether or not we feel its presence. At times, our inner goodness may evade us utterly or seem absent or lost. Indeed, aggression is evident in us from our earliest days; it too is innate. The good news is that we can believe in the enduring reality and primacy of our capacity for goodness, no matter what we may have done or how we may have lived until now. We may have to learn to show love, but the fact that the learning comes easily seems to point to love being a natural part of us. Love sits mindfully and immovably in us, all our lives, waiting for us to unveil it.

What keeps us from seeing our inherent goodness, from believing that we are good people? Our self-worth may have been wounded since childhood by pummeling criticism and the imposition of inhibitions. We take back the sense of our own value when we dispel our inherited false beliefs about ourselves. This is why we work on our past. By doing that work, we can find tools that help us open the treasure chest of love inside us. In fact, all the psychological tools we have gathered from the self-help movement in recent years were for this: to become lovers who stand expectantly at every door, flowers in hand.

As we look back on our lives and all we have learned until this moment, we may delightedly realize that it was all a transmission of teachings about loving without limit or restraint. What if all that happens to us is exactly what schools us in *how* to evolve in love in the course of life? That is the very definition of synchronicity, meaningful coincidence: Just the right events and people come along to allow us to articulate the love we are inside. All of them are emissaries of some nuance of light we need to let the full colors of our love appear in all their incandescence.

We learn to activate our potential for showing love in the same way we learned to use language, by imitating others and making our own efforts to expand our vocabulary. Our capacity to talk was not based on how our parents treated us, but our ease in using words may have been stunted if they ridiculed or silenced us. It is the same with love. Our capacity to love endures, though it may have been damaged by how we were treated. But just as we can learn to speak well at any time of life, we can always learn to let our love come through fully and volubly. We can refresh our capacity to love if it has been injured, animate it if it has been dulled, recover it if it has fallen by the wayside. Learning to do this is psychological work and spiritual practice at its best. In fact, it is the very reason we have a psyche, a body, a spirituality, a lifetime.

When we understand that love is native to us, we presume that there must be some help for expressing it. One reliable and powerful ally is our instinctive inner urge to fulfill ourselves. We do not have to rely solely on our own effort; we can trust that something inside us is helping us along. We have an instinctive need to love without reserve. That need is the archetypal assisting force, the reliable confederate, the unexpected resource, our own inner self, the interior Beloved that the mystics refer to. It is up to us in any given moment to act in accord with that inviolable and steadfast energy.

Two clues help us believe in our inner goodness: First, we can sense intuitively what the loving choice is in any situation. Second, we can become aware that everything that happens to us presents us with an opportunity to love more or better. This is because everything that happens is an evolutionary driver, a push toward more consciousness and more connection, the fruition of which is love.

The way we were first loved and the ways we have been loved ever since form our definition of what love means to us. Some people really feel loved when someone gives them a gift. Others experience it when people stand up for them. Still others feel loved when someone goes the extra mile to help them. If our mother showed love by holding us in our pain or joy, without engulfing or controlling us, that will be the behavior that always feels like love to us. We feel love now as we first received it; we give love the way others gave it to us. Thus, since love is unique to each person, we read and write love, receive and give it, in the style designed by our past experience. Yet, like good handwriting, our unique signature can be read by others.

At the same time, we have the option of expanding our definition of love. All our relationships give us the opportunity to open ourselves to ever-new forms of sincere love from others toward us and from us toward them. This is how intimacy challenges us to take a chance.

In the Christian tradition, the magi came to welcome the newborn Jesus with precious gifts. We can trust that many angels and buddhas showed up at our cradle to celebrate the thrilling and meaningful moment of our birth—the arrival of a new version of love. The gifts they brought us were not gold, frankincense, and myrrh. They blessed us with a capacity to love and to be loved limitlessly, an ability to show and receive love ingeniously, a desire to open to it endlessly.

Once we understand that love is our true identity, we realize that the skill of learning to love is mostly an undoing of the ego obstructions that have gradually overlaid our natural tendency toward loving. This means letting go of our ego entitlements and inflations. We then look for all the practices that can help that happen, especially those that release us from the grip of the main opponents to our happiness: our self-centeredness and aggression. The moment we loosen that grip will be the same moment that fear takes flight and all that is left of us is whatever can still lovingly open.

Being an adult in love means being adult about love and loving. Psychological adulthood—maturity—is letting love in carefully and showing it responsibly. Spiritual adulthood consists of expanding our love so that it is unbounded, a practice requiring recklessness. Since love sits in us someplace between trust and fear, a commitment to love requires both daring to trust and disregarding our fear, both risks we are willing to take when we love someone. Loving is often scary. This is why we have to become reckless in practicing it. *Recklessness* is defined as a letting go of concern about dangerous consequences to ourselves. We become reckless when we are so firm and focused in our intention that we are no longer held back by a fear of what seems threatening. This helps us give love unconditionally. (There is no such thing as conditional love—that is not love, only giving approval or showing that we are pleasing to the other.)

At times we are selective about showing the love that is in us, and here we see a contradiction in ourselves. We have no trouble committing to honesty toward everyone, unconditionally and unilaterally, no matter how dishonest others may choose to be. But we think of love as having to be meted out warily and promised only to very special people in our lives. We believe everyone is deserving of honesty, but we imagine that only certain people deserve our love. Would we be able to sustain the same commitment if we substituted love for honesty? It would sound like this: we have no trouble committing to being loving toward everyone, unconditionally and unilaterally, no matter how unloving others may choose to be.

It is, of course, true that discrimination in trusting others is necessary if we are to have quality relationships. Selectivity is important for our safety and security, because it means trusting only those who have proven their dependability. This makes sense but only in *how* we love, not *that* we love. Thus, our ways of showing love differ according to the commitment we have to various individuals in our lives. But our scope of love does not have to set or be set by limitations. We can be careful about our boundaries when others come close but free of boundaries in how far our love extends. There are boundaries in the topography of love but no barriers.

As an example, we can love our alcoholic spouse, but as long as he is abusive and refuses to seek help, we cannot live with him. Our love of ourselves does not permit placing our and our children's safety, health, and happiness in jeopardy. Our tough love for our partner does not permit us to enable him to go on destroying himself and others. So our love can remain as strong as ever but our way of showing it changes. It might no longer include sharing the same bed, but it would include supporting him in his recovery once he is ready for it. We have boundaries but have erected no barrier, because we remain open to full reconnection on his full recovery. We show our love based entirely on what has to matter: safety, security, health, and happiness for us and for those committed to our care. Yet we go on loving no matter what.

In a world in which we're scared of reckless loving, only those who please us or seem worthy deserve our love. In a world in which we're ready to be awakened, everyone deserves love because it is not based on merit, good deeds, or willingness to reciprocate, only on being alive. That kind of limitless love is what we mean when we talk about the fulfillment of our human mission, the maximum use of our human legacy, the full achievement of our life purpose.

Our love response is usually based on personal appeal. However, we can come to believe that the less lovable someone is, the more she needs—and deserves—love. We can learn to see lovability in everyone. Lovability is not earned. Our practice becomes welcoming everyone in our ever-expanding style of caring connection. This too is a subversive act, since we are overturning the usual sequence: We usually move toward those who are attractive and lovable and away from those who, in our opinion, are unattractive and unlovable. It is counterintuitive to love simply because of other people's existence rather than because of their winsomeness. But true love makes everyone irresistible.

To commit ourselves to loving everyone is certainly a subversive act, because it is an act of unconditional and egalitarian connection. It is up and running regardless of the qualities or the deeds of others. This is the love that honors diversity and excludes no one from its wide embrace. It is the love that ends every form of emotional apartheid, alienation, rank, and division. It is the love that can be unilateral if necessary. It is not based on likability or how others act toward us but on who we are.

This challenge is expressed strikingly by Lex Hixon in his book *Mother of the Buddhas: Meditation on the Prajnaparamita Sutra:* "Bodhisattvas do not become liberated from life, nor do they pursue any form of separate self-realization. They direct an ecstatic flood of love and friendliness toward all, connecting their mind streams as intimately with all beings as with their most cherished family member and beloved friend. This astonishing spiritual feat frees the bodhisattvas from every impure intention of harming, denigrating, abandoning, or even merely ignoring others." This book banks on a firm trust that we can all accomplish that feat or move in that radically spiritual direction, and it shows us how to do so while maintaining our boundaries.

We have a place in our lives for intimate relationships, with special ways of showing our love. We can have a place for the broader style of love too. When we "love all beings" without preference, when we extend love as caring and compassion to those least appealing to our ego, we are locating a new level of humanity in ourselves. We soon realize that those we come to love in this unconditional and unbounded way are transforming us by increasing our scope of loving.

In fact, every wounded person can be seen as the living incarnation of a bodhisattva, an enlightened person who has come to instruct us in the dharma, the enlightened teaching, of love. When we see that, it will not take us long to notice the trail of stars that follows his frail and disfigured body, now the light-filled radiant body of the Buddha.

We might say that everything we humans do is meant either to show love or to ask for it—often both at once. The asking can take many forms, charmingly pleasant or unskillfully unpleasant. When we maintain a deep dedication to love, any seeming unlovability in others does not become a reason for despising or hating but a stimulus to us to care more. In this liberated way of loving, the more unlovable people are, the more love we believe they need from us, so the more we give them. This is how we widen love without a frontier, unfazed by attraction or repulsion, able to open our hearts to new possibilities of caring. Indeed, caring connection can only happen when our hearts keep opening. As John Donne writes in his love poem "The Good Morrow,"

> For love, all love of other sights controls,
> And makes one little room an everywhere.

Buddhist teachings counsel us to watch out for attraction and repulsion. They lead to suffering when they trip us up or we are locked into them. We can be so attached to what we have that we cling to it, and clinging is a painful business. We can be so caught up in wishes for what we do not have that we crave, another painful act. Both these forms of suffering interfere with caring connections.

Our practice of universal love does not cancel out close attachments such as relationships with individuals. On the contrary, it offers us the resplendent alternative of expanding the reach, style, and direction of our love. The love we have for our one special partner becomes richer when we are committed to loving in the universal way. Our dedication to unconditional love teaches us to transcend ego restrictions, a boon in dealing with conflicts in relationships. Universal love is the most courageous and perhaps, to our materialistic society, the most foolish vow we can make. But the "I do" at the altar is surely deeper when it has already been pronounced to all our fellow earthlings as well.

The love that we are is ultimately a mystery to us. As a therapist and an author, I notice that I work from a structured framework of understanding about the psyche and the world. I appreciate the usefulness and common sense of a coherent perspective on life. I have gained that perspective from experience, from clients and students, from my own history, and from my spiritual teachers and practice. But I often remind myself not to believe that everything—anything—is pat, definite, fully explained, all wrapped up.

I want to remain loyal to my sense of mystery about human loves, human conflicts, human sufferings, and especially the here and now, the greatest mystery of all. We enter it fully only when we are free of preconceptions, final definitions, and perfect solutions. This reflects the Buddhist teaching about the void, the emptiness of definability in all that is. We realize that all we say about love is analogy not data.

I realize that my framework and set of practices in this and all my books is only an *approach,* a gingerly, tentative response to life's conundrums, not a final statement on the matter. I want to maintain my respect for the ever more evident grandeur of the human story. That story stumps any author or thinker who attempts to nail it down. (The nails would only be coffin nails, after all.)

Now I understand why Lao Tzu says that the essence of all liveliness cannot be adequately described in words. I am grateful that I have preserved my veneration of mystery, the last breath in any discussion, the ultimate reality behind our guesses, the Cheshire cat smile at all our formulas. I want the rest of this book to bow to and abide in that supreme radiance.

> The depths themselves remain uncomprehended. . . . This is the dark silence in which all lovers are lost.
>
> —JAN VAN RUYSBROECK

How to Be an Adult in Love

1

What Is Love?

You are as prone to love as the sun is to shine; it being the most delightful and natural employment of the soul.

—Thomas Traherne

Love is too elusive and individualized to permit a definition. However, we can ask, "What can love be?" This is not a definition but a request for an ever-renewed invitation, something we can keep daring to enter, like Alice persevering in her adventures in Wonderland.

We have described love by identifying its most basic ingredient: connection. The word *connection* is based on two Latin words: *con* meaning "together" and *nectere* meaning to bind or tie. The word was originally spelled *connexion* to reflect the past tense of the verb *nectere*, which is *nexus*. Love is a nexus that can happen along a wide spectrum. It can take many forms, from sending a kind letter to being sexually intimate to feeling a mystical oneness.

We are social animals, so connection is important to our survival. We imagine that connection can outlast our physical life, and thus it is usually included in our idea of a heavenly afterlife. We picture heaven as a place where we will be united with our loved ones. That makes hell a place of disconnection, exclusion, excommunication. We recall the words of Father Zossima in Fyodor Dostoyevsky's *The Brothers Karamazov:* "Hell is the suffering of no longer being able to love." This gives us an insight into the metaphor of hell: It is more about mourning our love failures than about punishment for not being loving.

Love is a connection that is caring, intended for good, respectful of freedom, and genuinely sensitive to another's needs, even making those needs as important as our own. This shift in attention to the needs of others deflates our own sense of self-importance. What power love has to help us let go of ego!

When love is reciprocal, we welcome positive connections from others and extend positive connections to others. A love relationship does not have to be reciprocal or symmetrical, however. It can be equal between two people or more intense in one person than in the other. A willingness to love someone who does not love us back equally is an example of the generosity of love. It is, indeed, a spiritual advance to make a dedication such as is expressed in these lines I composed as a personal affirmation:

> When love is not the same between us two,
> I'll be the one to show more love to you.

Loving will then not feel like a giving, as it does in the ego's world of *quid pro quo*. It will be my true self, love, simply being.

Caring connection includes altruism, fondness for someone, concern about what happens to her, wanting the best for her, being available to her in times of need, feeling and showing kindheartedness. All of this includes an openness to the possibility of some form of sacrifice of our own comfort for the other's well-being.

We ask four assurances of love from a partner or significant other. A yes to each of these questions gives us evidence of a caring connection. Each yes can become a commitment to the building of true trust and fearless love:

Are you there for me and how?

Do you care about me and how?

Do I matter to you and how?

Are you interested in me and how?

Loving also means putting ourselves in a vulnerable position; we show our love and hope it will be accepted. We bare our hearts and hope they will not be battered.

As love expands, it focuses on creating concord and reconciliation beyond our own relationship. Our concern may widen from interest in others' bonding with us to caring about the harmonious bonding among all our friends or all humanity. This altruistic concern can give us a sense of contentment, as we hear Edward IV express it in Shakespeare's *Richard III*:

> And now in peace my soul shall part to heaven,
> Since I have set my friends at peace on earth.

In addition, as love expands in our lives, it becomes a force for change. When we are stirred by love to pursue a goal, we are more likely to have a successful outcome. This is because situations and people respond best to love, a gentle but powerfully appealing energy. We see this in our personal relationships. Showing patient and enduring love helps someone change more than badgering or demanding ever will.

Likewise in the political forum, an antiwar movement makes more progress when those who are passionate about peace show that they are motivated by a genuine loving care for humanity rather than simply by their opposing stance toward a national policy. However, both in personal relationships and in political concerns, we do not use love as a strategy. That would be a form of manipulation. We simply notice that love has a power all its own. It is redemptive, because it forgives and thereby rehabilitates. It is transformative of hearts and of how the world works. It changes things.

Love is a force, but it is sometimes called a feeling. When we imagine that love is a feeling, we may be disappointed because we notice that we cannot keep any feeling up and running all the time. A feeling is an intense, immediate, sensate/physical experience. Feelings have a beginning, a middle, and an end; love is ongoing. Feelings are responses to specific stimuli; love is the stimulus and response at the same time. Love can be a state of being, a fond sentiment, an ongoing bond. All of these have an enduring quality. Thus, love, since it lasts beyond its instances of expression, includes and happens *with* feelings rather than *is* one.

Love can be understood in many ways, but six descriptors stand out: Love as capacity, as quality, as commitment, as purpose, as grace, and as practice.

Love as a Capacity

As a *capacity*, love is our potential to form connections and commit to them. Each of us has the faculty to love fully beginning anytime, especially now. We never lose our power and ability to let love into our lives and to act lovingly. The capacity to love cannot be canceled or erased by our past, no matter how damaging our experiences may have been. What can be damaged are our ways of showing love and our expectations of what it should be. How little we have loved so far does not predict how much we can love now or in the future.

Love as a Quality

As a *quality*, love is a way of acting toward others. It is not a noun referring to an entity or abstraction. We cannot reify love or any other quality. It is like an adverb in grammar. It shows *how* something is done. For instance, "I touched her lovingly" shows how I touched her.

The quality of our love increases as we show it more deeply and generously in our behavior. The quantity, or extent, of our love increases as we feel and show it to more people—from near and dear to far and wide.

There is no compassion, love, or peace in a stand-alone or abstract way. They are human qualities, and we are truly human when they are our natural style of being in the world. Our humanity is complete when we *are* compassion, *are* love, *are* peace. Then we automatically show them everywhere and to everyone. The mystic poet William Blake sums this up so beautifully:

> For Mercy has a human heart,
> Pity, a human face;
> And Love, the human form divine,
> And Peace, the human dress.

Love as a Commitment

As a *commitment,* love is likewise a verb. It shows an ongoing and enduring dedication to acting in a trustworthy manner and in the best interests of others. We are committed to loving unconditionally. Thus, we want the best for others no matter how they treat us, although our commitment to loving ourselves does not allow us to take abuse. Our commitment to loving in a relationship means keeping agreements, wanting the best for the other person, and working things out when conflicts arise.

Love as a Purpose

Love also serves as a life *purpose,* determining why we are here and how we fulfill ourselves. Our life purpose can be to show all the love we have in every area of life—to ourselves, to everyone we know, to everyone on the planet, and to the planet itself. Since each of us has a unique way of loving, our life purpose is to manifest our love in a style uniquely our own. In this context, love can be felt as a calling, an impulse from within and beyond us to make our personal contribution to the world.

Love as a Grace

We do not accomplish such a magnificent feat entirely on our own. Thus, love is also a *grace* we were given at birth, part of our human endowment, a gift that can be opened and reopened all through life.

Grace is the special help that seems to come to us from beyond our ego. Thus, it is from a source that transcends our powers of control. We cannot make it happen, but it can't help but happen when we are open to it.

In Sonnet 87, Shakespeare alludes to grace: "The cause of this fair gift in me is wanting." Grace is not based on our efforts or accomplishments; it comes to us freely. It is an unmerited resource that grants us more wisdom and courage than we have in our ordinary ego toolbox. Grace can be seen as an energy that helps us fulfill ourselves. In ancient mythology, Plutus was the god of wealth. Zeus blinded him so that he could give riches away indiscriminately without attention to merit. This myth reflects how grace is an entirely free gift, as well as one that comes from a transcendent source.

What can be said of grace can be said of our own commitment to showing universal love. It is a free gift from us to others regardless of their merits. It is transcendent in that it originates beyond ego and cancels all the ego's predilections, partialities, and restrictions. This is the best sense in which love is blind.

Love as a Practice

It is always up to us to expend the energy it takes to act with love in accordance with the grace we are given. Thus, love is a *practice*. We do not have to strive for love; it is in us already, but it takes practice to show it. Some specific ways of practicing love are by showing what I call the "five A's": attention, acceptance, appreciation, affection, and allowing. These are the components of love that make a relationship a truly caring connection. They can be directed toward ourselves and others.

- We pay *attention* with an engaged and sustained alertness to the needs and feelings of ourselves and others, both by listening and by awareness of nonverbal cues. We are genuinely interested in who we and others really are and what we/they feel.
- We *accept* ourselves and others just as we are, free of judgments or censure. At the same time, we are discerning. We acknowl-

edge the appealing side of ourselves and others all the way to the top and the unappealing side all the way to the bottom, while love continues unchecked and undiminished.

- We *appreciate*, or value, ourselves and others. To value people is to cherish their worth. It is an unconditional worth since it cannot be damaged or erased. It is not based on behavior, history, successes, or failures. Appreciation also includes acknowledgment of the good that others do and thanking them and of the goodness they are and praising it.
- We feel and show *affection* by caring for our own bodies and by respectful physical touching of and intimacy with others, according to what is appropriate within each relationship.
- *Allowing* does not mean granting permission to show personal liberty. It means welcoming the full expression of someone's deepest needs and wishes. We can do this for ourselves as well by making our own choices with unabashed alacrity. We are not trying to squeeze or squash ourselves into a persona—or a spiritual practice—that others may find appealing but does not fit us. Our practice is opening to who we are and what we are ready for.

We may wonder about the difference between allowing and accepting. It helps to compare their opposites: the opposite of allowing is controlling; the opposite of acceptance is rejection and judgment.

Allowing is supporting someone's choice even if we do not agree with it. Allowing does not always mean accepting, but accepting always includes allowing. For example, a father may not accept his daughter's eccentric, artistic personality, but he does not criticize her for it or stop her from pursuing it. He supports his child's choice to go to art school by paying the tuition, even if he would prefer her to have chosen a more conventional career.

Acceptance is about welcoming personality traits; allowing is about supporting the choices and lifestyle that follow them. Allowing also involves welcoming the full emergence of all that someone really is. Preventing full emergence results in more than a personal loss. It is a blow to the purposes of evolution itself, which requires everything each of us has in every era so it can progress.

Compassion, caring, respect, and all the other forms of love are not left out of our description. They can be described with the same five A's directed toward specific needs. For instance, compassion is the response of the five A's to pain. Caring is their expression of concern. Respect is the way they honor individuals and their boundaries. Trust is their expression of reliability.

We can use an analogy to understand the origin of the five A's. To have a healthy body, we require sustenance from food groups: whole grains; fruit; vegetables; dairy; and protein from meat, fish, or other sources. Each of these groups targets different systems in the body, such as muscle, skin, blood, bones, and so forth. Each is a necessary building block of a healthy body. If one is missing, there is a deficiency that can cause illness.

Likewise, we require specific forms of love that build the systems in our psyche. The five A's, like the food groups, are not arbitrary. Each of them is a specific and necessary building block of our psychological makeup. If one is missing, we feel the deficiency, and a part of us suffers. Here is how each A contributes to our psychological health:

- *Attention* is necessary so that we can be known. This makes it possible for us to express our needs and have others understand them, early in life by our caregivers and later by our partners or loved ones. If people did not pay attention to us, we would feel isolated, and we would not trust ourselves to show others what we need and receive appropriate responses. Attention from others supports our sense of being recognized and having power.
- *Acceptance* is necessary so that our unique qualities, both positive and negative, can be granted hospitality. Without acceptance, our true self has to go into hiding. We doubt our talents and singular gifts. We also doubt that our shadow side can be befriended and become a source of creativity. Our self-esteem cannot grow unless our full self is validated. Acceptance by others supports our trust in ourselves as having a lot to offer the world.

- *Appreciation* is necessary so that our contributions can be recognized and received with gratitude. Without appreciation, we feel that we are taken for granted. Our actions and words fall flat and have no impact. This damages our sense of power and self-confidence in the world around us. Appreciation from others supports our sense of our own value.

- *Affection* is necessary so that our bodies can feel held, honored, and cherished. We know that physical holding contributes to the development of the brain in early life. We also know that touch gives us pleasure and comfort throughout life. Without holding and affectionate touching, our bodily sense of self-worth suffers. Affection from others, caress by caress, supports our pride in our body.

- *Allowing* is necessary so that we can experience the freedom to live in accordance with our deepest needs, values, and wishes. Allowing also shows us we can move out on our own when the time is right. In adulthood, allowing means being able to pursue our dreams and move as we wish in the world without being judged, controlled, or inhibited by others. Allowing by others is what supports the journey archetype. An *archetype* is a familiar and universal theme in the collective consciousness of humankind, expressed in stories and myths, that describes a human energy, potential, and purpose.

It is curious to note that the plots of fairy tales often hinge on deficits of the five A's in relationships. For instance, the story of Sleeping Beauty is based on a lack of attention to one of the princess's godmothers. Hansel and Gretel lack acceptance by their stepmother. The Beast in *Beauty and the Beast* lacks affection. Cinderella lacks appreciation. Snow White is not allowed to be as beautiful as she is and live. In each example, the story has a happy ending, because someone comes along who makes up for what was missing. As adults, we understand that we are primarily the ones who must serve that purpose. We cannot expect to be rescued, but there are wonderful people who love us by showing us the five A's that save us from isolation and despair. The one thing to remember is that those who *give* us what was missing in our past also *show* us what was missing. That combination of fulfillment and grief can be hard to hold, so we have to be patient with ourselves.

Kinds of Love

Ancient Greek philosophers delineated four main types of love: *storge, eros, philia,* and *agape. Storge* is family love, especially between parents and children. This love can endure even when there is neglect or abuse. For instance, we know we love our relatives, even though we do not always trust them to give us the five A's. A family bond can offer safety and security but at the price of having to camouflage part of who we are. Thus, our loving connection within our family sometimes transcends even the importance of self-emergence. Signs of love may not be apparent in our relatives' behavior, but we still know they love us and we love them; our mutual loyalty remains. In our affection for our family, we certainly learn how to practice unconditional love.

Eros is passionate love, which we experience most potently in the in-love state. Eros includes, but is not limited to, sexual passion. It is often initiated or sustained by an attraction to physical qualities. The erotic love we feel for a special someone in our lives may be part of a committed intimate bond. It can also be a feel-good attachment in the moment that will not be sustained. Eros can be both a longing for and a union with the beloved. This is because eros includes pleasure from both fulfillment of our longings and our longing for fulfillment.

Eros also refers to the sensuous, passionate, lively, and creative dimension to human life in general. It can therefore be active between friends or in any relationship without being manifested sexually. Carl Jung, in *Dream Analysis: Notes of the Seminar,* said, "People think that Eros is sex, but not at all; Eros is relatedness."

We can appreciate intimate love as more than erotic, and it can include friendship. *Philia* is friendship that combines affection and admiration. This is also known as platonic love. Like all forms of love, it can include an erotic element, but it is not usually sexual. Authentic friendship-love is unconditional. It makes the interests of the other equal to our own, does not keep a record of faults, does not retaliate, does not compete, is not predatory, includes both liking and loving, restores itself easily after conflicts, and is transparently vulnerable. These qualities are difficult challenges for an ego that has to have everything even steven.

Friendship thrives on companionship, which is not necessarily a form of closeness. For instance, playing computer games together includes companionship but happens without eye contact. Team sports are forms of connection that give companionship but do not include sharing on a personal level. In full companionship, friends share life events and their reflections on them. They are happy about one another's success and are supportive in helping each other navigate sufferings and losses. The friendship style of relating often seems more sustainable than bonds based only on romance.

The Greek philosopher Aristotle proposed three bases for friendship. A friendship can be based on *utility,* as in being friends with our next door neighbor whom we may need someday. A friendship can be based on *pleasure,* as happens when we have a buddy whose company we enjoy and with whom we have interests in common. And a friendship can be what Aristotle calls *noble,* when it is founded on encouragement and support of one another toward moral progress.* In an ennobling friendship, friends help each grow spiritually. To accomplish this, they need to be able to accept constructive feedback from one another without defensive ego reactions. That is a quality of both true friendship and intimacy.

In the biblical book of Sirach, we see a reflection of what we know from science today, that friendships boost our immune system: "A loyal friend is like a safe shelter; find one, and you have found a treasure. Nothing else is as valuable; there is no way of putting a price on it. A loyal friend is like a medicine that keeps you in good health."†

Friendship is indeed one of the most satisfying forms of love, because it allows for uncomplicated pleasure as well as unconditional

---

* Aristotle, *Ethics* 8, ch. 3.

† Sir. 6:14–16.

support. I notice as I age that my circle of friends increases, but the number I choose to spend time with decreases. I appreciate them all, but certain ones stand out as totally comfortable to be with for many reasons. For example, maintaining the bond is effortless. We have come to trust each other implicitly, especially in a pinch. We can share anything about ourselves without fear of shock or judgment. We can say anything to one another without fear of offending. Occasional long silences are not uncomfortable. And most of all, the same things strike us as funny.

Xenia, or hospitality, is related to *philia.* In ancient times, this referred to a more formal style of friendliness offered by a host to someone he did not know. The host provided meals and accommodations at his home for the guest. The only response expected from the guest was thanks and respect. Reciprocity was not required, but it was expected if the tables were turned.

Agape (pronounced "ah-gah-pay") is selfless love that gives with no expectation of reciprocity. It is not based on a need or attraction but entirely on our own dedication to generous giving and sincere concern. Since early Christian times, *agape* has been understood to be impartial rather than preferential; it is universal in extent. This ideal of universal *agape* was not the style in the ancient Greek world, in which *agape* was considered sufficient if it extended to the population of one's city-state.

Agape can be present in all forms of love, since its energy is possible in any caring experience. Love resembling the *agape* model is promoted as an ideal in a variety of cultures and religions. For instance, in the fourth century, a Chinese philosopher-ethicist, Mozi, offered an alternative to Confucius's narrow accent on loyalty to family and clan. He proposed *jian ai,* impartial caring and concern for everyone, which we can understand as universal love. This is caring connection not based on levels of closeness or family relations. It is extended equally to friends and strangers. This can be the ideal of unconditional love that is not tied to reciprocity. *Jian ai* became associated with finding enlightenment.

In the Islamic Sufi mystical tradition, we see love portrayed as *ishq.*

Here, love is the essence of God reflecting himself in the universe. Thus, when we show love, we are acting according to divine intent.

In Hinduism, *kama* is sexual love chosen legitimately for personal pleasure. *Karuna* is compassion and mercy; *bhakti* is devotion to the divine; and *prem* is ideal, selfless love, which is closest to *agape*.

In Buddhism, love is based on nonattachment, nondualism, and nonseparation. Thus, true love does not include clinging to someone as a refuge, and the lover and the beloved are one.

The Buddhist practice of loving-kindness, by extending love to all beings, is a form of *agape*. Here are the four qualities of love and of the enlightened person in Buddhism:

Maitri: benevolence, good-heartedness, loving-kindness

Karuna: compassion

Mudita: sympathetic joy at the success of others

Upeksha: equanimity, even-mindedness, imperturbability (that is, freedom from being destabilized by feelings or predicaments)

To love ourselves or others is to want all four of these in everyone's lives. We want ourselves and others to experience loving-kindness, compassion, success, and equanimity.

The Buddha taught the practice of loving-kindness, *metta,* as an antidote to fear. We will explore loving-kindness practice at the end of this chapter. It involves aspiring to the four immeasurable qualities of our higher-self-than-ego, our true nature, not only for ourselves and people we know, but for all people. Fear fades in that fourfold light.

The *metta* practice is like *agape;* it is about extending love in an unconditional and universal way. We know that everyone wants to be loved, but some people have given up hope of finding or showing it. We restore hope to others by our unilateral and wholesale outreach of love. We see and trust that everyone has an inherent goodness and that being loved by someone can help activate it. *Agape* makes us want to be that someone, no matter what the consequences or concern about whether our love will be greeted with appreciation or rejection. This is a radical alternative to our usual, carefully selective way of loving. Now there are no holds barred. This *agape* fostered by *metta* practice combines caring about, altruism toward, and service to others. It is loving because we are love, not because we have found a reason to love.

Spiritual refers to the transcendent, that which is more than what meets the eye and in all that meets the eye. Since *agape* transcends the usual limits of loving, it is the spiritual dimension of love. As we have seen, love itself is spiritual, because any kind of love shows that we have gone beyond ourselves, transcended ourselves. In her Sonnet 43 ("How Do I Love Thee?"), Elizabeth Barrett Browning expresses this transcendent quality of love: "I love thee . . . when feeling out of sight / For the ends of being and ideal grace."

From the mystical perspective, all that is forms only one reality. To say that there is unity in multiplicity is another description of this connection. Such a belief in oneness can make love more likely. The more we identify with our fellow humans, the more our compassion increases and the more altruistic our choices become. In addition, our sense of connection with nature deepens. Since love is connection, all this is love in bloom.

We also see the *agape* style in Jesus's call to "love thy neighbor as thyself." It is necessarily unilateral; we do not wait until others love us first. This ethical practice can be understood dualistically, from subject to object: "I love myself, and I love my neighbor in the same way." It can also be perceived as an expression of mystical oneness: "Love is my focus, since I and my neighbor are one and the same." This kind of love is an ideal to attain, a destiny we were born to fulfill, the evolutionary purpose we seem to be on this planet to achieve. We all have the capacity for *agape*, but it takes practice to activate it.

To love our neighbor as ourselves includes honoring the dignity of others and their freedoms—just what we want for ourselves. In our society, concerns like these have become political issues when they are really challenges to love the human family generously: universal health care, women's right to choose, gay marriage, and the abolition of torture and wars for corporate gain. When *agape*, universal love, is our commitment, we uphold—with unstinting compassion—the rights of all people to life, liberty, and the pursuit of happiness. These words are no longer political but descriptors of everyone's commitment to love.

> Nothing could satisfy me that was not on the scale of the universal.
>
> —PIERRE TEILHARD DE CHARDIN

Compassion

Another form of love is *compassion.* Concern for others' pain helps divest us of ego-centeredness. This is why compassion can so easily be a bridge to the *agape* style of loving.

In my own life, I noticed an advance in compassion in a singular way. I saw a film version of *Macbeth,* and instead of my usual dislike of the main character, I felt compassion for him. I saw how caught up he was in ambition and fear, and I felt sorry for his woebegone state. I did not condone his murderous behavior, but I appreciated his plight in a more humane way than I had in previous readings and viewings of the play. Something had happened in me; there was a new judgment-free openness, a way of connecting to others, even when they were not very appealing. That was a sign that I was moving more in the direction of *agape,* which is always a move away from judging others. I have gradually realized that openness is how love happens.

In this context, compassion is not based on pity for someone's plight. It is not top-down but nondual. Indeed, compassion is not a virtue that we may or may not have. It is the way love, always in us, responds to others' pain. That pain tugs at us because of our natural bond in the worldwide human family. To forgo a compassionate response is to contravene a natural inclination. Compassion in this sense is not just feeling sorry for the suffering of others. Rather, it is self-investment to relieve suffering and, if possible, to change the conditions that led to it.

As our circle of compassion widens, we begin to appreciate suffering not just in particular humans but in the human condition. We are touched by what Virgil, in *The Aeneid,* called "the tears in things." We appreciate that built into all existence is a grief about impermanence; a vulnerability to disappointment, hurt, and loss; a resignation to suffering. That touches us both as participants in the givens of the human story and as loving witnesses to it.

Hamlet says, "Use [practice] almost can change the stamp of nature." We know that the practice of showing love and compassion transforms our hearts. We are thereby somehow changed deep within. That change is a richer relatedness to the human family, the essence of *agape:* "You belong to my heart." Eventually that solidarity helps us realize that our shared givens of pain and impermanence are not predicaments we put up with but the very essence of our connectedness—and a path to our enlightenment.

The ancient Roman Jewish historian Flavius Josephus realized that love was the point of religious practice: "I suppose it will become evident that the laws in the Torah are meant to lead to a universal love of humanity."* For "the laws of the Torah," we can substitute our spirituality, our psychological work, our religion, our schooling, our political party, our nation, our family, our relationships, our commitments, our birth, our death, our breath, or our life span. In fact, there is nothing that does not have an ever-widening love as its purpose.

> May I be a guard for those who need protection,
> A guide for those who journey on the path.
> For those who wish to cross the water,
> May I be a boat, a raft, a bridge.
> May I be an isle for those who yearn for land,
> A lamp for those who long for light.
> —SHANTIDEVA: *The Way of the Bodhisattva*

Liking and Other Connections

Other sensations can be confused with love. *Liking* is regarding someone as pleasing and preferred over others. We use the word *love* some-

---

* Flavius Josephus, *Contra Apionem* 2:146.

times when we mean *like*. For example, we say, "I love lemon meringue pie. I love Hawaii. I love Mozart." The pie, the state, and the composer do not represent caring, but they are pleasing and preferred over others. We enjoy them.

Love is an unconditional positive regard with or without continuous liking. Love is like grace; it does not have to be earned. Liking is like approval; it does have to be earned. Liking people happens in response to their persona, the way they look, the way they act. This changes throughout the day. Love happens in response to the real self, the deep reality of our humanity, where we are unchanging. The word *deep* is a metaphor for the underlying reality of something, its essence, what is required for its fulfillment. Love is our essence, because love is connection, and we remain connected to one another and to all of nature beyond like or dislike, birth or death, damage or despair.

To say that love is our essence has a consoling ring. But it can fill us with terror when we feel unloved. Not to be loved or responded to as lovable then becomes the equivalent of having no essence, being all alone in the world.

We can confuse loving (always) and liking (sometimes). When we say, "My mother loved me, but it was conditional," we may mean, "My mother loved me but did not always like me. She loved me wholly but liked me only when I was behaving in ways that were satisfactory to her."

We may also confuse love with *loyalty*. Without realizing it, most of us were imbued with a deep loyalty to our families, schools, and churches. In the child's view, loyalty is directed toward institutions or families and the authorities who lead them. In the adult view, our loyalty is to the meaning and purpose of an institution. Thus, we are loyal to our families when they provide safety and security. We are loyal supporters of our government's policies when they reflect the principles of the Constitution. We are loyal to our religion when its teachings honor its founder's principles; encourage our full self-emergence; and help us cocreate a world of justice, peace, and love.

On an interpersonal level, we might feel loyalty to a partner and imagine that to be love. We might stay in a relationship that has lost its liveliness or has become intolerable in many ways. We remain because of allegiance, not because of mutual happiness and affection. Then our work is to undo the inappropriate identification of loyalty with love. For instance, we can remain loyal to someone by preserving a caring connection, but that does not have to mean living under the same roof.

Infatuation is attraction to and fascination with someone and involves a strong erotic component. When our hormones are activated by the woman across the room on some enchanted evening, we lose our ability to distinguish real love from immediate desire and enthrallment. We might then be seduced by our own fascination with her. In an authentic intimate relationship, romance turns into selfless love and then into egoless commitment. *Agape* frees *eros* from being stuck in infatuation. Our journey then goes from enchanted evening to enlightened dawning.

The in-love state is caring connection with dollops of adrenaline for excitement and oxytocin for pleasure. When only the caring connection remains, we say we love someone but are no longer in love. This may be the result of noticing that our partner no longer, or only occasionally, arouses our sympathetic nervous system and increases our heart and breathing rates. We may mistake such physiological arousal for love when it only ever signified fascination. This happens because our brain is not sophisticated enough, without careful training, to distinguish subtle hormonal messages. Since both falling in love and falling into fascination have exactly the same physical components, we can confuse them, especially when that first kiss makes us feel like we have at last come home, found what we always wanted, entered nirvana, and found our soul mate. Given the ecstatic feeling, it is understandable that we are not sure what is really happening.

"I need someone" plus "You are desirable and available"
can feel like:
"I am in love with you."

To fall in love is often to fall for an apparent, but not necessarily accurate, matchup of our own need and our discovery of a person who will fulfill it. In the in-love state, we see a reflection of our own pleading longing in the other's smile.

Adults will not trust their hormones until they align with good sense. An adult knows it will take much more than a welcoming or come-hither smile to make the case for real love, a love that is an enduring commitment. A bond based only on sexual excitement can't sustain itself through the vicissitudes of adult relations. We need a deeper resource than honeymoon energy to stay connected through the thick and thin that we'll be going through.

Even in our infatuated state, we may realize that this is not the right relationship for us, that it has no future. Yet we often can't let go. We may refer to this inability as our heart speaking, when it is actually our adrenals. We are under the influence of our own adrenaline, the hormone that keeps us attached whether or not our feelings are real or a relationship is good for us. In the world of drama and adrenaline, a relationship begins with infatuation. In the adult world, relationship begins with investigation. We recall the humorous lyric from "At Long Last Love" by Cole Porter: "Is it a cocktail, this feeling of joy, or is what I feel the real McCoy?"

Infatuation and fascination are sensations—legitimate, enjoyable, but temporary. They can be phases in a burgeoning relationship or flashes in the pan. Real love includes romantic fascination but then moves on through conflict to commitment. It is not always pleasurable, but it is reliably enduring. Infatuation craves exhilaration as well as safety and security; love provides them through sustained trustworthiness.

Fascination includes erotic attachment that can become compulsive clinging, an addiction, a form of consumerism for something more or different. The mature alternative is a connection that feels good without the stress, compulsion, and restlessness that are so prominent in addictive attachments.

To project is to imagine that someone has qualities that we may not have. We see in another the reflection of our own desires, beliefs, feelings, needs, and fantasies. An example of this projection is a *crush*, a usually short-lived infatuation. We can tell the difference between this hot, stressful reaction to someone and a warm, serene affection. The

former is like an active volcano; the latter is like green pastures and rest-
ful waters.

We can also tell the difference between being really loved and being
the object of a crush. Mature adults will not find the latter ersatz projec-
tion-love appealing, nor will they take advantage of it for their own benefit. In fact, a crush is painful, so in spiritual consciousness, we may feel
compassion for the person who obsesses about us in that way. When
we know we have no interest in reciprocating, we feel uncomfortable
and sorry for the other person.

A Buddhist teaching is that being caught in attachment is a cause
of suffering for us. Yet it is also a form of suffering for others who become obsessed by their attachment to us.

In this and all the charts that follow, keep in mind that between each
column are many gradations of possibilities depending on each individual's unique feelings, thoughts, and behavior. There are no either/
or's in human experience.

Projection/Crush On Us	*Authentic Love for Us*
Is based on a subjective assumption	Is based on the reality of who we are
Can end as quickly and as irrationally as it began	Begins and lasts through the vicissitudes of relating
Remains firmly entrenched not matter what we do	Is responsive to changes in us
Idealizes us, failing to acknowledge our shadow side	Remains aware of our shadow side and works with it creatively
Comes from a unilateral need	Is about mutual fulfillment of needs
Becomes an obsession	Takes our presence or absence in stride
Is aroused and maintained by adrenaline	Leads to serenity
Can be followed by hate or indifference	Can only turn into kindly regard even while letting us go

Heart-Centered Feelings

William James, in *The Varieties of Religious Experience,* makes it clear that there is no discrete stand-alone "religious experience." Rather, a religious sentiment can be part of any feeling. He says there is "religious fear, religious awe, religious joy." Religious love is "only man's natural emotion of love directed to a religious object. . . . Religious awe is the same organic thrill which we feel in a forest at twilight . . . only this time it comes over us at the thought of our supernatural relations." James adds, however, that religious emotion is "a higher kind of emotion," so for him, it is qualitatively different not merely different by reason of its lofty object.

Likewise, love is not a feeling in itself, but every feeling can happen with love:

- We can be *sad* and show it in a loving way by feeling it without self-pity and with compassion for all who suffer as we do.
- We can be *angry* at someone but still love that person. We show this by expressing our anger without blame, violence, or intimidation.
- We can be *afraid* for someone's safety because we care so much about him or her.
- We can feel *joy* in such a way that we pour it out to others and are enthusiastic about sharing it with them.

Finally, all our feelings can be experienced at either of the two levels we find in our own psyches: ego-centeredness and self-giving. For instance, joy can be experienced in an ego-only mode or in full-self mode. We feel joy at the egocentric level when we are exulting only in our own personal satisfaction. We feel joy at our fully giving self level when our own experience of pleasure gives us a sense of connection with the wider world, and we wish others could feel as we do in that moment.

Melodramatic, operatically expressed emotions are drenched in ego desires and adrenaline. They commandeer our attention by their plea to our most superficial or sentimental emotions. They play on our "heartstrings" (adrenals again). They seduce us by inveigling us into drama. Emotions that tap into our deep, existential experience in the human community draw our attention by their sincerity and authenticity. They touch our hearts more than our adrenals.

We can look at specific feelings to understand what they look like in ego-centered mode and in their higher self-giving mode, where love happens most easily:

Feeling	Ego-Only Level	Full-Self Level
Sadness	Self-pity, caught up in our own story, especially as victims	Grief that combines our own sorrow with a compassionate awareness of how others suffer as we do
Anger	Aggression arising from a sense of personal affront	Displeasure at an injustice, without violence or the need to retaliate
Fear	Worry about danger or threat to ourselves	Worry about danger with a terror of disconnection
Exuberance	Pleasure in having what we want	Joy in sharing and in our sense of connection

What It Takes to Love

I recently bought a faucet set. On the box was a list: "Tools you will need to install this faucet properly." Fortunately, I had all the required tools on the list. I had gathered them over the years—one of them inherited from my dad and one from my grandfather—not realizing that on this particular day I would need them all.

I mused to myself later, "Too bad our bodyminds did not come with such clear listings of what we would need to have in place if we were ever to install love in our lives properly." Then I realized that just as I had gathered my hardware tools without knowing their full potential benefit, I had been gathering psychological and spiritual tools in the same way. In fact, many of us have. The collecting began in childhood, with parent and grandparent contributions, and has continued in each of our relationships. In addition, from the time we were introduced to the self-help movement and first became acquainted with spirituality, we have been assembling the necessary tools for loving. It was all synchronicity, the meaningful coincidence of gaining just the right skills and tools that could be used later in the tasks of love.

For instance, the early self-help movement focused on helping us become more and more aware of our bodies, feelings, and motivations. We may not have realized back then that when we were learning the importance of awareness, we were finding ways to be on the lookout for the primitive, aggressive reactions of our reptilian brain, the part of us that will do anything to survive. The meditation suggestions we received about how to notice what is happening in the here and now therefore qualify as crucial instructions about how to love.

Carl Jung helped us realize that each of us has an unconscious side that he called the negative shadow. This "dark side" contains the disavowed or repressed, unacceptable parts of our personality. We tend to see them in others rather than acknowledge them in ourselves. Now we realize that while we were learning about our shadow side, we were finding out how we project blame onto others, which is an obstacle to loving them. Jung showed us how to look more deeply into our own inclinations and behavior. That would give us an opportunity to work on ourselves and love ourselves.

When we listened to and were moved by the speeches of Martin Luther King, Jr., we found out how to trust the power of nonviolent love to overcome injustice and hate, no matter what the odds against us.

At the same time, love requires setting limits *while* remaining heart-centered. For this, we needed some help from psychology. Perhaps the assertiveness training we went through years ago was equipping us to know how tough love sometimes has to be on others and ourselves.

In recent years, we have become aware of how the Buddhist practice of loving-kindness can help us be more heart-centered. That, too, was about a bigger way of loving, one that legitimates our love for ourselves and extends the possibility of loving to strangers. The fact that we responded was an indicator that we were ready to upgrade our ways of loving. Later in this chapter, we will explore this practice and how to use it effectively.

Another example from Buddhism helps us see how we are becoming prepared to love. It is *bodhicitta.* This Sanskrit word refers to a longing to be enlightened and to help others find that same enlightenment. From the perspective of *bodhicitta,* we can say that we are not complete until we share ourselves. Since love is our deepest identity, that means showing our love.

Bodhicitta is the awakening of *agape* within us, since it arises from caring about the spiritual welfare of others. Our yearning in *bodhicitta* is to free others from the suffering of being caught in fear and ignorance. It is unconditional, unrestricted, and universal, so it actually represents a commitment to love fully.

Bodhicitta also brings out the love that is in us, because it is an aspiration for the transformation of ourselves and others. Love always includes that desire. This is how we know, for instance, that retaliation is not compatible with love; it seeks not transformation but retribution, a concept that is not found in the lexicon of love.

In *bodhicitta,* our loving intent in embracing our own suffering is always to end that of others too. We do this when we remember that our sufferings and challenges here and now are simultaneously the same as those of people all over the globe. *Bodhicitta* causes us to feel akin to them, to offer our suffering on their behalf. It causes our love to expand to become universal. Our awareness of others' sufferings and our effort to help frees us from some of our own suffering, because suffering is diminished by a sense of affiliation. Concern for others is thus a path to our own bliss. Indeed, the wider the scope of our love, the more benefit we receive from loving. Thus, it is important to welcome both the comforts and challenges of life as the essential ingredients of the nourishing bread of love. A life of comfort with no challenges would not give us enough grist for the mill of love.

Bodhicitta, like all forms of love, is accessible to everyone; it is not a special calling for only the few. It becomes possible for any of us who practice repeated acts of kindness, who can enlarge our awareness of suffering, and who take some action—no matter how small—to alleviate it. In *bodhicitta,* our personal efforts and practices matter to everyone; no being is left behind.

Bodhicitta is not just about us and our calling. Its benefits come to us from others. Many saints and bodhisattvas are already dedicating their lives to *our* enlightenment. Like Sleeping Beauty, we don't realize that, in our darkest dungeon and deepest slumber, a prince is on the way to awaken us. In that story, we also see another wonderful hope for ourselves, since the prince of awakening comes not because of a list of our good deeds but because of his own vow to find us.

What It Takes to Practice

> Although this inconceivable Dharma is abundant in each
> person, it is not actualized without practice.
> —EIHEI DOGEN ZENJI

Before beginning the first practice in this book, let us explore what is meant by a spiritual practice. It is not an exercise—that is, an action or movement that produces a skill we do not yet have or increases a skill we are learning. A spiritual practice is an ongoing dedication to a way of living that reflects a quality we *already* have. We practice, not to become something, but to manifest our true nature as enlightened, loving beings. It is not that our true nature has love; it is love. Thus, to act with love is to act according to who we truly are. Success is in the sincerity of our intention, not in getting it right every time. So even if we often fail to live up to our goals, as long as we keep returning to our efforts, we are living enlightened lives.

We can trust that when we hold to our practice, our practice holds us. It gives us a framework of mindful awareness to place around our straying thoughts. We can pause and observe our mind's reactions. We can choose not to act from ego but from our enlightened, loving nature. Holding to the path of practice gives us liberating alternatives to the habits we learned on the street. We have something to fall back on now; we are not just out there with no support. With a program that upholds us, we are not compelled to do things the same old way. We find safety and security in having an inner handbook of useful precepts that show us how to be loving and wise in any moment, in any predicament, and in any relationship.

This does not mean we are living an ideal life. We still make mistakes. Someone gets on our nerves, and we mentally dub him a jerk. When we notice that aggressive judgment and call ourselves on it, we are still doing perfect practice. We corrected ourselves when we noticed our slip. Our unskillful thoughts and actions helped point us to more practice. All our thoughts and actions are portals to enlightenment, as long as our intention remains pure. Purity of intention means we really want to redirect our thoughts into the light. We really want to show our love. Then all that we think or do from an inflated and frightened ego is thrown onto the bonfire of *bodhicitta,* its flames lighting up the darkest night.

All we are giving up are the permits to build more additions onto our house of misery. Once we are no longer living at the tyrannical address of ego, we can identify instead with our enlightened nature. A list of spiritually mature alternatives to our ego habits can be found in Appendix 1. Use them as guidelines or work with them as commitments as you read on in this book.

Keeping a journal may be a helpful adjunct to the practices. You can record your reflections about the ideas in this book, write a poem about what touches or excites you, and notice and record synchronicities and dreams that relate to the themes in the chapters. It is certainly useful to write out the practices in your journal and then look back at them to remind yourself of the commitments they suggest.

Use your own timing when tackling both the psychological and spiritual practices in this book. They are stated and described baldly and directly. But they should be approached as gingerly or briskly as your needs or style can accommodate. Some of the practices can evoke fear or reluctance. Stay with those feelings to see what they reveal about you.

Do the practices only in the way that seems to work for and help you. The more you can improvise from them, the more beneficial and entertaining they will be.

Finally, keep in mind that we are all self-seeking at times. That is human. Love is how we make the radical shift into self-giving, which is also human. In childhood, you may have been told you were too self-centered. In relationships, you may have been told you did not really know how to love. You yourself may suspect or be sure that you are narcissistic, self-seeking, and not really a loving person. None of that makes any difference whatsoever. Here and now, no matter what, you can start a practice of love. You may feel phony at first; that is normal. Your loving acts may feel like acting, but just keep acting. Gradually, loving acts will become real love, and its power will repeal the fears that held it back all these years. You will see that your love was just waiting for its chance to make a personal appearance. Saint John of the Cross said it best: "Where there is no love, put love and then you will find love." We can restate this as, "When you believe there is no love in you, put acts of love out there, and then you will find the love in yourself." Maybe all those other people whom you see as so sincerely loving got there by this very same route.

> The degree to which our experience is productive of practice shows the degree to which our experience is spiritual and divine.
>
> —JONATHAN EDWARDS

PRACTICES

TRUSTING OUR ABILITY TO LOVE MINDFULLY • Trust yourself to know how to love. Ask yourself what you need to do or be to show your love in the specific occurrences and encounters you expect to happen today. Check in with yourself in the same way at the end of the day regarding how you responded to what actually happened. Record all this in your journal. It may help to share it with someone you love. You can then ask for feedback about how well you showed the qualities you listed early in the day.

In this book, we use the term *mindfulness* in its usual modern meaning to describe staying in the here and now, noticing our mind's chatter without joining in the conversation or dismissing it. We simply notice it with bare attention and keep returning to the present moment by focusing on our breath, what is real right now.

In mindfulness, we are so attentive to our thoughts and reactions that we see precisely where they lead and how they do or do not produce suffering for ourselves and others. This awareness is what helps us understand others' feelings and reactions. Mindfulness is useful, because it is a way of observing without prejudice or the need to repair or restrain events or people. We thus become more skillful in how we express our compassion, the enlightened alternative to judgment. It will be enough for us to be present courageously (that is, without criticism or even recommendations for a solution) with others in their crises. This is a noninvasive way of loving. We will be there for others as we are now here for ourselves, fully present, calmly witnessing, not rushing in to fix or control.

We sometimes confuse making assessments and being judgmental. To assess is to critique, or to comment on the value of something in an objective and disinterested way, such as reviewing a movie. We evaluate its acting, script, and direction. This is not personal but informational. Mindfulness shows the legitimacy of assessing; it requires constant assessment so we can label thoughts and feelings to see how they differ from what is real in the moment.

To judge, in the negative sense, is to criticize, to censure, to make someone wrong or bad. Usually, this is a reaction to someone's behavior or words that we do not like. In loving-kindness, we assess rather than judge: "Their means are unskillful," not "They are bad." The following chart helps us see the difference between judgment and assessment.

Being Judgmental in the Negative Sense	*Making an Assessment*
Based on prejudice	Based on unbiased inquiry and resultant evaluation

From a reactive, spinning imagination	From an intellect that remains simply present
A reaction to our own projections, taking things personally	A response to what we actually see, coming from an objective, neutral stance
Possibly including ridicule, scoffing, and scorn	Respectful
Censorious, a verdict	Aware of accountability, a communication
Acting like a jury	Being a fair witness
Caught in mind-sets	Mindful
Likely to come across to the other as being told (talked at)	More likely to come across as a helpful suggestion (talked with)
Harsh/scolding tone of voice/manner	Kind, mild tone of voice and manner
Blaming, making the other wrong or bad	Being aware of limitations and flaws but taking it all as information
Including criticisms meant as put-downs	Includes critiques meant as commentaries
Usually instant	Based on time for discernment
Often hard-hearted	Usually compassionate
Often motivated by the desire to punish the other	Motivated by a desire for the transformation of the other
More apt to lead to defensiveness or hurt feelings in others	More apt to encourage attention and improvement in others
Excludes the other so love is not possible	Understands the other so love is easily possible
Archetype of the judge	Archetype of the mentor, the assisting force, the friend

Our spiritual practice of mindfulness can help us move from judgment to assessment.

In mindfulness practice, we certainly notice that it is difficult to turn off our ongoing inner monologue. We learn soon enough that putting effort into stopping it is useless. So we give up trying to change anything. The point of practice isn't to demolish the train of our thoughts, and we miss the point if we stop our practice because we are not successful in quieting our minds for long. Practice is about surrendering to the way things are inside us. Our success is in noticing how our mind works and in coming back to our breath whenever we become aware of our distractions. Our success is in continuing to show up, not in being utterly free of distracting mind-sets. We notice that pure mindful awareness is generally a momentary thing; it's impossible to maintain it in a constant state. The words of William James are encouraging to consider in the face of mindfulness's fleeting nature: "Attention cannot be continuously sustained. . . . The faculty of voluntarily bringing back a wandering attention over and over again is the very root of judgment, character, and will."

Simply acknowledging our powerlessness to stop our chain gang of thoughts takes effort. That effort is the calming practice of accepting how our mind works, a major feature of true mindfulness. This is useful in learning to love, since love flourishes in an atmosphere of utter surrender to the way things are. Love comes to its full actualization when our surrender leads us to persevere in our healthy efforts to return again and again to a focused presence, just what love entails. And, of course, love is like mindfulness practice, because we get it wrong almost every time but never give up.

To keep returning to mindful awareness is to be ready for love. The easiest way to see the connection between mindfulness and love is to understand the five A's as prerequisites for loving. Record in your journal how the five A's are happening in your relationships and how you are giving them to yourself. Reply to the questions in italics that follow each of these descriptions:

- Attention can happen only with a commitment to hear the other without our add-ons of judgment, comparison, fear, or attachment to being right. *Can I take leave of my own thoughts and needs long enough to take an interest in and pay close attention to someone else?*
- I attend to my inner world, who I deeply am, when distracting and ego-constructed thoughts clear off my psychic property. *Can I focus on my own needs and appreciate their legitimacy?*
- Acceptance requires a freedom from any sense of threat by the other and in an absence of judgment or blame of someone. *Do I accept others just as they are, or do I judge them?*
- When I accept myself as worthy, I can recognize the other's worthiness as equal to mine, not as above mine. Only that equality lets love thrive. *Do I accept myself as I am?*
- Appreciation takes a recognition of the essential goodness of others, their unconditional value, untrammeled by their history or behavior. *Do I notice what people do for me and then remember to show appreciation?*
- When I value myself, I grow in appreciation of others' love for me. *Do I appreciate myself?*
- Affection can happen by a here-and-now, caring connection shown with physical closeness and touch but without clinging to summon the comfort we experienced in childhood embraces. *Can I show affection in physical ways that do not lead to sex?*
- When I take affectionate care of myself, I learn to love myself. *How can I take care of my body and mind as a way of loving myself?*
- Allowing means letting others have their own voice and being open to hearing them, no matter what their message to us may be. This takes mindful awareness of another person's needs and feelings and a letting go of our own ego investments. *Am I able to allow others to live in accord with their own deepest needs, values, and wishes, or do I try to control them?*

- I can grant myself the irrepressible freedom to live in accord with my own deepest needs, values, and wishes. *How does my life reflect who I am rather than what others have wanted or want me to be to please them?*

The practice essential for all of these is mindfulness.

To look for the reality behind external appearances and internal perceptions is the ongoing task—and joy—of mindfulness practice. We do not lose hope, however, as we realize that love, whether given or received, is rarely free of projections, personal meanings, memories, and feelings. That is the natural state of any mind. But there can always be A+ moments when we are really there (or, rather, here) for ourselves or someone else. There can be moments when we really see ourselves just as we are and love ourselves that way. There can be moments when we see others just as they are and love them for being that way.

Like enlightenment, full-on love happens only in moments, here and there, now and then. But we can increase the number of moments by our commitment to a mindfulness that helps us be more present. That is the same practice that helps us love more.

The Chinese characters for mindfulness signify presence and heart. Mindfulness is, indeed, a heartfelt practice. It is not a cold inquiry into the workings of the mind; it is a lead-in to loving-kindness. We become fully present only so we can find the hiding places of love and make them gloriously visible.

EXPANDING OUR CIRCLE OF LOVING-KINDNESS • All the practices in this book can begin with loving ourselves, as in the first part of *metta* practice. This is a meditation method in which we mentally wish happiness to all beings, beginning with ourselves, using a system of repeated phrases that extend this intention toward people of various categories. We begin by wishing ourselves happiness. We extend our aspiration to those we know and then to those we do not know, and so forth, until we include all beings.

In Buddhism, enlightenment is our awakening to the here and now with no need to judge, define, or analyze what is happening, with no attachment to a particular outcome, and without fear or craving. In other words, with freedom from what William Blake called our "mind-forged manacles."

This is possible because our natural state *is* enlightened. We all innately possess the four limitless qualities of enlightened living, what we affirm for ourselves and others in the loving-kindness practice: universal, unconditional loving-kindness; compassion for those who suffer; joy for those who prosper; and the equanimity to accept reality evenly and serenely so we can maintain the stability to engage in the other three.

Loving-kindness is a frame of mind or, rather, a frame of heart. With it, we see people's pain with compassion. We feel joy at their success. We find ourselves more at peace, because we trust that we are learning to accept the events of life with equanimity. We do not carry ill will or vengeful thoughts about others. *Thoughts lead to actions, so cultivating loving thoughts is a step toward showing love.*

Stress and drama can interfere with our ability to give ourselves unreservedly. As we grow in equanimity within the loving-kindness practice, our stress level is reduced. Thus, equanimity can help us love. Since equanimity is a surrender to the way things are, it is a path to contentment—if we accept everything as it is, we need nothing else. Equanimity is the feeling of even-mindedness in the face of both suffering and joy, in all circumstances, toward both friend and foe. It is the ability to regard all beings with loving-kindness and without partiality or bias. This protects the purity of our loving-kindness, because our love remains unaffected by what happens or what other people do. Our equanimity keeps us stable, and our love follows suit.

An essential practice for achieving equanimity is letting go of our ego, the part of us that feels entitled to respect and goodwill from everyone. With equanimity, we do not take social disappointments so personally, which is the main source of our pain when people or events do not turn out as we expected. With less ego interference, we no longer become so upset when people fail to acknowledge or please us. Less ego means less reaction to other egos, no matter how abrasive. This is how equanimity helps us extend our love in *metta* practice to those with whom we have difficulties.

In the practice of loving-kindness, we expand our circle of love to its full circumference. This is how practice helps us make the journey of a lifetime from common courtesy to unconditional love. As we move from self to others in loving-kindness practice, we expand our own identity as we extend our circle of love. The full human path goes from being egocentric to other-centered to cosmocentric.

The more we practice loving-kindness, the more we realize that everyone we encounter helps us find love's path. Indian Buddhist teacher Shantideva says in *The Way of the Bodhisattva,* "Because of those whose minds are full of anger, I engender patience in myself. They are thus the cause of patience, fit for veneration.... Thus, the state of Buddhahood depends on beings and the Buddhas equally.... Beings are Buddha's very self."

Loving-kindness is not simply done in a time set aside each day to enumerate aspirations. It is an entire lifestyle, yet one that happens in particular moments. A practice moment can happen when we make a choice to be kind to our body by choosing a healthy food at a restaurant. A practice moment with a partner can involve focusing fully on the story of her day, picking up on her feelings, and holding her in them.

A practice moment of loving-kindness can happen when you see a crowd of people and wonder, "How would I ever be able to love all these people?" Try answering this way: "I can't make contact with everyone, but I can always show kindness, courtesy, and respect to everyone I meet. I can, right now, include everyone in my spiritual practice of loving-kindness by wishing everyone happiness and enlightenment. May I and they find ways to love with all our might." This combines the elements of caring connection with a realistic sense of our mutual human limitations.

Here is a simple set of aspirations you can repeat every day to get started with a loving-kindness practice:

- May I love myself as I am today.
- May I be happy and healthy.
- May I be free of the suffering of imagining I am separate.
- May I be safe and secure at home and work.

- May I harbor no unkind thoughts or engage in aggressive actions.
- May I be even-minded and serene, no matter what happens to me today.
- May I keep practicing loving-kindness, compassion, joy at others' success, and equanimity.

Repeat some or all these aspirations, or similar ones, first for yourself, then for those you love, then for those to whom you are indifferent (acquaintances or people you may meet during the day but do not know), then for those with whom you have conflicts, and finally, for all beings everywhere.

This practice shows us the concentric circles in which love travels. We begin with ourselves, then some others, then all others. We are spiritually adult in our love when it is not limited but goes in all directions. We love ourselves without feeling egotistical about that commitment. We show love to our families, in our intimate relationships, and in our friendships. We extend the wish for happiness and enlightenment to those we may not like or who may not like us. We love all beings with a caring compassion. These are unusual and radical challenges for most of us, but we dare to embrace them.

The loving-kindness practice shows us how to love unconditionally, since we include people with whom we have difficulties and conflicts. This includes those who have hurt us or who are hostile to us. When we think about how badly they behaved toward us, we do not hold rancor but feel sad for how they missed out on an opportunity to love.

The practice shows us how to love universally, since we extend loving-kindness to people we do not know. The known/unknown distinction no longer holds, because our goal is a wide reach of love, not the near reach based on narrow preferences. Here, there are no preferences; everyone receives the exact same aspirations for well-being. This is how our hearts stretch in practice to the size they truly are inside us.

Finally, this practice is not accomplished only by aspirations but by daily actions that *show* loving-kindness to others, compassion for their suffering, joy at their successes, and equanimity about what comes to us from them.

If you now beheld them, your affections
Would become tender.
                    —WILLIAM SHAKESPEARE, *The Tempest*

WORKING WITH OUR FEAR OF LOVE •

Although I love you, you will have to leap;
Our dream of safety has to disappear.
                    —W. H. AUDEN

Most of us fear love as much as we want it—sometimes less, sometimes more. We fear both the receiving and giving of full-on love. The engaged focus of loving eyes can feel invasive. Those who want our love can seem to be asking too much of us. The vulnerability inherent in loving and being loved can be quite daunting. We want love to happen on our own terms. We want to show love only in the way that feels safe to us. We want full control of the love we parcel out: how much, how long, how deep. To be loved requires vulnerability in three forms of willingness: to show we love someone before he shows he loves us, to be seen at our best and worst, and to show our needs.

There is a direct proportion between vulnerability and courage. The more vulnerable we are willing to be the more courage do we have. Fearless, go-for-it love is reckless, not careful; it takes a chance rather than playing it close to the vest; it is open and spontaneous, not in tight control. Those options can strike terror into our hearts, which have been burned so often for doing these things.

When we feel needy for more from someone while also fearing more closeness to her, a tension arises in us. *We feel anxious because we fear what we want and want what we fear.*

The components of both giving and receiving love are the five A's. They seem, at first look, to be quite desirable. But we can also see how they may evoke fear or suspicion.

When we give our love, each of the five A's can feel threatening. We cannot trust others to receive our love in the limited way in which we offer it. We may feel that too great a follow-up commitment will be expected of us if we accept others' love. We do not feel safe and secure in showing attention, because we may see feelings that will evoke feelings in us, and that is scary. We may fear showing acceptance, appreciation, or affection because we have noticed that they lead to a closeness we are not ready for. We may fear allowing others to make their own choices, since we will then lose the control we want to have over them.

When love is shown to us, each of the five A's can feel untrustworthy, interfering with or canceling our sense of safety and security. Attention can feel as if someone is scrutinizing us too deeply, invading a part of us that we are not ready to reveal. Acceptance, appreciation, and allowing can come across to us as obsequiousness, arising from the untrustworthy motive of trying to manipulate us. Physical affection can have a sexual or overly friendly connotation that may be unwelcome, transgress our boundaries, or feel premature, so we are mistrustful of it.

Fears thrive on the primitive emotions in our brain's limbic system. As we use the awareness factor of our orbital and medial prefrontal cortex, we make accurate evaluations of situations. Now our anxiety can be overridden more easily. When it does arise, we can calm it with assurances that we can deal with whatever happens. This self-soothing builds our trust in ourselves, which is the first step toward loving ourselves. Since fear thrives on making us feel trapped or cornered, fear is less likely to get the better of us when we see new options.

Our main conflict in life is often between choices made by the unaware amygdala and the aware prefrontal cortex. A full release from fear would take a major restructuring of the amygdala—a daunting task. But there is hope. With mindfulness as our practice, we can be on the lookout for primitive fears and use bodymind techniques to alter and disable them. For instance, we can use deep breathing exercises and access mindful awareness.

We can use the 4A technique of admitting, allowing, acting, and affirming to release ourselves from the grip of fear of loving or of being loved:

1. We *admit* we are afraid and assess that our fear is not rational or truly dangerous.

2. We *allow* ourselves to feel a little more fear than we can usually stand, while reminding ourselves that it is arising from habit and is not a reality to take too personally. We hold ourselves as a kindly parent would, letting it be all right to have our fear but assuring ourselves that all will be OK. In this part of the practice, we choose our response. This cancels out the style of being victims who are forced to feel afraid, hijacked by the amygdala that makes fear seem so insuperable. With a paradoxical intention, we gain mastery because we are in charge in a very real sense. "Bring it on" has courage in it. We allow the full release of a virtue that is inherent in our hearts. In fact, the word *courage* means "heart."

3. We have chosen to feel our fear and to *act* as if it has no power to stop us from doing anything or to drive us to do something. To act courageously is to be courageous. The practice is both cause and result. This is not acting in the sense of pretending but of behaving in a new way. Ralph Waldo Emerson wrote, "Do the thing you fear, and the death of fear is certain."

4. We design an *affirmation* that sums up our practice and that we continue to use. An example might be, "I let my fear pass through me and am free of being controlled by it."

Our most useful spiritual tool in freeing ourselves from the power fear can have over us remains loving-kindness practice. Joining daily metta to the 4A technique combines psychological work and spiritual practice, producing a formidable force.

Fear thrives on isolation, so we also ease our fears through contact with those we trust. Thus, every time we feel safe support from others, we become more able to approach danger rather than having to run or dissociate from it. We thereby lessen its power over us.

I recently heard a radio interview with a man who had been a student protester in the 1989 Tiananmen Square uprising in Beijing. The topic was how empowering it was to be standing shoulder to shoulder with other students who were so like-minded and similarly committed. When asked if he was afraid of being killed, he firmly and serenely replied, "My fears were gone, and it no longer mattered whether I lived or died." This is the power of affiliation to free us from fear. True connection casts out fear.

In addition, others' empathy toward and support of us helps rebuild our prefrontal cortex. This restructures our neural circuitry so we can regulate our limbic, emotional, and impulsive responses to what happens. Now our cortex and limbic system work together.

This also happens when we receive the five A's in healthy relationships, grieve our losses and let go, and make a unilateral commitment to a life of love—all the practices we are exploring in this book. The brain is not hermetically sealed, so our chances for improvement are good. We have a brain that can use social engagement and personal commitment to health, happiness, and personal growth to rewire itself.

At the same time, our commitment to these practices shows us the power we have, on our own, to rewire the circuitry of self-rebuke and fear so we can maximize the present. We love ourselves more when we arc present to ourselves in such a loyal way.

We can examine our fears about love in close relationships by looking at what happens at gatherings of our immediate and extended family, such as Thanksgiving. What happens between us and family members can give us information about how love is shown or limited, both from and to us in a group that is generally considered to have close ties:

- Do we all genuinely like one another?
- Do we communicate honestly about our lives, feelings, and concerns?
- Do we care about one another's health, happiness, and success with no competitive element interfering?
- Do we enjoy one another's company?
- Do we show respect toward one another?
- Are any of us there out of obligation, or do we genuinely want to be there?
- Do we look forward to the end of the visit less, more, or as much as to the arrival?

- When it is over, do we have to recover from the stress of our time together?

Consider how family members stack up on this chart, using the five A's as a barometer of fearless love.

With Fulfillment of the Five A's	*Without Fulfillment*
Sincere *attention* shown by extended periods of listening, eye contact, and awareness of feelings	Continual distraction, especially by excessive focus on the children, the game on TV, texting, and so on
Full *acceptance* of each person, with all of his or her quirks, welcomed with curiosity and amusement	Judgment, ridicule, censure, shaming
Real *appreciation* of each person's story, limits, suffering, needs, and talents	Disregard or discounting of the contribution each person makes (Does each contribute?)
Affection shown in continuous contact and respectful, friendly touching	The required hug at arrival and departure and not much more
Allowing them all to be themselves during the visit, without shaming or blaming them for their behavior or their occasional need for time alone	Criticism or attempts to control behavior

Love thrives on quality time together. Tending relationships, both familial and intimate, requires personal and in-depth sharing. Discomfort with direct, feeling-laden, face-to-face communication is fear of closeness and full-on loving.

This final question about family meals may help us see if we are inhibited in expressing the five A's to one another: At the end of the meal, do the adults sit around the table and have a serious conversation? The alternative is constant focus on the children—or other stimuli—before, during, and after the meal. In that scenario, the adults talk to one another in a catch-as-catch-can manner, perhaps a good description of the only kind of closeness they are prepared to show.

I recall a custom in my Italian childhood that I do not see performed much in present-day families. All the children were certainly present at the table with our extended family at holiday dinners. But after the main courses, we were sent outside to play while the adults had their coffee. (That beverage, since it is not suitable for children, ensures adult space.) The whole ritual allowed the adults to converse without us around to distract them from face-to-face contact, something they weren't afraid of. And we children were given the opportunity to socialize with each other, something being sent to watch television or play video games does not offer.

2

How We Can Love Ourselves

I bless the vicissitudes, the good fortune, the misadventures of my career. I bless my own character, my virtues, my faults, my blemishes. I love my own self in the form in which it was given to me and in the form in which my destiny molds me.

—Pierre Teilhard de Chardin

Self-love is self-caring. This is not selfishness but a wise tending of our bodyminds, a loving-kindness toward ourselves. We love ourselves effectively when we organize our relationships, our diet, our lifestyle, our work, our pastimes, and our choices in such a way that they lead to and protect the three goals of self-caring: health, happiness, and personal growth (which refers to both psychological and spiritual progress).

These three are the criteria for all the wholesomeness in our decisions. They are important in any choice, whether about a hobby or a partner: "Is this good for my health, my happiness, and my growth?" Growth-fostering choices are those that maintain our sanity and serenity. When we take care of ourselves by sticking with those norms, we begin to trust that we really are friendly toward ourselves.

We love ourselves when we do not make choices that compromise our health, no matter how pleasurable or exciting. We love ourselves when we take our own happiness into account rather than making pleasing others the motivation for our actions. We love ourselves when we do what builds and stretches our psychological and spiritual potential.

We love ourselves when our criteria for an intimate relationship are health, happiness, and personal growth. We do not find someone appealing who does not want to join us in reaching those goals. Our commitment to self-care becomes more important than having a relationship. Our health and sanity become primary.

Part of loving ourselves is learning to be cautious about the motivation behind others' attraction to us. We can tell if someone wants us because of who we really are or if, instead, he wants us because of what we look like or what is in it for him. This clarity also immunizes us from being swayed by praise from someone who is trying to reel us in because he is needy for company or sexual relief.

We recognize that flattery can be about the other person's neediness or strategizing rather than a response to our authentic charms. We love ourselves when we welcome prospective partners who are healthy enough to offer mutual need fulfillment. We protect ourselves from letting anyone get close who is not like that, no matter how appealing the sweet talk. We are always aware that any and all of the five A's can be forms of seduction.

It is also up to each of us to recognize our own motivations and intentions when it comes to being attracted to or accepting attraction from a potential partner. We trust our own value and have identified what we consider to be traits of a healthy relationship or partner. Therefore, we are not apt to buy what someone may be trying to sell us, so to speak. Rather we are able to identify authentic motivations in ourselves as well as in a partner whose potentials are congruent with our own.

We all have love—and aggression—in us, but we learn how to express these inclinations by having them modeled. We learned how to love ourselves from our caregivers in early life and in later relationships when partners showed us the five A's. Anyone who loves us now is a model too.

No one was or is loved unconditionally all the time, nor do we need that to develop from childhood to adulthood. But repeated attunements of our feelings make us feel understood and loved for who we are. Encouragement from others to take care of ourselves helps. We come to see that self-care is not self-centeredness. That means a lot in laying the groundwork for loving ourselves. Attunement to ourselves means tracking, moment by moment, our feelings, our body, our needs, memories, beliefs.

Self-love actually grows exponentially when we are loved by others. This is not only based on realizing that if people love us, it must follow that we are lovable. It happens at a deeper level as well. We knew that we made the transition from childhood to adulthood when we assumed the functions of our caretakers. One by one, we did for ourselves what they had always done for us, everything from dressing ourselves to comforting ourselves. Likewise, whenever others love us, we begin to give ourselves the same diligent care we receive from them. In other words, we don't just soak up the loving attitudes and behaviors of others toward us. We let them soak in so we can love ourselves as they love us. We don't just love ourselves with our own love. We love ourselves with the love others have for us that we have now internalized. Letting love into our lives is practice for loving ourselves.

Here is an example of how being loved by others shows us how to love ourselves. We may have felt loved by those who supported us when we were dealing with difficult feelings and predicaments. As adults, we can commit to staying with ourselves as we go through things. The love that came to us from others is now the love that comes to us from ourselves. Using our example, we can do this by giving ourselves the five A's, accompanying rather than abandoning ourselves, in the midst of any predicament we are going through:

Attention: "I am paying close attention to what I feel, how I talk to myself, how I judge myself. I am letting go of what holds me back and focusing in an engaged way on who I am and how I am responding to this moment."

Acceptance: "I accept what I feel in this moment without passing judgment on myself or inhibiting my choices or liveliness."

Appreciation: "I value and congratulate myself on how I am handling things so far. I don't expect perfection, only to keep persevering. I appreciate how I turn to resources that can help me."

Affection: "I feel affection for myself in this predicament. I show myself loving-kindness by taking care of my bodymind. I care for and tend to my health and my growth as I go through this."

Allowing: "I allow the chips to fall where they may, and I trust myself to pick them up and make something of them. I am giving up control in favor of openness to what may come from all this."

Our core imprint will also point to our central fear in relationships. If our core love imprint is related to the idea that someone must stay with us as we go through things, we may fear abandonment or indifference keenly, because in our personal lexicon, it represents a total loss of love.

The core imprint of what love feels like to us may also color our ideas of what a higher power is like. If our model of love is feeling accompanied, then Psalm 23 might have a particularly special meaning for us when it avers, "The Lord is my shepherd." And we might have a crisis of faith when we encounter the theme of Psalm 22, which begins, "My God, My God, why have you forsaken me?" Adult faith is flexible and expansive enough to trust accompaniment even when we do not feel it happening.

A distorted imprint is one that includes abuse or disrespect of our freedom. For instance, we may have been imprinted with the feeling that a father or husband truly cared about us because he controlled us. Or an alcoholic mother may have entangled us in her emotional needs but showed us she really cared about us too. Thus, drama and entanglement in a current relationship may feel like closeness.

If there was abuse in our alcoholic home in childhood, we may be carrying an imprint like this: "Something terrible is happening to me, and I can't leave." As we work on ourselves, the imprint can be rede-signed: "When something terrible *may* happen, I'll leave." Such pre-empting is a sign of the self-caring that is self-love.

It is instinctive in us to flee abuse or at least react with anger and self-protection. When, in adult life, we are so afraid that we override our natural instinct, we can suspect that the issue goes back to childhood. In this instance, the imprint has gone on printing rather than simply becoming a reminiscence.

Here, our work is threefold: we examine each of our imprints and look for healthier ones to replace the damaged originals; we attempt to resolve the past by grieving it; and we regain our connection to our natural instinct for self-preservation and for showing appropriate anger. This "connection" is a way of loving ourselves. The practices in this book can help us get there.

It is wise to notice also that a predator is a connoisseur of imprints or of a canceled instinct for self-preservation. He will easily locate the vulnerable place in our heart and exploit it. We love ourselves when we stay on the lookout for such tricksters and run the other way when we see them.

Early in life, others may have shown us love in a distorted extreme, as outlined in the far right column of the following table. In these instances, our parents' positive intent of love interfered with our health, happi-ness, and personal growth. The center column shows what healthy love looks like both in childhood and in adult relationships. It also outlines how we can love ourselves as we befriend our shadow side.

The Five A's Shown to Us in Childhood or in Adult Relationships	*Expressed Positively and Appropriately*	*Pushed to Extremes, Distorted, Reflecting the Shadow Side of Love*
Attention	Engaged focus on our feelings and needs, taking an interest in who we are	Scrutiny of us ostensibly to protect us from the world but actually to control us

Acceptance	A welcoming approval of us just as we were, while giving helpful feedback when appropriate	Treating us as if we were perfect so that we believed we could do no wrong when we needed feedback to help us appraise our talents and limits realistically
Appreciation	Acknowledging our gifts with gratitude and our struggles with compassion, valuing us	Overvaluing us or setting us above others, as if we were entitled to special treatment and were excused from accountability
Affection	Showing love physically by frequent and appropriate touch and holding	Smothering or intrusive physicality so that our boundaries were not honored
Allowing	Honoring our deepest needs, values, and wishes and our right to pursue them without force or inhibition	Ignoring our choices and our whereabouts, making no attempts to guide us or to set reasonable limits that might help us structure our lives so we could find our own path

To Be Myself and Love You Too

Scottish philosopher David Hume, in *A Treatise of Human Nature*, stated, "For my part, when I enter most intimately into what I call myself, I always stumble on some particular perception or other." A way to approach loving ourselves is to see that we have no separate self. We know this because we notice that the self never appears alone. It is always experienced in connection with someone, something, an idea, a feeling, a mood, a condition. There is no naked I. There is only I as the one who is here rather than there, I as the one feeling this not that, I as the one in relationship to a specific someone or something. There is really no "I and you." "I-with-you here now" is the only I there is. There is no self without connection. This is another clue that love is what we are.

This mirrors the Buddhist teaching that there is no separate self. *Separate* in this context means not existing independently but being entirely interdependent, not freestanding but contingent on, connected to, everything else. We have a unique personality, body, and ego, but they too are interactive and interdependent. We are separate bodymind beings but are not separated from all other beings. We have to speak of ourselves and others to make useful distinctions. To awaken is to penetrate more and more deeply into the truth that there ultimately is no "me" or "other." In the *Diamond Sutra*, we read, "Although the Bodhisattva saves all sentient beings, there are no [individual] sentient beings to save." The word *self* is, after all, merely a useful designation, not an indicator of a separate existence. In fact, our sense of separateness is our central illusion. It opposes connectedness, which is what love is all about.

When we adjust our perspective in this way, we understand that we are not isolated selves but selves-in-relationship—which is love. Our suffering comes from believing that we are separate, which is the opposite of love, a contradiction of our real nature. Our sense of an enduring autonomous self is nonetheless understandable. It happens because of the continuity of our name, our body, our memory, our personality, and most of all, our thoughts. In this sense, René Descartes's statement "I think, therefore I am," is actually "I think, therefore I think I am."

Love as compassion for others also presupposes our seeing clearly that we are not separate. This is why in Buddhism, *prajna* (wisdom), our direct perception that we do not have a separate existence, is necessary if we are to feel compassion. When we are not isolated from others, we are responsible for them, connected to them.

Psychologically, we have two basic drives: to be independent and to be interdependent. We want to be alone *and* with others. We want relationships in which we can maintain our own individuality while we connect intimately. We do not want to lose ourselves in order to relate to others. We do not want to lose our relationships in order to preserve our autonomy.

Our fondness for the companionship of pets tells us a lot about being alone-and-with. A man is sitting and reading with his dog quietly lying by his side. Whether we are introverts or extroverts, we appreciate non-interfering companionship: Our pet is present but not making demands, passing judgments, or interrupting us. Not everyone wants a partner, but we all want companionship of some kind, at some time, from people or pets. This need is yet another indicator of our interdependence. Through it we find what we are: love.

Thus, true love requires that we surrender any attachment to rugged individualism and total independence. It means gladly embracing the teaching of universal interdependence, which is what we discover in spiritual consciousness. We can see, therefore, why love develops optimally with a spiritual practice. Our higher self—the no-separate self—is ready for that development. It is usually our ego, frightened by surrender of any kind, that puts up a fight. When our very identity is equated with control, the prospect of giving it up can infuse us with panic. To let go of control can feel like dying, like not being anybody anymore. An unconditional yes to the unpredictable givens of life is a radical leap for an ego that has nothing to fall back on but its habit of controlling.

Any work we can do on letting go of that fearful ego is therefore an act of great self-love, because it readies us for caring connection. We work on our ego so it can leap into the arms of our higher self—that is, our real self, or enlightened loving nature. We will explore this work in a later chapter.

Embracing the teaching that there is no separate self shows us our place in the human community, equal in stature to and just as lovable as anyone else. The sense of coherence we feel as we maintain our own identity while loving others makes us more likely to love and trust ourselves. This will be quite a task to an ego that has to be superior.

Once we affirm that we were made for love, it becomes easier to love ourselves without feeling that we are being selfish. That bias was introduced to us by family or religion or whatever source feared our full emergence. When we don't love ourselves, it is not because we are unlovable but because we were repeatedly taught not to.

Early in life, we might have noticed we were different: "I am like this; everyone else is like that." That semicolon stood for immense disconnection, a loss of the chance to be included, placing in jeopardy the only way we knew of feeling loved. The cost to join may have been our true self. "If I remain what I am here, I am in danger of disconnection, so it is better to be like everybody else." As we mature, we cherish our uniqueness and offer it to those who can receive it. That is how disconnection begins to feel like connection. Now the semicolon joins.

Any of us may doubt that we are lovable: "If they knew me, they would not love me, because I am not like them, as good as they are, and so on." The irony is that we become lovable to loving people when we show ourselves to them just as we are. Opening our unique qualities to them is seen as a gift, not a reason for excommunication. Those who have love will love us for who we are, no matter how different we are from the mainstream. Those who don't love us for who we are deserve our compassion for missing a many-splendored thing.

PRACTICE: GETTING UP WHEN WE ARE PUT DOWN

Our primitive ancestors had to recall negative experiences more than positive ones so they could stay on high alert and thereby survive. It was more important to remember the close call with the saber-toothed tiger than the brilliant sunset. At the tribal level, we still have that inclination to recall, grab on to, and maintain negative memories, often more firmly than positive ones.

Self-loathing may have its origin in childhood, when we may not have been shown the five A's. We may, instead, have been held in contempt, humiliated, neglected, or abused. If we followed the example of parents who disliked us, we may now dislike ourselves. To have a contrary opinion about ourselves from that of our parents would have disconnected us from them, made us orphans. It was safer—since connection, not happiness, is always our primary need—to join them in turning against us. A sad loyalty indeed.

In the socializing process, an inner critic is necessary to keep us in line, reminding us about what works and what does not in society so that excommunication can be avoided at all costs. One of those costs is ongoing self-loathing. It takes us a while to realize that the voice of the inner critic is imitating other voices. It is not a determinant of or an infallible guide to what is true about us. It would be better to have an inner lover who keeps reminding us of how loving we are/can be than an inner critic who puts us down. We learned to listen to the critical voice; we can practice learning to listen to the loving voice.

Throughout this book, we have been using and will continue to use the 4A technique (admit, allow, act, affirm). It is one of the most useful practices I have for making changes, because it does not simply demand a reversal of unwanted thoughts, feelings, or behaviors. Instead, it honors all that we think and feel while offering a behavior that frees us from what may be interrupting our growth.

The 4A technique begins, as any recovery does, with an honest admission of what is true rather than a denial of it. We then let ourselves feel our feelings rather than look for an escape. Finally, we act in accordance with what is best for us, no matter how we think or what we feel. This very doable technique involves the use of paradox, the poetic path to truth, an unfailing tool for healing.

Here is how it works. When we hear an unfairly critical or self-loathing voice within us, we apply the 4A technique:

1. We *admit* our pain about the verdict that was passed on us in the past and that we are now passing on ourselves.

2. We *allow* ourselves to feel that pain and hold it in a cradling way, compassionate toward ourselves now for repeating it inwardly. We are also compassionate toward those who first pronounced the verdict because of their ignorance or malice, which were forms of pain within them.

3. We *act* in the opposite way to the voice's dictates. For instance, if the voice says, "You are selfish," we show some form of generosity at the first opportunity that comes along. This shows us that the critic's judgment was not correct.

4. We design an *affirmation* that congratulates rather than disparages us. We repeat it, silently and aloud, throughout each day. An affirmation keeps our practice in our awareness and reminds us to continue it in everyday experience. Using our example from the last step, we can affirm, "Each day I grow in generosity, and I love myself more and more

for being like this." (The steps of acting and affirming can also be re-versed.)

The 4A approach lays down new neural pathways in our brain that override old ones. We can trust that we are truly moving from self-negation to self-affirmation. This is a powerful way to unseat original limbic, primitive emotional programming.

There is one caveat when using this practice. We cannot fully allow our feelings to emerge if we find that they flood or overwhelm us. In that instance, the allowing can so traumatize us that it is not safe. We are not resolving our feelings, only crashing. We can only use this practice if we can modulate or manage our feelings so that we feel only what we can handle.

What would it take to desensitize ourselves so that we could contain rather than be possessed by our feelings? We would have to work, usually in therapy, on building our inner resources. This includes an unconditional yes of acceptance of ourselves as being just as fragile as we are. How hard something hits us is directly proportional to how much control we are trying to exert over it. This paradoxical and humbling practice of an unconditional yes to how limited we are is a path to healing. It is a long road, but it does not have to be a discouraging one. We should never be ashamed of being sensitive.

A final word on what makes this practice work. Our inadequacies are not to be construed as proof of how bad we are but of how human we are, the best position to be in for loving ourselves. When you hear yourself say, "I am so messed up," say instead, "This too is workable, since my inner inclination toward healing is stronger than any fault I may believe I have. I have, right here and now, everything required for my three goals of health, happiness, and growth." This is how your programming changes. You are no longer tied to the judgments others have made about you. You are now committed to trusting your inner goodness. It is this alignment to your goodness that makes you more apt to love yourself and others. To recognize this inner goodness as buddha nature, God within, and a higher power than ego is to latch onto spiritual support for your work—what we all need so much.

Loving ourselves is how we become ourselves. Fear of loving ourselves is how, understandably but devastatingly, we may still be submitting to the abusive voices of the past. Thus, self-love will require the work of becoming assertive. We will no longer be prisoners of our past, but mutineers in it. Our practice will be to stand up for ourselves, proclaim our valid place in the world, our equal standing in the human family. Indeed, loving ourselves is more than just self-care or liking our own company. Self-love is actually a giant step in the direction of our own full emergence.

Loving ourselves began in early life easily and naturally when our full identity was welcomed not stunted, shown unconditional positive regard not shaming or judging. Self-love resulted from such lovingkindness, our birthright, our due. Our self-love now is a mirror of the love that identified us as lovable. It was and is being enriched by every person who loved or loves us. Thanks to our practice, we join in that recognition of our worth, our right to be ourselves, and our unconditional lovability. The wonderful thing is that belief is all it takes for these three to become real: When we believe we are worthy, we are. When we believe we have a right to be ourselves, we have it. When we believe we are lovable, we are.

> The part of us that wants to become is fearless.
> —JOSEPH CAMPBELL

Befriending Our Shadow Side

Our life began with connection. Our survival depended on the approval of our caregivers. When we noticed that certain behaviors or personality traits were not approved, we repressed or disavowed them. Our need for connection took precedence over our need for individuality, for our full emergence. It was not only our negative traits that went into hiding. Sometimes our wonderful gifts and talents were scoffed at or discredited, and they too had to be concealed for the sake of safety and security.

We do not realize how much goodness, how much talent, how much love is in us. We also do not realize how selfish, greedy, or mean we can be or are. There is an "iron curtain" of unconsciousness separating us from our full selves. But it lifts easily when we acknowledge that we may possess any human quality, both positive and negative. In that sense, to accept that we can be like the best or worst human we know is a way of seeing our connection to all humanity. As we bring our dark side into the light, we feel kinship with all beings—a giant step toward love.

Since our psyche keeps yearning for wholeness, our shadow seeks ways to let us know about itself, our self. An inherent drive toward self-emergence opens the door of our inner life and urges it into the light of awareness. This is why our shadow side appears in dreams. In its negative form, it sometimes appears as a monster or a wild, out-of-control character. We may also dream of characters who are much more virtuous or talented than we believe we can be. These figures, usually of our own gender, may be pointing to shadow qualities that are ready to emerge into consciousness. They are usually not to be taken literally; they are symbols of useful but still-veiled strengths. Thus, dreaming of ourselves being aggressive might symbolize our need to be assertive, a healthy management of aggression. Dreaming of being a concert pianist might mean we wish to use our unique artistic talents that hitherto have been unrecognized or discounted.

Another way that our shadow reveals itself and tries to enter our consciousness is by projecting itself onto others. In other people, we see the traits that we cannot admit are in ourselves. As Jung said, "Projection makes the whole world a replica of our own unknown face."

Regarding the negative shadow, projection takes the form of strong *dislike* of someone. We are actually turning against the very traits that lie hidden within us but do not emerge so obviously as they do in the person we find repellent.

Positively, projection takes the form of strong *admiration* for someone. The qualities we marvel at in others are in us. They can be exactly the same characteristics or similar ones. They are in us, however, as potentials. In those we hold in awe, these potentials are activated. Ken Wilber wrote in *The Spectrum of Consciousness:* "We build pedestals out of our own potential." In other words, we deduct from our own powers by the excessive admiration we have for others.

To love ourselves means that we love all that we are, conscious and unconscious. To love ourselves means befriending our shadow, our unconscious side. To befriend means that we do not cancel or root out our negative characteristics; we come to terms with them. The more we trust them as useful, the more we discover their creative energies. Indeed, every negative shadow trait holds a kernel of value. For instance, we may acknowledge that we are controlling. Within that unacceptable trait is the ability to show leadership and organizational skills, the ability to get things done. The aggressive controlling tendency can be tamed and managed so that its central value, organizational and leadership skills, comes to the fore.

Every positive shadow quality indicates a potential in us that mirrors the person we admire. For example, we respect courage in others. This is a sign that we have courage waiting to be activated. We befriend our shadow as we begin to act more assertively, and gradually we awaken the bravery that is within us. We affirm a virtue and take the risks that help us put it into practice. It is then easy to love ourselves because of the courage we find in ourselves. This is an example of how befriending our shadow encourages self-love.

When we take back our projections of our own qualities from others, we find our secret self. Then we acknowledge more and more of ourselves just as we are, with no fear of what we may find out. The parts of us we project onto others are the ones we never learned to love in ourselves. Now we can.

When we see the shadow of ourselves and realize its origin in repression and fear, we love ourselves compassionately. Thus, love replaces fear. In addition, as we show ourselves as we are, we love ourselves more, because we notice that people are more impressed with our honest self-presentation than the mask we donned to please them.

An example of withdrawing our projections is when we feel envious of someone's success or skill and, based on our loving-kindness practice, we say, "I am happy for her." Gradually we will indeed be happy for her. Likewise, when we strongly dislike someone, we can say, "I believe he can be transformed." Gradually that will become our sincere wish. This also helps us see why learning not to give up on anyone helps us love more.

The psyche is like a compass. As a compass always points north no matter where we are, so the psyche is always pointing to our work no matter with whom we are or what we are facing. We encounter exactly the people and events that show us where our shadow waits for the light. That is an example of the assisting grace of synchronicity in our lives.

> There is some soul of goodness in things evil
> When men observingly distill it out.
> —WILLIAM SHAKESPEARE, *Henry V*

How Our Brain Helps

Recent brain research has made us more conscious of mirror neurons in the brain. *Neurons* are cells of the nervous system that give and receive signals neurochemically. Each cell is a system of energy and adapts to changes in its environment. Mirror neurons kick in when we see someone doing something, using a tool for example, and we automatically imitate the action. Our mirror neurons fire both when we observe a behavior and when we imitate it, hence the word *mirror*. Mirror neurons connect neural networks of perception and movement, so they help us with learning and remembering. When we imitate goal-oriented behavior, our prefrontal cortex is activated. This is the part of the brain that can remember how a behavior can be useful in the future.

Mirror neurons make it possible for us to see the world with the motor folds in our brain. We use the part of our brain that has to do with movement rather than cognitive learning. This might apply to spectator sports, where we actually learn to play the game we are watching. The same thing may happen at a play or film. Aristotle proposed that we feel pity and fear at a play. We can feel these for the actors and for ourselves. By the end, we experience a catharsis, a physical and emotional release, a resolution of conflict. By watching with mirror neurons firing, we are learning from the actors' behavior what works and does not work in human choices. The players on the gridiron and the actors on the stage are models, not just athletes and entertainers.

Mirror neurons also help with empathic attuning, so we can know what someone is feeling. By mirror neuronal connection, we can know the other from within ourselves rather than as an object outside ourselves. Then we can more easily attune to that person's feelings or pain and be compassionate.

Our bodies are wonderfully constructed to tell the story of love in our lives. They were sometimes held with kindly affection, sometimes battered with violence—both of which remain registered in our every cell. The positive messages make us ready for love or sometimes exaggerate our expectations of it from other adults. The negative messages take their toll on our love for ourselves and present their bill of self-reproach until we have processed and resolved them—which is difficult to achieve fully. Recent neurobiological research confirms that we store the memory of ancient betrayals and consequent self-negating messages mentally *and* somatically. Sooner or later, we realize that there is more pain from our childhood stored in our bodies than our adult mind can remember. This realization can foster compassion for ourselves.

The latest research on neuronal rewiring, however, shows that we can recode our patterns of beliefs and feelings. The brain can be reprogrammed to change a long-standing set of messages; its habitual coding is disabled, and a new code emerges. Modern science is helping us see that the neurochemical patterns in the brain by which we hold and process our emotions are elastic. They can be altered to work in favor of health, happiness, and personal growth. Negative self-talk can be reprogrammed by the practices we have been exploring. Our brain can help us love ourselves, though it is up to us to rewire it.

There is a direct connection between healthy early experiences and the development of the parts of the brain that help us live and love effectively. For instance, the insula (also called the insular cortex) is found in both hemispheres of the brain. It is part of the cerebral cortex and is involved in maintaining consciousness. In people who have had secure attachment experiences, especially in early life, the insula makes associations between the sense of self and feeling loved by others. It also regulates our bodily states and emotions and allows us to identify them. Our sense of being lovable is part of such self-awareness. This leads to trusting that all's right with the world, that good will triumph over evil, that things will work out somehow, that we will be able to deal with whatever happens. Thus, early loving embraces lead us to hold ourselves that way and to trust that we live in a world that holds us too.

Likewise, the prefrontal cortex develops when we receive the five A's in infancy. As a result, our ability to trust is installed, our self-esteem grows, we can handle our emotions, we can adjust expectations to fit reality, and we can deal with problems and predicaments efficiently. Prefrontal cortex development helps us maintain a sense of self and others at the same time, so we can take other people into account in our decisions and interactions. Thus, we can love more effectively. Both the insula and prefrontal cortex can help us trust ourselves and thereby live more serenely and confidently.

The prefrontal cortex does not mature fully until age twenty-five. Nature has arranged for us to have plenty of time to develop the circuits in our brains that make for such skills as self-soothing in the midst of anxiety and self-restoration after a crisis. In fact, throughout life, our brain retains its ability to create and restore neurons that rewire our circuitry beneficially. For instance, feeling loved generates endorphins that act on the reward/pleasure centers in our brain. This makes us more apt to love ourselves.

New neural pathways can thus replace the old superhighway of habit. A lifelong "I can't win" belief can become, with the same insistence and fervor, "I love to cooperate; it's the best way to win." "If people knew me as I really am, they wouldn't like me," can become "If people knew of the love inside me, they would want to bond with me." And "It's selfish to love myself," can turn into "The more I love myself, the more generous I become toward others." We can also lay down new pathways in our brain to increase our self-love by starting and ending each day with this affirmation, which is helpful at any time of day: "I am love in the form of [your name]."

In Henry Harlow's famous 1950s experiments, young monkeys separated from their mothers and paired with wire and terrycloth mannequins became autistic and socially fearful. When normally raised monkeys were introduced to them and continually cuddled them, they evolved from their self-centered, autistic style and began to trust. This transition from fear and isolation represented a rewiring of their brains as a result of behaviors associated with love. We are reminded of the biblical statement that true love casts out fear.

From an anatomical point of view, there is a lessening of activity in the amygdala, the primitive part of the brain that keeps us on guard and is overly alert to fearful stimuli. When we are loved, we feel safe and secure; the higher levels of endorphins and dopamine quiet the amygdala and thus offset primitive anxiety.

The amygdala is geared to identify danger, even if it is not real. This part of the brain is not nuanced and sophisticated but grossly survival-oriented. It bases its reactions on memories of past fearsome events rather than immediate reality. Thus, fear instantly arises, even when it is unnecessary. For example, an experience of being held too tightly in infancy so that we felt we might suffocate can evoke fears of engulfment when someone hugs us firmly in adult life. We might say that the amygdala cannot understand that what happened before won't necessarily happen again. It sees us as victims, because we were victims in the past. It is noteworthy that the amygdala has been shown to be larger than usual in children with an anxiety disorder.

The amygdala registers an angry word or face as dangerous, but the higher, rational centers of the brain do not. This happens because the survival instinct takes precedence over serenity. With our present understanding of the neural plasticity of the brain, we can learn ways to redirect our response to angry faces or hugs. In a way, this requires redirecting the whole course of a lifetime, which is why it takes a long time to free ourselves of irrational fears.

We must keep in mind that the entire limbic system is not a "bad guy." It is valuable in maintaining our emotional vitality and in providing immediate intuition about survival and pleasure. But since it can throw us off course, it requires a helper, so the cerebral cortex steps in to help regulate and redirect—which we all need from time to time.

Our Chemical Conditioning

The space between humans is like the synapses that transmit necessary chemicals between neurons. We might say that cells are social. Thus, relationships are important to our brain development, because they transmit information and feelings, or develop the brain itself.

Our parents attuned to our needs through the five A's. A partner or friend may do that for us now. Attunements give us a physical sense of being held lovingly. That sense of being loved, combined with security, makes us able to trust ourselves as lovable. This boosts our self-esteem and fosters a sense of safety and security within ourselves. The resultant self-trust is the same as self-love.

Our ability to love ourselves increases rapidly when we receive the five A's from someone in a reliable way. That will be the person who helps upgrade our sense of self in our prefrontal cortex so that self-doubt is no longer at the helm. Our healthy relationships can even work backward and make up for some of what we missed out on in the past. Thus, people are implicated in the conditioning of our brains, for better or worse. In primates (like us), the ratio of the size of the cerebral cortex to the rest of the brain will increase in direct proportion to the size of the social group. It is clear that our brain is connected to others for its full development, just like love itself.

Oxytocin is a hormone, a chemical released from a cell or gland that can affect other parts of the body. It is also a neurotransmitter, a chemical that transports communication between nerves. It promotes a sense of safety and security, the foundations of trusting. Oxytocin and vasopressin (another hormone) figure in bonding and affiliation, so they can help us be more open. Dopamine (a neurotransmitter) is associated with reward and pleasure, and it conveys safety and security.

Oxytocin makes us more likely to respond with a "calm down and make contact" style rather than the fight, flight, or freeze responses that happen when our cortisol (a stress hormone) kicks in. When we feel held, loved, and cared about, oxytocin flows and we relax. Our stressful feelings are regulated, and we can protect ourselves from any damaging impact our feelings might have on us. Thus, love from others has the power to protect us from stress by giving us a sense of equanimity as we face life's predicaments. We grow in self-confidence as we achieve that serenity. Self-confidence is a bridge to self-love.

A mother who knows how to regulate her own emotions helps her infant develop emotionally. She models how to find composure and how to recover after stress or a crisis. Her child learns this when held safely and securely in her arms. The mother knows how to restore her baby's equilibrium with her warmth, touch, and comforting words. The older child gets the same experience from her words of comfort and sometimes explanations about how the world and human psychology work. Still later, the grown adult learns to find it in self-soothing, self-loving practices.

When our early relationships lack the five A's or include abuse, our oxytocin receptors may not mature fully. Then it becomes difficult to trust others when we grow up. But it is never too late to rewire those receptors by being loved and cared about by other adults. Even one moment of oxytocin inflow can recode our brain. Perhaps this is what psychiatrist Rachel Naomi Remen was referring to in "Giving Darshan": "One moment of unconditional love may call into question a whole lifetime of feeling unworthy and invalidate it." This may be because the physiological element of love generates the release of oxytocin that lowers our hypothalamic-pituitary-adrenal cluster response, the underpinnings of stress.

> Healers in most traditions recognize that the power of love is the most potent healing force available. Effective healers from any culture are those who extend the arms of love, gratitude, acceptance, recognition, validation and acknowledgment.
>
> —ANGELES ARRIEN, "FOUR WAYS TO WISDOM"

PRACTICES

GIVING TO OURSELVES WHAT WE GIVE TO THOSE WE LOVE • This practice is best done using your journal. Begin by thinking of the person you love most in the world.

First, write what you want for this person. For instance, you want him to be happy, healthy, and continually advancing in personal growth, the three central goals of a wholesome, consciously evolving life.

Describe how you hold him in your heart. This includes what you feel about him, what you think of him, and what you admire in him.

Imagine how you would try to work things out with him if he were to hurt or disappoint you. Notice the extent to which you are willing to forgive him. To forgive is to let go of resentment and retaliation. To forgive opens the door to compassion that cannot exist in an atmosphere of resentment and retaliation. In his "Love Your Enemies" speech, Martin Luther King, Jr., said, "He who is devoid of the power to forgive is devoid of the power to love. It is impossible even to begin the act of loving one's enemies without the prior acceptance of the necessity, over and over again, of forgiving those who inflict evil and injury upon us."

Now list the ways you show love to your beloved. Make these entries specific. Include how you would or do go out of your way to be there for him.

Finally, how do you encourage him to be himself; to let his full self emerge; to show his qualities, interests, values, needs, wishes, and talents without shame or inhibition. This is the allowing element of the five A's.

The following list of questions summarizes these points:

What do I want for him?

How do I hold him in my heart?

How easily do I forgive?

How do I show love toward him?

How do I keep encouraging his full self-emergence?

Now take each of these responses, and ask if you treat yourself with equal affection. Make specific commitments to see yourself as you see your beloved, to act toward yourself as you act toward him, to be there for yourself as you are for him. Write these commitments in the form of affirmations in your journal; write them on a separate sheet of paper and place it where you can see it daily.

Finally, ask yourself how you can expand your love and attitude to show those same forms of love to others in your life. When we imagine there is only one special person, we lose sight of the fact that our love is a banquet table at which all can be welcome.

You may also want to think of the person who loves you most. Ask yourself these questions and write your responses in your journal:

What does she want for me?

How does she hold me in her heart? What is her opinion of me?

How does she handle my inadequacies?

How docs she show her love toward me?

How does she encourage my full self-emergence?

Now ask yourself if you are showing appreciation for her love, or if there is something you both need to work out.

Apply what you gain from this part of the practice to how you can love others more.

ADDING A TAIL TO OUR TALE • We can adopt a kind attitude toward our life story. We can learn to hold our disturbing memories, regrets, and mistakes without letting them pull us into despair or push us into guilt or shame. Our stressful or pessimistic memories can be given calming or optimistic add-ons, or "tails."

We actually began using this technique in fourth grade when we learned the times tables. We always said, "Four times four is sixteen." We did not say, "Four times four is . . ." without adding the tail "sixteen." This practice made the answer stick in our mind as a unit, not a separate question and answer. In fact, it is impossible now to think "four times four" without its permanently attached tail of "sixteen." We can use this same skill in working with our memories.

Here is an example of adding a tail to a thought when we have boundary issues with how much someone asks of us: "I make myself available in any way I can for her, *and* I let go of having to be sure it comes out right for her." Here, we show our original concern but with the addendum about letting go. Thus, our concern is followed by release from being overly responsible for someone.

We used complete statements for the times tables, but psychologically we often learned only half-statements. In the preceding example, we learned that it was important to give but also that giving has to happen within boundaries.

Using the same add-a-tail technique, we can also alter the impact of our negative memories by joining them to positive memories. When a negative memory arises in our mind, we can add on something positive. For example, we may recall our father blaming us for something, but we make sure we also recall him (or any father figure) praising or caring about us. We make it a practice to recall a positive example every time we recall an instance of blame. The original regretful memory will soon come with its complementary tail every time. We will have added a caboose to our train of thoughts.

With this practice, every coin in our psyche is now valuable, because it contains both heads and tails. As the positive message becomes more prominent, it gradually infuses the negative message with positive tones. Then the negative material is reconsolidated as neurochemically positive in our brain.

Here is another way this practice can work. Pause and savor positive experiences, especially examples of the five A's that you receive. Gradually, you will build a storehouse of positive memories. Use them to heal past memories by inserting them into any critical voice or negative story from your past. Now you can hold what was originally archived in a new way. For instance, whenever you recall being told you would never amount to anything, you recall a friend's compliment about the good work you are doing now. In this way, the old message is drowned out with new and more positive information. You say, "That judgment of me turned out not to be true, as the recent record shows. Mother said I would not amount to anything, but my friend Harry showed me otherwise." Try to say this to yourself with no resentment toward or blame of your parents or whoever instilled the original negative message in your mind. All that matters now is that you love yourself and everyone enough to upgrade your mutual story.

We now understand that neural plasticity is possible through the power of our thoughts and choices. The more time we spend on any one negative focus, thought, or emotion, the more power we give it in our brain circuitry. As a result, our brain requires less effort in running that program. It becomes a default setting, an easy port in any storm. As we redirect our thoughts and feelings positively, we notice new programs awakening in our mind. Along these lines, we may recall that in Romans 12:2, Saint Paul said, "Be transformed by the renewing of your mind."

To appreciate the brain chemistry in this exercise, consider this: The hippocampus stores explicit memories but is open to new learning experiences all through life. It upgrades itself with each new experience. For example, I don't have to keep fearing that I won't know how to use my new computer once I notice that I am actually learning to use it more effectively day by day.

The amygdala's memory is enduring, generalizing anything to a similar original negative event or experience. It does not upgrade easily. We might say that it thrives on obedience to entrenched memories. When it signals danger, we cower, which reinforces its hold on us. Our work is to bring the amygdala's messages to the intelligent realizations of the prefrontal cortex.

The hippocampus upgrades itself continuously as it receives new information. We reinforce its assistance when we add a caboose to the old memories and messages. I use this analogy because the original function of the caboose was to afford a safe space to the train's crew. From the caboose, they were able to disembark and inspect the train, its cargo, and its equipment. The crew decorated the caboose with personal objects, such as photos of their families. So it is a meaningful analogy for how the psyche finds its own safety, keeps itself moving, and cherishes its past. It also recalls the journey archetype, the central focus of every human life.

A personal memory is not static and unalterable like a times table. A life story memory is plastic and porous according to its connection to the circumstances in which we are recalling it. Thus, we may use this practice to reconstruct an incomprehensible or traumatic memory and make it work for us in the moment. This would be like telling the story of Snow White to a child who is frightened by the witch with the poisoned apple. We help calm her when we add that this is Snow White's way of warning all of us of the danger of taking fruit or candy from strangers. We have added a tail to the tale that shows a caring connection from the heroine to us. Every character in the story of our lives can do that for us.

Loving ourselves is loving our story, our memories, and our personality. Each is unique and has contributed to making us individuals. Today the emphasis, especially among young people, is on electronic connection, whether it involves computers, cell phones, or iPads. Love is indeed connection, but this kind of connection can alienate us from who we really are. We are dodging the time alone that is required to get to know ourselves. We love through connection, but we individualize through solitude. If we lack the long interludes of solitude and silence that go into people-making, we may lose access to our own identity. Then how can we love ourselves?

AFFIRMING THE FIVE A'S • We can apply the five A's to the events that have happened and continue to happen to us. This has a spiritual dimension, since it leads to trusting that the universe is somehow helping us love ourselves. The following affirmations can be helpful no matter what situation you face:

> Everything that happens to me gives me an opportunity to pay attention to myself.

> Everything that happens to me gives me an opportunity to accept myself.

Everything that happens to me gives me an opportunity to appreciate myself.

Everything that happens to me gives me an opportunity to care for myself.

Everything that happens to me gives me an opportunity to be free.

I am thankful that everything that happens to me gives me an opportunity to love myself.

These same affirmations can be used by partners in a relationship:

Everything that happens in our relationship gives us an opportunity to pay more attention to one another.

Everything that happens in our relationship gives us an opportunity to accept one another on a deeper level.

Everything that happens in our relationship gives us an opportunity to appreciate one another more.

Everything that happens in our relationship gives us an opportunity to show more affection to one another.

Everything that happens in our relationship gives us an opportunity to honor one another's freedom.

We are thankful that everything that happens in our relationship gives us an opportunity to love one another with more caring, compassion, and joy.

> No form of love is wrong, so long as it is love, and you your-self honor what you are doing.
>
> —D. H. Lawrence

3

Our Need to Be Loved

We are spiritual beings who need love as much as we need food. . . . Survival of the Most Loving is the only ethic that will ensure not only a healthy personal life but also a healthy planet.

—Bruce H. Lipton

WE WERE BORN WITH FOUR WORDS engraved on our bodies and in our hearts: Love me, hold me. We always knew they were in us, though we may not have had permission to say them out loud. Now we may be looking for the one or ones who can read and understand the words without our having to say them out loud. We may be asking and receiving a no. Or we may have given up on finding someone we can trust to give or even understand those four little words.

Our first experience of being loved leaves an imprint. That defining moment will, ever after, be what love feels like to us. Our original experience of being loved becomes our personal way of reading and *needing* love for the rest of our lives.

An example of a core imprint of feeling loved is being accompanied, having a backup, someone who stays with us through thick and thin. Staying is certainly a way to show love, but in the mature version, we see it as flexible, happening sometimes, missing the mark sometimes, not constant but reliable overall.

It is important for us to keep in mind that our original way of being loved might have included a negative element as well. The one who loved us so strongly in childhood might also, for instance, have been overly possessive or controlling. These traits are the opposite of the allowing component of healthy love. Now we may perceive control or possessiveness in an adult partner as indicators of love. Likewise, we ourselves may be possessive or controlling toward those we love, such as our children. We imbibe and then model both sides of the caring connection, light and dark. It will be up to us to detect the subtle shadow side of love in ourselves and others—no small task. (We find help for this work in the "Befriending Our Shadow Side" section of Chapter 2.)

As an aside, a parent who cares about her child wants him to grow up, to move from dependency to greater independence with every passing year. As long as a parent includes possessiveness and control in her love, a child's launching out into the world will be a serious threat to her. Such a parent will feel a disconnect, an abandonment, and a grim loss when the child flies the nest. This same parent may attempt to keep the adult child dependent in other ways, such as monetary indebtedness to her or her need for constant caretaking. This parent's love has become synonymous with maintaining dependency, that is, it has not become adult.

Another problem in an adult relationship may be that we will settle for nothing less than that special childhood way of being loved by our partner—without letting her know what we need. To expect an adult partner to come through as absolutely reliably as Grandma did can keep us tied to a child's version of being loved.

Speaking of Grandma, I recall that when she made eggplant parmigiana, she baked a separate little batch, just for me, with only Parmesan cheese on top, because she knew I did not like mozzarella. I think back and realize it was another way she had of making me feel special, this time by remembering and honoring my preferences. In that separate Pyrex casserole dish, I saw more than eggplant. It was love. I got myself in trouble later in life when I turned Grandma's way of loving me into an expectation. Future women were to pay similar homage to my special predilections. It did not take long to get my comeuppance and learn that the world didn't revolve around me anymore. And it is also good to know that now I can make my own eggplant just the way I want it.

The issue here is that we all want love, so we may manipulate others into serving it to us in the ways "Grandma" did. To use a reverse example, if we experienced love by having things given to us, we might learn to act in ways that manipulate people into giving us what we want now. This can often be confusing to the ones we love. For instance, we may not give to others until we are given the things we want. We will seem stingy when we are simply trying to feel loved by getting others to give and not expect as much in return. Comeuppances will certainly follow that attitude. When we learn from them, we grow and change. When we dig our heels in and hold on to our existing beliefs, we wind up alone.

Finally, our need for love is reflected in the gods and helpers we choose to believe in. Bodhisattvas keep coming back for our enlightenment. Angels stay by our side to guard us. God creates the world for us. Christ dies for us. Humans have always had a need for the love, accompaniment, and protection of transcendent sources. This love is caring to a heroic and reliable extent; the accompaniment is connection even if unseen; the protection is safety and security beyond what humans can offer. These are the deepest longings in our hearts. We want them from human and divine sources—which we ultimately realize are all one.

In Buddhism, Jizo Bodhisattva is honored as an enlightened saint who understands with great compassion how hard it is for us to let go of our attachments and find contentment. These are the vows he makes for our sake. They show the heroic and loyal love we hope for:

Only after all beings reach enlightenment will I myself realize it. Only after the Hells are empty am I willing to enter full enlightenment.

—Jizo Bodhisattva

We notice a similar vow from someone in the Christian tradition:

I asked for the grace of not entering Paradise until all my spiritual children have entered first.

—Padre Pio

How We Know We Are Loved

In an episode of the television series, *All in the Family,* the neighbor Louise is moving away and has come to say good-bye to Edith. As they stand in the kitchen together, Edith touchingly asks Louise if she ever told her that she loved her. Louise answers, "In every minute of every hour we've ever spent together." It is not only when we are being told or shown affection that we know someone loves us. Love comes through to us in the other's every word and deed.

The two best ways to have others love us are to love them unconditionally and to be ourselves transparently. Both of these qualities appeared in the characters of the two women in the television series.

Love can't be overlooked; it can't be hidden. We will know when we are loved. It will feel like a welcoming. Being loved awakens the secret inner core of our self and tells it that it is safe to come out. We know we are loved when we can let our guard down because we know we are permitted to be ourselves, no matter how numerous our faults. The more supported we feel, the more we learn the art of self-support. We can appraise our traits and choices in kindly ways, see dangers as opportunities to evolve, and feel confident about handling whatever may happen to us. This is self-regulation: we are no longer overwhelmed by emotions or circumstances. Being loved thereby contributes to our equanimity.

Our ongoing contact with those we love contributes to our confidence that we have value and that our life has meaning. Being loved helps us preserve our trust that we live in a world in which our deepest needs and longings can be fulfilled. This is why we feel such panic at the prospect of being rejected or feeling isolated. Rejection and loss trigger the same circuits in the brain as physical pain.

Turning to others for fulfillment is not a sign that there is something wrong with us, nor is it a regression to childhood. Our problems arise when we expect *all,* rather than *some,* of our fulfillment to come from other adults.

We then overlook two important facts of life. First, some of what we need is in ourselves, nature, spirituality, career, and other sources beyond individuals. Second, the existential reality is that all human experience and relating is limited. Our deepest needs may never find adequate fulfillment. It is a given that life and people are unsatisfactory in many ways. A yes to this makes us less likely to complain when we do not receive all the fulfillment we seek. We then let the imperfect be alright with us, including our imperfect selves.

The one who loves us does not kill our demons for us; he stands watch at the mouth of the dragon's cave while we go in to face it. From that position, he pays close attention to our battle. He shouts encouraging words to cheer us on. He knows we have to struggle on our own, but he will not let us be destroyed. And he is there when we come out. This is what a parent-child bond, a friendship, or an intimate relationship can be. Sometimes love's leap means simply standing very still. As John Milton said, "They also serve who only stand and wait."

Those who loved us in childhood cherished our uniqueness and encouraged its evolution rather than manipulating it. At the same time, they respectfully shone a revealing light on us when we betrayed our potential. This feels like, and is, love: caring comfort combined with caring challenge—just what we need to develop early on and evolve all through life.

Feeling loved can only happen when we believe we are worthy of it. For some of us, not feeling loved may have become the standard, as if it were justified because we were undeserving. To have accepted that predicament as suitable became the equivalent of a lifelong belief that we were not really lovable or worthy of the five A's. Here are some behaviors we may have learned to help us cope with feeling unlovable:

- We learned to use posturing as our way of garnering *attention* and *acceptance*. If it did not work, it at least made us look independent, and we could hide our vulnerability.
- We sought *appreciation* by focusing on skill, prowess, and accomplishment, always believing that only doing, not just being, could work for us.
- We later identified the *affectionate* holding we so desperately needed with sexual activity or addiction.
- We gave up on being *allowed* to make our own choices and went to the extremes of either rebellion or submission.

A child excitedly shows his mother what he made at school. He says, "Look at me; see what I did." He means, "Love me." We know this because he is asking for the five A's: "Pay attention to me; accept me; appreciate what I have done; show affection; and allow me to go on doing this without interference or interruption."

Love is a mystery so it can't ultimately be limited only to the five A's. Some people just aren't built to show love so openly. Indeed, most of us did not consistently receive the five A's in childhood from one or both parents. Yet we realize that our parents did love us nonetheless. The love came through in ways that were perhaps more inconspicuous than demonstrative, more indirect than engaging, more practical than emotional. So we knew they cared about us—in their own way.

PRACTICES

HOW WAS I LOVED? • There were moments in our childhood when we needed one or more specific A's. For instance, we came home from school and told our mother that the kids made fun of us. In that moment, we needed her to hold us with affection. We needed to be assured of her acceptance of us. We needed to be valued rather than ridiculed. We wanted to be told that to know us was to love us.

Recall specific times in your own childhood when you felt a need for one or more of the five A's and ask yourself, "Was my need honored and mirrored in that moment? How did my caregivers fulfill or fail my acceptance moment, my attention moment, and so forth?"

British child psychiatrist D. W. Winnicott said that mirroring, or attunement to our feelings, is the equivalent of physical holding. How were your feelings received? How safe did you feel in showing them?

Recall specific need-moments in past or present relationships, and ask yourself the same question about the fulfill-or-fail response. This will, of course, elicit a whole spectrum of responses, some fulfilling or some failing.

When we were ignored, neglected, or abused in childhood, we may have numbed our feelings or dissociated from what was happening. That made sense at the time, because we had so few options and no escape. Write in your journal about whether and how you notice yourself reverting to those types of behavior in your present relationships or any stressful situation. Write a note to yourself affirming that you were wise to go numb in the past. Make a commitment not to go numb in the present but to interpret the inclination to do that as a signal of what is missing or problematic in your relationships now: "I went numb when I was not seen, so if I go numb now, it may mean that I feel I am not being seen. I will open a dialogue about that with the person who seems not to see me."

Ask your present partner or a friend to tell you about the times when he or she needed you for an A moment and about how you responded. Listen with your heart so you can respond without ego-defensiveness. Make a commitment to being aware of others' needs so you can step up to the plate for a partner or family member or friend with an A+ response. Pay closer attention to your own needs so you can come through for yourself with an A+ too.

From now on, find ways to let others know very directly what you need from them. Because it is grounded in the present moment, mindfulness as aware and reality-based communication is the language of our true nature. It has never been damaged by trauma, nor can it be silenced by our negative experiences. Mindfulness helps us identify our thoughts and feelings for what they are. We can bring that style of practice to our relationships and foster a wholesome assertion of our truth to others.

Finally, ask yourself if the people you believe love you today generally meet the following criteria. No one will meet them perfectly, but being able to recall some instances of them is certainly revealing about how much or whether someone loves you:

- They consistently give and can receive the 5A's: attention, acceptance, appreciation, affection, and allowing.
- They genuinely care about your welfare.
- They feel joy at your successes.
- They are there for you in good times and bad.
- They give you a sense of safety and security when you are together.
- They joyfully join you in and encourage your enthusiasms.
- They find you lovable when they see your vulnerability and never take advantage of it.
- They do not respond to your love or generosity as permission to be "takers" or to absorb your energy.
- They are respectful of your limits of responsiveness to their needs and accept the kind and amount of love you offer rather than demand more or resent you for offering too little.
- They do not base their love for you on exchange. (Reciprocity is important in close relationships. But a person who loves you does not keep track of how much you give him compared to what he gives you: "After all I did for you, you should at least do this for me." An expectation like that is about owing and being owed. The generosity of love is missing. When someone loves you, he gives of himself with no cost to you.)

- They always want the best for you and always want you to be happy even if, in a relationship, that means letting you go because you chose someone else as a partner.

CHILDHOOD'S INFLUENCE • We know we are resolving our childhood issues when we become less needy, attract a healthier level of partner than before, and have fewer expectations of partners or relationships.

Ask yourself these three searching questions:

1. What forms of love did I receive in childhood and now seek from others? This question leads us to appreciate our parents for what they did provide. It also leads us to grieve for what was missing and let go of blaming them for their deficiencies or neglect.* Then we become more adult, because we are fulfilling the inner urge that all humans were born with: to go on a heroic journey, to move on rather than stay stuck. Where we are is not our fate. It is where we can best begin the journey.

2. How have I given this love to myself? This question leads us to find ways to take care of ourselves. We will pay attention to our bodies, our feelings, and our needs instead of minimizing them or demanding that others fulfill them. This gives us a sense of agency, or ability, skill, and power, in our own lives. We become more adult because we take care of ourselves as parents or partners of ourselves. As we become successful in fulfilling our needs, we can ask others to join us, but we no longer ask them to "do it for us."

3. What forms of love have I been giving to others as a way of showing them what *I* want most? This question shows us how difficult it is to present our deepest vulnerability, our need for others. We may have been afraid to ask for what we needed directly from a partner, so we showed it by example. We gave to others what we wanted from them, hoping they would follow suit. That can change to a practice of asser-

---

* My book, *When the Past Is Present: Healing the Emotional Wounds that Sabotage Our Relationships* (Shambhala Publications, 2008), has practices that can help in this area.

tiveness in which we present our needs to another openly yet without demand or manipulation. This is showing what we want without embarrassment or manipulation.

As we become more willing to be vulnerable, we can accept the fact that some people can and will join us in fulfilling our needs, and others cannot or will not. We accept the former with gladness and let go of making demands on the latter, without blame. We do not abandon them, only reconcile ourselves to their limits. We have become mature enough to accept what we have no control over and still ask for what we want.

When we have no voice because we do not speak up for ourselves, we create a vacuum. Controlling people steps right into that space if we are not careful. The archetype of the predator is part of the controlling style.

These three questions and the three practices that follow from them result in a new way of seeing current or prospective partners. They are no longer the be-all and end-all of need fulfillment. They reduce from giants to life-size, even pygmy-size sometimes. They drop down to a lower position in the lineup of resources for love. We no longer desperately seek the one who gives love in that special way that rings our bell just right. We no longer give any man or woman that much—too much—power. Now we are first in line. Those we trust because they have never failed us come next. The third place is for a partner. That person moves up in line as the record shows he or she is trustworthy, but we are never supplanted from first position. Self-love is first in loving-kindness practice and in psychology.

As we reconfigure our lineup so that self-love happens more and more, we may notice something very gratifying. We begin to take better care of ourselves. Little preferences begin to shift. We start enjoying and preferring juice over soft drinks. We give up substances and behaviors that can harm our health. We love our bodies. We stay away from people who hurt us. When we notice an attractive person, we simply appreciate what we see without sorrow that we don't possess him or her. We love our peace of mind.

SHE LOVES ME, SHE LOVES ME NOT • As we learn to love ourselves more, the reactions others have toward us no longer carry as much weight. We appreciate those who choose us, like us, and love us. We notice those who do not, but we are not devastated by them. Our emphasis is no longer on how people see us or what can make them want us, but only on how we can grow in integrity and loving-kindness in all our dealings with them.

In the childhood game of picking the petals from a daisy, we said, "She loves me," in the same tone of voice as, "She loves me not." Only at the last petal did our voice change to a jubilant or somber tone. Can we extend our equanimity now in adulthood to all the choices others make about us, whether for more closeness or less? Can we become witnesses of others' acceptance or rejection, mindfully observing without becoming devastated or overexcited either way? To do that perfectly would be a lot to ask of ourselves as ordinary humans, but we can practice moving in that direction by becoming more accepting of the choices made for or against us by others. We can take the givens of acceptance and rejection in stride. They do not have to influence our mood quite so much—though great jubilation and grief are always legitimate when appropriate to the circumstances.

Our statements might then sound like this:

- Now she likes me and wants to be with me, and I appreciate and enjoy that.
- Now he does not want to be with me, so I release him with love and am open to what may happen.
- I accept that people have reasons I don't always understand or am not allowed to know. I say yes to this given of uncertainty.
- What role did I play in this, especially if it has been a pattern between other people and me?

This practice can only work when our ego is tamed enough not be aroused or affronted by other people and their choices. We then break the connection between "They don't like me" and the sense of insult because "I deserve to be liked and loved by everyone." We are not destabilized by a rejection. We have learned to hold that experience with equanimity and without a sense of personal injury—in other words, without ego. *Such letting go of ego is healthy self-love.* We become witnesses, not victims. We can use the analogy of watching a movie: When I watch a movie, I am a witness of what the characters are doing. I have feelings, but I keep my seat, and I don't try to influence or interfere in their behavior. I look for how the unfolding story can be entertaining on its own.

This practice won't work if we still have not let go of the need to retaliate: "I'll show her! I won't call her either." Or "His relationship with his new partner failed, so I gloat in triumph. He got what was coming to him." Instead we might say, "I feel genuine compassion, because in loving-kindness practice, I have trained myself to want everyone to be happy."

We may feel we have been disrespected when the other person silently withdraws with no explanation. The silent treatment is a choice for disconnection, the opposite of love. That can hurt, but with this practice, we no longer become distraught. We no longer ask, "Why is she doing this?" or "How dare he do this to me?" Instead we say, "This feels like disrespect, and I can say, 'Ouch!'" We can also say, "This is a loss, and I need to grieve. In this way, I diminish the power of rejection to stress me. I take it in stride and find ways to deal with its sting. The more comfortable I am with myself, the less affected or injured I am by what others do, say, or think of me. I am thankful for this result of letting go of my ego entitlement."

We will be referring to the exclamation *Ouch!* throughout the rest of this book. A healthy "Ouch!" is a cry of pain. It can be followed or happen simultaneously with an expression of anger, defined as showing our displeasure at what we believe is unfair. A healthy "Ouch!" represents anger without the will to retaliate, without resentments, without blame, without holding a grudge—anger with an ultimately forgiving spirit. A healthy "Ouch!" does not include such ego arousals as "How dare you treat *me* that way? I will get you for this." We are basically saying, "This hurts," which is our experience, not "You hurt me," which is accusatory and can open the door to punishment of the other person.

We can also practice becoming lightning rods as we respond to people and events. We fully allow our feelings to happen, imagining them flowing safely through our bodies, from head to toe, then going into the ground. We remain grounded, no longer thrown off course by events or by our reactions to them. We do this because we love ourselves and honor our three wholesome priorities: our health, our happiness, and our personal growth.

In the instance in which a family member or friend, without explanation, does not return calls, does not want to see us, or refuses to talk to us, we contribute to our equanimity with the following Respect Choice practice:

1. We make one attempt to connect.
2. We feel our grief as mentioned earlier. We don't speculate on why this is happening.
3. We compassionately include the person in our loving-kindness practice.
4. We do not react in kind.

We may be open to reconnecting if the other initiates it, in which case, we can ask for an explanation.

Finally, it is normal to speculate and wonder why someone wants to be with us often at first and later wants to see us only once in a while if at all. Emily Dickinson, in "The murmuring of bees has ceased" states, "As accent fades to interval / With separating friends . . . we speculate."

Our practice then is to notice our speculations, identify them as thoughts, and let them go rather than trying to deny, silence, or entertain them. Gradually our conjectures, all forms of "Why?" fade to "Yes to my not knowing why." Then all that matters is that our self-respect and generous love keeps us from hurting others in the same way.

WHEN THE ONE WHO LOVED US DIES • We can be aware of two styles of grief: lamenting and accepting. The grief of *lamenting* that someone is gone is for the loss of how that person loved us. We are disconsolate because now there is a hole in our life.

We experience radically *accepting* grief when we mourn the person's passing while reconciling ourselves to a lower dividend of love in our lives. We accept this with an unconditional yes, a radical acceptance. This leads us to a wonderfully consoling realization: We can imitate the person's ways of loving us and give them to ourselves. We notice that his love is working within us as part of our love for ourselves. We still miss his love, but we are not so utterly bereft as in pure lamentation. Our grief is a beautiful nostalgia for his specialness and a tender gratitude that we had him in our lives as long as we did—and now carry him inside us. The poet Sir Philip Sidney said it well: "My true love has my heart and I have his."

Acceptance with an unconditional yes is a useful practice when we experience any loss, such as when we find that our age prevents us from doing as much as we once did, getting the kind of job we once had, or attracting the partner we had hoped for. We can lament, or we can accept the given of change with the yes that includes reconciling ourselves to less. That will open the door to new kinds of "more."

Lamenting, ironically, is a grief that keeps someone totally absent from us. Acceptance keeps the gift of love the lost one has given alive in our hearts, and it now works in us as a way of keeping him alive in a touching and enduring way.

Does Someone Who Abuses Us Really Love Us?

We so need connection that when we know someone loves us, we may become willing to put up with some hurts. However, abuse is never legitimate. Love cannot be real when it includes abuse, which breaks the caring connection or shows it was never there to begin with. To most of us, connection matters more than happiness, which might cause us to tolerate abuse even though it is never deserved or appropriate, no matter what the provocation.

Occasional mild abuse in childhood is complex and does not have to represent a lack of love. Severe, unremitting abuse can never be an expression of love. To believe that a parent loved us "deep down" all the time he was abusing us does not make sense. It lets a perpetrator off the hook and keeps us in the victim role. Abuse can be physical, emotional, or sexual.

We may hold on to the opinion that Dad did love us anyway, because that belief dulls the impact of his cruelty toward or humiliation of us. Our endurance of his abuse can also be dangerous, in that it can legitimate the violence we were required to tolerate. The "love" in a parent is real only if it comes with accountability toward the child. Love is not abstract. Believing this requires freeing ourselves from Plato's view that there is a realm of reality made up of pure and abstract forms and sentiments. That view doesn't apply to love. Love doesn't exist in some vague, disembodied never-never land.

When we are grounded in adult reality, *love* as an abstract noun is insufficient and, indeed, impossible. Love is real when it is consistently respectful and repeatedly shown in actions that demonstrate caring connection. Violation is hurt no matter what the presumed underlying "sentiment" or how much it was meant "for our own good." A cruel father does not love us as long as he is cruel. If we add, "He was sick," we really mean he was too sick to love us. When we honor that distinction, we gain the wisdom to see that love is real only when it looks like love, acts like love, and feels like love all over.

How I myself let my own parents off the hook all these years came through to me this week. With an Italian family background, I watched an Italian movie with a non-Italian friend. The main character, a twelve-year-old boy, is slapped around by his father throughout the film. I saw this as no big deal, since it reminded me of my own upbringing and was certainly considered legitimate in our Italian-American culture. Our immigrant, working-class parents did not have child-rearing skills; they simply repeated what had been done to them in their own childhood. I chalked up the abuse in the movie to culture and inadequacy of parenting skills. I saw the beatings, sometimes severe, as harmless because they were not malicious, as excusable because "that is how it was back then." The abuse was shown in a quasi-comic way, with no indication of any actual harm. This showed me that perhaps the director himself was excusing the child abuse, especially since he also made sure to show that the father ultimately loved his son.

Watching the movie, I took all this in stride. But my friend, also a therapist, showed me I was justifying behavior that is not right no matter what the culture. This helped me see how I had been excusing my own, often abusive parents. Each of us can benefit from asking ourselves if we are making such excuses and how. We may still be afraid that if we admit our parents did not always love us, or love us at all, we will be orphans—a worse fate than living with the truth.

Finally, most rooms in the house in the film had a crucifix on the wall. For those of us brought up with a crucifix facing us at home and in church, we have to wonder about what might have been registering in our bodyminds as we looked at it. Yes, we were taught to believe it showed how much Christ loved us. But it might also have been saying something more sinister: "This is what a father is allowed to do to you when he loves you."

The same message might have come through to us from the Hebrew Bible story of Abraham being willing to sacrifice his son, Isaac, since God asked him to do so. At the last minute, God reversed his order. The father was asked by the Father to perform the grisly deed, because both were believed to have power over life and death.

Our self-confidence in adult life is directly proportional to our ability to allow ourselves to have clarity on this crucial topic. As long as we let our abusers off the hook, we cannot come into our full power as people. We are still tied to a loyalty that allows others to hurt us with impunity, whether that other is a parent on earth or a Parent in the sky.

When we are brought up with abuse on a regular basis, we lose sight of alternatives: "This is all there is, and I have to endure it." This makes sense in childhood. In adulthood, if someone is abusing us at home or work, we have other options: "This is not acceptable, and I don't have to take it anymore."

We may love those who hurt us as Desdemona did in Shakespeare's *Othello*:

> His unkindness may defeat my life,
> But never taint my love.

That love can be noble and show a spiritual commitment to loving-kindness and compassion. It never justifies abuse, however, so our best response is to run for cover and not come back until it is safe to do so—which Desdemona did not do and paid with her life. Love becomes codependency when we stay and endure. Then our affection is misguided and misdirected. Real love from us to others never puts us or keeps us in danger.

If we adapted ourselves to a childhood in which our little hearts or bodies were plundered, we can still survive. But we pay later, because our adaptation to that atmosphere interferes with our healthy development. In psychological evolution, the "survival of the most loved" is a more accurate phrase than "survival of the fittest."

When we are abused, we are in the world like the frightened and defenseless villagers menaced by the dragon, not as Saint George with sword in hand. However, after he slayed the dragon, he cut it up and served it as food to the villagers so they could absorb the dragon's power and never need a rescuer again. This story is symbolic of how we sometimes need help and that the best help makes us more capable and apt to help ourselves.

Therapy is an important option along these lines. Appendix 2 of this book offers a questionnaire that can help in deciding whether therapy might be useful for you. The healthier you become the more effective is your love for yourself and others.

The practices in this book can help us to grow beyond our past. So can a spiritual program. But even in conjunction with therapy, self-help, and reliance on spirituality, it is a long and tedious journey. Yet we know, no matter what the roadblocks or how long the path, that we can become independent enough to give love and interdependent enough to receive it.

We can trust an innate self-caring that helps us respond to a loss or lack of love. We can grieve, let go, forgive, and move on. The ability to mourn is a necessary skill in a world in which love is not always actualized, rejection and betrayal are always possible, and disappointments are certainly inevitable.

Our evolution as fully adult humans proceeds on a continuum of developmental tasks. When we are held and nurtured, we can face life's givens and adversities with courage. When our connection does not grant safety and security, our wounds may keep us from handling life effectively, even into adulthood. We all received conditional acceptance and enough love for sufficient development, since we have ample opportunities for connections throughout our life span. Much depends on childhood, but not everything.

We can still love our parents while being honest about their inadequacies. We can still believe they loved us. But it is important to acknowledge that when they were beating us, humiliating us, or hurting us, they were not loving us. They showed love on Monday when they acted lovingly toward us. They did not love us on Tuesday, when they hurt us.

Nonetheless, a loving bond can always begin or be revived, because the capacity to love remains intact. An abuser can change and show regret. He can make amends. All this helps the bond resurrect itself. Of course, it will take a surrender of ego on the abuser's part, a hard-won path but a transformative one all around.

PRACTICE: WHAT WE TOLERATE

Is the following statement familiar from childhood or from a present relationship? *If the caring connection is to last, I have to be on my best behavior.* The unspoken beliefs implied in this statement are as follows:

- There is no safety and security for me in this relationship.
- I lack a foundation for trust in this relationship.
- I have to appease this parent or partner.
- If I get on her wrong side, I am in trouble.
- I am always on guard here, never just hanging out as I am.
- I can never do enough for him or fully please him.
- I don't measure up; I am always lacking in some way.

These self-diminishing beliefs do not tell us how to behave, but they show us the reasons for saying, "Ouch!" and taking action for change. *Where do you stand in this?*

An intimate, caring connection is real when it is unconditional. If it includes a list of self-negations that contradict the five A's (like the preceding list), it is a connection but not a caring, let alone an intimate, one. A person whose early family life imposed the same list of beliefs is a sitting duck for a relationship with a bullying partner. *Is this happening to you?*

Part of healthy self-nurturance is protecting our delicately balanced hearts. We can steel ourselves to abuse, endure it, and thus *harden* our hearts, the very meaning of the Latin word from which we derive *endure.* This is like choosing to live in a dangerous part of a city where we have to watch our step every minute, stay on guard at all times, and never let down our defenses. We may succeed in remaining safe but at the cost of closing, rather than opening, our hearts. That is too high a price to pay when love is what matters. *What price are you paying to maintain the familiar relationships and lifestyle that go on hurting you?*

4

Neediness-Driven Drama versus Serene, Contented Love

What I needed most was to love and to be loved. I rushed headlong into love, eager to be caught. Happily I wrapped those painful bonds around me; and sure enough, I wound up being lashed with the red-hot pokers of jealousy, suspicions, fear, bursts of anger, and quarrels.

—SAINT AUGUSTINE

I love thee to the level of every day's
Most quiet need . . .

—ELIZABETH BARRETT BROWNING

WE SOMETIMES CONFUSE LOVE with finding a port in the storm of our own neediness. We may identify love with drama—a relationship full of volatility, hot-bloodedness, explosiveness, clinging, uncertainty, fear, and desire all at once. The intensity of drama can make it feel like we are loving deeply and enduringly. Dramatic desire can be confused with pity for someone, sexual desirability, or a promise of rescue. We might be so plagued by loneliness that we think the one who saves us from it is the one we love.

As an aside, there are many forms of loneliness. Two stand out: We can be lonely because we lack company or connection. This is boredom-based loneliness. We can also be lonely because we miss or fear to lose someone who is immensely important to us. This is fear-based loneliness. We feel ourselves sink into what feels like an irremediable powerlessness. Our safety and security is tied to someone who matters to us so much that we have no identity without that person.

This abandonment-loneliness is the scariest option for beings like us, who so passionately choose to stand alone but so poignantly require caring connection. The practice of embracing our bereftness—facing it head-on and letting it pass through us—can help us survive it. Then embracing our loneliness rather than trying to gain control of it or cancel it becomes an empowerment. Our practice of embracing, our yes to our loneliness, is our refuge and protection.

Fear-based loneliness can diminish or demolish our sense of self. It is terrifying to contemplate the prospect that we may not really be anybody, have no real identity or substance of any kind. Our fear of not being someone leads us to take control in every area of life. We imagine that if we are in control, we are definitely somebody. But someday we may realize that the control is all there is to our identity. So we are back where we started—no-self, as Buddha declared all along. To rest in that no-self as a spaciousness within, rather than to run from it into control, is freedom from fear.

We use the word *love* in this section. Neediness-driven love is not actually love but a dramatization of it. In the context of neediness, a mutual experience of safe and secure intimacy is impossible, even if some affection is shown. Neediness-driven love is like sugar; it is a food, but it's not good for us.

The healthy parent-child relationship is about needs and their fulfillment. There is a universal assumption built into that combination: our parents love us, and we love them. From our earliest days, we associate need fulfillment with love, whether or not they really happen together. In an adult relationship, when one of our needs is fulfilled, we may imagine that is all it takes for love to be present too. We needed our parents and could not always tell the difference between needing and loving. We may still mistake need for love.

If love was shown to us in a household that was full of chaos and uproar, we were most likely programmed into associating love with dramatic excess. This misprogramming makes only drama-drenched love seems authentic to us. Intellectually, we know this is not true, but knowing it does not liberate our bodies from its emotional mistake. The identification of love and stress has been lodged deep in our psyches and our cells. Here, *deep* means so hardwired into us that it is hard to dismiss. What we were taught can be relearned easily; what was conditioned into us requires long, difficult work to undo. Unconscious programs keep running in our bodyminds. Their undertows affect our choices and behavior until we become aware of them and take action to disengage from them. The practices in the previous chapters have helped us lay down new neural pathways that lead to such healthy disengagement.

Neediness thrives on internalized beliefs from childhood that feel like verdicts with no chance for an appeal. Here are some examples: "I don't matter." "I am invisible." "There is something wrong with me, and I don't know what it is, but everybody else does and it can't be fixed." Whenever a need possesses us, whenever it feels rigid and intractable, whenever we feel helpless in the face of it, it is usually about something unresolved from childhood.

As children, we often dealt with our parents' unresolved issues that were foisted on us. Since we did not yet have boundaries, we could not discriminate between what was theirs and what was only ours. Childhood magical thinking made it seem that it was appropriate for us to feel responsible for our parents' well-being, because we could not do what the healthy ego does and separate others' conflicts from our own.

The familiar messages from our parents can make it seem as if we have a real bond with a partner if we are repeating our past with him or her. This is an insidious effect of internalized beliefs. We often stay in a relationship simply because it replicates our relationship with our parents or our parents' verdicts on us.

The events of childhood strike us the way a hammer strikes a bell. The vibration can last a lifetime, depending on how hard we were hit. We are not responsible for the strike nor fully for the choices that happen because of its ongoing vibration in our bodyminds. But we are responsible for the consequent choices we make.

As we mature in spiritual consciousness, contentment becomes more valuable than gratification. We prefer meditative moments to operatic acting out. Our happiness is in the equanimity of "green pastures and quiet waters" more than the stress of ongoing turbulence.

If we were brought up on drama, such serenity can seem boring and unappealing. We may not even know what it is or how good it feels, since all we have been exposed to is the stress based on continuous uproar, with no predictability or security. We may think that is how love in an adult relationship should be, because that is the way it happened in the house of those who certainly loved us.

A Frustrating Search

The natural sequence is to feel a need and to look for a way to fulfill it. A *need* is defined as a requirement for what seems necessary or useful. A need ends when fulfillment happens, and the result is contentment. For instance, I am hungry at lunchtime. I need to eat. One restaurant is closed, so I go to another. When I have finished lunching there, I am no longer hungry and I feel satisfied:

Need → fulfillment → satisfaction
or
Need → not fulfilled → look elsewhere → satisfaction

Sometimes, however, we feel not simply a need but neediness. Neediness is a desire without the capacity for fulfillment. It does not end in contentment like an ordinary need. In fact, it does not end at all, even when all the elements are in place that would ordinarily satisfy it.

A true need is for something outside ourselves. Neediness is a sign that we need *ourselves*, usually to give ourselves one of the five A's.

An ordinary need is a desire that may gnaw at us for satisfaction. Neediness is a form of pain, because it feels interminable. Thus, I am hungry for a snack at night, but when I eat it, I am still not satisfied. Four oatmeal cookies satisfy authentic hunger, but I am still looking for another snack, which again will not be enough—in fact, nothing will be:

Neediness → find what we wanted or close to it → remain unsatisfied → keep looking for more

The need was never for cookies, but for comfort in my loneliness and release from my boredom. Food easily steps in to those needs as a consolation prize.

Once we find what we need in ourselves, a shift happens in how we need others: we find that we may not need them quite so desperately. Working in reverse, we can say that desperation is a signal that we have not taken full advantage of all we have going for us within ourselves.

When we are needy for relationship, we may seek connection, but lacking the capacity for fulfillment, our approach to others can come across as clinging or aggressive. Our panicky neediness can have an insistent tone that sounds pushy, even intimidating, to the other. When we are needy, we may be crestfallen if the other does not love us. If the other does love us, we may find it difficult simply to appreciate it and hold it gently. We want to grab and cling, a style that will not go over well with a healthy adult with boundaries. So the other backs away.

It is often a losing game to seek someone who will love us, since that seems to work best when it happens on its own as we meet people in the ordinary course of life and work. It can also happen suddenly by synchronicity, a meaningful coincidence of our openness and the appearance of someone who takes to us. This is more likely to happen in a healthy way when we are open rather than needy.

Our needy search for love can become addictive when our way of relating to someone becomes dependent, clinging, possessive, insatiable, or volatile. An addiction is about the thrill of satisfying ourselves, unlike true love, which is about creating mutual, contented satisfaction. A truly intimate relationship is not addictive. It is not dependency-oriented but interdependent. We don't cling. Instead, we hold and release in accord with what the other offers. It is liberating rather than possessive, satisfying rather than insatiable. We are not obsessed with the other person, only present to and with her. We are coming not from "must have" but from "open to," not from "can't live without" but from "it would be enjoyable to have."

As we let go of addiction in favor of true intimacy, our understanding of the source of safety and security is upgraded. At first we thought, "He will provide the safety and security I need so badly." As we grow in self-trust, we say, "I welcome the safety and security he can provide while I focus on providing safety and security for myself. Now I don't need it so badly from someone else." When our need was insatiable, our implicit statement was sadly, "I am trying to get a safety and security from him that I can't receive, because I lack the receptors for satisfaction."

As an aside, we can say that a person approaching others with this skewed energy will be attractive mostly to partners with little or no safety and security within themselves. They can't give what they don't have. They can't fully show up in a relationship; they run from conflict and from feelings. Thus, the chances of a successful relationship are minimal all the way around.

In an addiction, we are ultimately seeking safety and security in something we believe can take us beyond our immediate circumstances and limits, something transcendent. We soon realize that addiction provides a temporary escape but not a solution. Pierre Teilhard de Chardin characterized our predicament well: "We find ourselves in the grip of what we thought we could grasp."

In addition, we soon notice that the object of our addiction, what we believe will be reliable, is actually precarious. Recovery from an addiction therefore requires a spiritual program that offers access to that which is *reliably* transcendent, a higher power than what can be found in any object of addiction.

In addictions, we do not quite notice that we are compelled to do what is to our detriment, so we may deny our need for help from a twelve-step program. How ironic that we seek security in something that cannot provide it and avoid the program of healing that can. Our resistance to repair shows that an addiction has a life of its own, one that it wants to preserve. So, for instance, an alcoholic may not want to commit to Alcoholics Anonymous *because* it really works.

As we admit our own powerlessness and embrace a program of recovery, more happens that just sobriety. We no longer thrive on adrenaline. Then the caring connection can happen, without clinging or fearing, and lead to contentment. Even our description of love will be transformed from thrilling rush to contented connection. That depiction of love lands with sound sense in our wounded but healed hearts.

Someday we will understand that we are not seeking what we *think* we need. The one doing the seeking is the one we are seeking. The journey was always to finding ourselves.

Clinging When We Find Someone

Once we find someone, our drama can keep us caught in what is called codependency. We cling to those who give us nothing in return or hurt us again and again. As mentioned earlier, we have an instinct that does not serve us well: we remain attached to those who do not treat us well, because we crave connection more than safety and security.

This unstable connection can include hurting one another. Gordon Clifford states the case well in his lyrics for "I Surrender Dear": "Those little mean things we were doing must have been part of the game, lending a spice to the wooing." Dogs, interestingly, have the same misdirected instinct. They stay with us no matter how badly we treat them.

A connection becomes stressfully dramatic when we don't believe we have what it takes to keep someone interested in us. We may thrive on the suspense of what may happen next in our ongoing drama. A healthy relationship is not suspenseful. We can trust its past, present, and future. Suspense has a place in life; it drives drama, sports, and entertainment. We enjoy a play, a movie, or a game *because* we are kept in suspense.

A healthy person does not find suspense in a relationship entertaining or tenable. We want the safety and security that builds trust and peace of mind. When we want serenity more than suspense, our love matures. We can then rest in love as a soothing experience, a source of safety and security. We limit drama to the movie or television screen, never seeking it beside us on the sofa or bed.

In conclusion, we can say that when we are truly held and loved, we may move in one of two directions. We may receive the love and holding appreciatively and take it as a model for how to love and hold ourselves and others. Then the fulfillment of our needs is not only a joy but a learning experience with many benefits.

The second option is to cling and keep clinging, not a helpful style for people who are born with an inclination to go on a journey. Our mistake is to keep wanting *only* from others what we can learn to give ourselves. A central feature of becoming an adult is to accept and appreciate all that is received from others as a teaching about self-care. This is how we learn that others participate in our love story rather than being the source of its success.

PRACTICE: DRAMA OR LOVE?

Where do you see yourself on the following chart?

Neediness-Driven Dramatization of Love	*Authentic Love*
Based on unfulfilled childhood needs that we are still trying to fulfill through someone else rather than in ourselves first. This is only possible when we have grieved the deficiencies and disappointments of childhood.	Our childhood needs have been fulfilled in a good enough way, or we have done the kind of work on our childhood issues that readies us for healthy relating now.
Exhibits theatrical "passion" that masks a fear of real intimacy.	Exhibits comfort with intimate contact and commitment to increasing it.

Fueled by stress hormones such as adrenaline, norepinephrine, testosterone, and cortisol. The pleasure and trust hormones may briefly and occasionally be accessed.

Thrives consistently on pleasure and trust hormones such as dopamine, oxytocin, vasopressin, and endorphins. Stress hormones may briefly and occasionally be released.

Includes lies and betrayals, so safety and security are impossible. This means that trust, the basic building block of love, is missing.

Based on mutual honesty and trust, an atmosphere in which love can thrive and mature.

Involves secrets.

Involves openness that is appropriate to the occasion or the boundaries in the relationship.

Restless and compulsive.

Calm and freely chosen.

Impulsive, chaotic, ambiguous styles of behavior that keep the relationship in an uproar and suspense.

Consciously chosen ways of establishing and maintaining safety and security within a basically reliable bond.

Focuses on immediate gratification, a superficial style.

Focuses on growing in ego-sacrificing love, a style of depth.

Comes from an inner emptiness that must be filled.

Overflows from a plenitude that wants to share itself.

Craving without a capacity for satisfaction.

Ability to be satisfied with moderate need fulfillment.

Lack of resolution; resentments hang on.

Commitment to address, process, and resolve conflicts to whatever extent possible.

Exhibits sporadic, intense closeness, toggling between fears of abandonment and engulfment.

Exhibits an ongoing, mutual expression of the five A's: attention, acceptance, appreciation, affection, and allowing.

Equal excitement in connections and disconnections, since what matters most is that someone is responsive to us.

Satisfied only with ongoing positive connection, according to the definition of authentic love as a caring connection.

Ego-centered; our own desires come first, and the partner is there to fulfill them.

Mutual desires with mutual fulfillments: dispossessing ourselves of ego for the sake of building a successful relationship.

Characterized by sex that is intense and obsessive, yielding thrilling but temporary relief.	Characterized by sex that is exciting and brings joy and abiding contentment.
The "love" can easily turn to hate.	The intensity and expression of love may change, but it endures.
Can include abuse and revenge.	Committed to nonviolent communication and reconciliation rather than retaliation.
Physical appearance matters too much.	Priority is given to inner appeal.
Power is in one person or continually moving back and forth from one to the other.	Both partners share power.
Often described as codependency in one or both partners.	Described as an ideal relationship in which committed partners work toward maintaining it in little ways each day.

This chart is not about a distinction between bad and good, either/or. We honor the survival functions of our needy, clinging side while welcoming the adult side that regulates and manages it.

Finally, we can tell the difference between need-love and pure love. We think back to a relationship or friendship with someone from whom we kept wanting something, such as sex, but he or she refused to give it. We recall the drama we brought to the relationship: demand, expectation, disappointment, and resentment. Now that need is gone, and we love that person in a serene, genuinely caring, respectful, and supportive way. We show him or her the five A's with no demand for anything. This is how we know we can love and what love is.

What It Takes to Change

Neediness leads to dissatisfaction on both sides. We feel we are never getting enough, and our partner feels that too much is being asked—especially when it is asked in a demanding or petulant way. That approach won't get us very far. There is a step we can take, albeit not a very appealing one when our needs are clamoring for fulfillment. The work when we are needy is to stay away from partnering until we deal with our own neediness. We commit ourselves to do the work that readies us for a healthy relationship. That work is more likely to attract a healthier partner.

Making the choice to work on ourselves before embroiling others in our dramas is an act of love toward them. We want to save them from the pain that will ineluctably arise for them in a frustrating relationship while we remain so unready.

To work on ourselves in the ways described in this book's practices helps us make the journey from neediness-driven love to healthy, adult love. It means gladly leaving the opera house and going to the meditation hall.

The work moves forward when we realize that behind every form of neediness is an early life deficit of need fulfillment, a missing out on one or more of the five A's. Thus, neediness indicates our need to grieve what was missing, not our need to find a better version of our parents. We know we truly need someone when that person is not a substitute for anyone. For instance, mature adults do not need partners to substitute for their parents. But moments of fatherly and motherly love from others are certainly welcome—and important—all our lives. We never grow out of wanting both those kinds of love, and we can always give them to others.

Grieving for our past unfulfilled needs begins with three feelings: We let ourselves feel *sad* about our lack of need fulfillment, *angry* that we missed out on it, and *afraid* that there is no way to make up for it. Our feelings do not reverse our loss, but we forge a new relationship to it: we *let go* of our blame for our parents for not caring about us more than they did, and we *move on* in self-caring ways. We know we are moving on when we have more compassion than resentment for our parents. We have accepted the reality of missing pieces as a bare fact, not as an accusation. At this liberating point, we ask only, "So now what?"

We begin by understanding that childhood is important in the shaping of our adult relationships. In the course of life, we keep discovering new ways that this is true. These discoveries of new layers of meaning are like what happens with progressive readings of Shakespeare. We may reread or see *King Lear* in each decade of our lives, finding deeper layers of meaning and more telling insights into the human story each time. But Shakespeare's plays have more levels of meaning than we have decades in our life span to plumb them. Likewise, with respect to our childhood, we can't expect a final grasp, a full resolution of what happened to us. One lifetime is not enough, since so much remains stubbornly unconscious even while it so strongly affects our conscious choices. But we can trust that if we stay with our work on ourselves, we will eventually become healthier. Our past will no longer interfere with or vitiate our relationships.

The work of dealing with our neediness also includes becoming able to do the following:

- Settle for nothing less than relationships that foster the three goals of wholesome choices: health, happiness, and personal growth
- Give and receive the five A's
- Be free of addictions
- Accept and embrace our own and others' vulnerability
- Show our feelings and be open to those of others
- Be able to deal with conflicts and endings
- Be perfectly OK with or without a partner
- Accept the things we cannot change, change the things we can, and have the wisdom to know the difference.

This work is painful to do. We should not be surprised if we feel things we don't want to feel or become skittish about relating at all. That fear will pass. However, because we are taking the bull by the horns, we can expect that he will surely toss us and perhaps gore us too. But we have it in us to subdue him. Our wounds will become openings to new powers within ourselves, new ways of loving ourselves. We will be stronger because of our fight and proud of ourselves for not running away. This happens because we are no longer seeking something outside ourselves but trusting an inner plenitude that is waiting to be discovered and uncovered.

In a personal example of synchronicity, I was editing this section the same day a client asked rhetorically, "When will I be ready for the love I deserve?" I came up with the preceding list later in our session, and as he was leaving my office, he said, "You want me to take the bull by the horns, don't you?" So there it is.

Open to Finding

Freedom from neediness is the journey from "I am incomplete and need you" to "How can you and I cooperate in fulfilling our mutual needs?" Our challenge in any relationship of love is to cocreate a holding environment of safety and security. A *holding environment* is any household, social setting, or relationship in which the five A's are reliably given, it is safe to have needs and feelings and to express them, and we are personally supported in being who we are.

Then a new energy emerges from within us. Our focus is on *being open to finding* rather than on *needing to find.* Connection is then something we are receptive to, and we keep our eye out for it. This is an aptitude for discovery, not a craving for satisfaction. Like Columbus, we are not on our voyage because we need a new world; we are only intent on finding one when the horizon presents it.

One way to know whether we come from natural need or neediness in a relationship is to ask what we do when our partner is away. Does our life proceed with its usual healthy choices and routine responsibilities? Or do we think of ourselves as seriously incomplete and seek compensatory satisfaction by returning to an addiction? Does our diet go out the window? Do we spend time engaging in online porn? These may be signs that our dependency on our partner is extreme. He or she has become the source of stabilization for us. Without him or her, we fall apart or fall back into harmful habits. This is because we are using our partner to do what only we, a full support system, a higher power, or our spiritual practice, were meant to do.

Our partner is not a mother, father, coach, rescuer, or sponsor who is always on hand lest we descend into disarray. Such dependency on a partner is a clue to our neediness. Dependency itself can feel like connection, so some people remain needy precisely to experience that feeling, a poor man's version of being loved.

At the same time, a needy person is also an angry person. We always resent someone on whom we are dependent. Our ego, out of its sense of entitlement, seeks full attentiveness from a partner. Yet our ego's insistence on self-sufficiency asks, "How dare someone be that important, have that much power over me?" Deep down, our ego resents people *because* we need them. In addition, we resent them for not loving us exactly as we want and in precisely the way we believe we deserve. The level of grand-scale, unconditional love we want is perhaps reflected in the early caregivers who made a fuss over us and lived to fulfill our every whim.

We do not have to blame ourselves for our need of or neediness toward others. We do not have to reproach ourselves for giving them power over whether or not we are happy. If the relationships in our early life were not safe and secure, our connections to others later in life feel insecure. We find it hard to believe that others love us as we are. We believe our purpose is to please and appease if the other is ever to trust us. We then read the frown on someone's face as a sign that we did something wrong and will have to pay for it. As we trust ourselves more, we read the frown as pain within that person, without self-referencing. We then wonder how we can help. Now we are free to show compassion, which is what love looks like when the other is in pain, and we are not caught in blaming ourselves because of it.

In any case, our human psyche is not like a statue, sturdy marble on a sturdy marble base. It remains flexible, vulnerable, and sensitive to every smile or frown, no matter how much work we do on ourselves. That is not a sign of weakness, only of human responsiveness to whether a connection is secure or threatened. I recall a plastic toy from my childhood, a giraffe standing on a round base. When I pressed the base button from underneath, the giraffe broke down in a seemingly unfixable collapse. When I let go of the button, the giraffe reassembled itself and stood up again. This is a fitting metaphor for human stability. We too can collapse, but we can restore and reconstitute ourselves. Sometimes it only takes letting go, as with the toy, and sometimes it takes more, but it can happen. Notice in the toy metaphor the paradox that with pressure we collapse, but with letting go, we get back on our feet. Transformation requires a period of deconstruction, as any caterpillar now flapping powdery wings can surely and exultantly affirm.

It is particularly difficult to be without a partner when we were cut out for relationship; relatedness is our innate orientation. Our patient affirmation can be, "I accept and trust what is for now, and I am open to what may be." We show we take this affirmation seriously when we neither seek nor avoid the possibility of a relationship. We trust the universe to send someone our way when the time is right. That attitude creates a nonclinging serenity that is visible in our whole body and attitude and makes us appealing to others. The paradox is in the fact that our acceptance of what is and our openness to what may be, with no attempts to control or force any outcome, makes us *content while not having to be fulfilled.* What an empowering feat! When we grab and cling, we lose our chance to experience that wonderful paradox.

We cannot clearly know our needs when we do not live in accordance with our own truth. For instance, in a loveless, sexless, futureless marriage, in which neither partner wants to seek help, the truth is that we are not really married; we are alone. If this empty marriage leads to divorce, it may be that, alone in our apartment for a while, we find out what we really need or how we can survive without having what we always thought we needed. A truth about our real needs may have been trying to come through, but it couldn't until this happened. Now we forge a new relationship to our life story and our feelings, because we are only who we are, not who we are in relation to the someone who became so excessively crucial a player in our drama.

Now it is our healthy ego that motivates us, our appropriate pride in our right to thrive, to expand our potential, and to grow in self-esteem. This ego strength helps us take necessary but scary risks in new relationships. We become more assertive. We present our needs and ask for what we want. We appreciate a yes reply and draw near. We move on without resentment when the answer is no. This leads to a new, more caring connection to ourselves. That caring connection, missing elsewhere or before, is another way we learn to love ourselves.

We can relate love to the attitude taken in Zen Buddhism toward meditative sitting. The practice is not meant to be about gaining enlightenment. We sit because we are already enlightened, and this is what enlightened people do. We sit to observe the mind and its machinations and to see through its obscurations. Love is just like that. We act lovingly because we are love. We love others, not to gain love from them to staunch our neediness, but because that is what our love does—show itself, not play hide-and-seek.

Out in the open at last, we come to love ourselves, and our needs assume the more reasonable and calm position they were always meant to be in. They are landscape, or "inscape," not the whole picture.

When We Can't Get Enough

A childhood in which our needs were honored and fulfilled grants us a capacity for fulfillment later in the moderate ways that are appropriate to adults. A childhood in which our needs were not met but scorned or denied may leave us with no or very little capacity for fulfillment later in life. We missed out both on the experience of satisfaction and the capacity for it. Thus, when adults offer moderate need fulfillment (the adult dosage), we cannot read it as enough. We seek more than healthy humans offer. Our needs become insatiable, bottomless pits, like those in an addiction.

We also may become confused about our needs. We may need healthy holding and touch but imagine them to be about sex. We then keep seeking sexual contact in which at least physical satisfaction may be possible. We have not identified our real need or the way it can be fulfilled. At the same time, our physical satisfaction is just gratifying enough to make us continue our pattern. Unfortunately, such gratification is brief, so we soon seek it again.

We cannot allow ourselves to trust anyone to be fully loving or loyal to us. We also know how hard we are hit by abandonment. In fact, we interpret any move away from us as an abandonment. This makes us wary, not only of trusting others, but also of trusting our own needs.

Since human meaning is so closely tied to intimacy, this makes life terrifying, because it feels so futilely empty and pointless.

With this frustrating pattern going on inside us, we may repudiate our need for closeness, because we are so afraid of being rejected that we have to deny wanting it. We become intimacy-phobic while desperately wanting intimacy. What a sad and painful position to be in.

We find love difficult even in its skeletal form—welcoming and extending a positive connection. We cannot welcome love into our lives because of our lack of trust. Our history of disappointments makes us doubt those who sincerely offer their love to us now.

We want to have someone, and we fear having someone at the same time. But we cannot admit that to ourselves because we are so stuck. As Shakespeare's Juliet says, "Bondage is hoarse and may not speak aloud."

We cannot fully control our emotions. We feel ongoing anger because of our frustration that others back away from us. Yet, at some level, we know it is based on how difficult we are to be with. We keep asking others for closeness but do not have the capacity for fulfillment when we receive the amount of intimacy they offer us. At the same time, we are afraid of closeness, because it was associated in early life with abuse or betrayal. This adds to our frustration. We can't get enough of what we fear to have. We fear to find what we need most.

The left column in the following chart shows the intimacy-phobic/intimacy-craving personality characteristics and their effects. The right column shows the healthy alternative, the difference in the way crises are eventually handled when our sense of self is basically stable.

Intimacy-phobic/Intimacy-Craving Ways of Thinking and Behaving	*Goals for a Healthy Sense of Self*
Our present crisis seems to be insuperable, irremediable, and permanent.	We trust that this will pass and that we will recover. The crisis is a setback, not a disaster.
Our moods are unmanageable and change rapidly for no apparent reason.	We are aware that our moods and biorhythms are temporary, and we take them in stride.

We experience deep loneliness with a sense of emptiness that seems deserved and inescapable; time by ourselves is difficult.

We accept lonely times as a given of life and know it is not a judgment against us; time alone is difficult when we are lonely, but we may find out more about who we are that way.

We have to have approval.

We want to be attuned to.

We want closeness but are simultaneously terrified of it.

We want closeness and may simultaneously fear engulfment, but we come to terms with it.

We cannot tolerate separations or any forms of distance, since they feel like abandonments, even when they are not so intended.

We are upset by separations but do not have to construe them as abandonments; we survive them by grieving and letting go.

We panic when there is even a hint that others may leave or reject us.

We are saddened by the fact that some people reject us, and we may even be depressed for a while about the loss, but eventually we accept the undesirable reality and do not take it so personally.

We sometimes have paranoid thoughts.

We may harbor suspicions and doubt that others like us or wonder about how they see us, but we let it all go after a while.

Major issues cannot easily be distinguished from minor ones.

We can tell the difference between major and minor issues, and we can line up our priorities.

Anger or rage keep arising in us, even when there is no apparent reason for them.

We may become angry or enraged in reaction to certain stimuli, but our feelings soon blow over.

We may physically harm ourselves, or we may say we are suicidal, often to dramatize our distress and frustration.

We have found self-soothing options that help us get through hard times.

We act impulsively and addictively, as in overspending, acting out sexually, overeating, and so on.

We may sometimes be impulsive or addictive, but not for long and not in ways that get us into trouble or seriously harm us.

Our relationships are unstable, are usually short-lived, and may be full of uproar.	Our relationships tend to last, though they may certainly become tumultuous or confusing at times.
We become possessed by our dramas; our predicaments become sources of obsession and lead to compulsive reactions. We make decisions that lead to continual uproar and stress.	We can become caught up in drama, but we find ways to work through it. We genuinely seek serenity.
We stay stuck; we do not work things through. We tend to keep things incomplete, uncertain, and unresolved.	We may get stuck sometimes, but then we attempt to address, process, resolve, and integrate our issues.
We have an either/or way of seeing things and are not negotiable or cooperative with others.	We are able to see gradations in ideas and behavior and become flexible in how we respond.
We see people as all good and then as all bad, so we love and dislike or hate them in turn.	We realize that people have both good and not so good qualities, so we neither idealize nor demonize them.
We may dissociate from what is happening in the moment.	We can be distracted but generally remain present in the moment.
We likely experienced severe sexual, emotional, and/or physical abuse in our childhood, and it remains unresolved.	Some abuse may have happened to us in childhood, but we are finding ways to deal with it.
People with this personality disorder have some, but not necessarily all, of these traits. The symptoms of this insecure, anxious attachment are destabilizing, long-standing, and pervasive, but they can be managed—especially with mindfulness training.	A person may show any or all of the intimacy-phobic/intimacy-craving traits at one time or another. However, the symptoms can be dealt with and resolved, and they lessen and then disappear when circumstances improve.

In loving-kindness, we will feel compassion for people who are like this. In loving-kindness to ourselves, we avoid trying to establish an intimate relationship with people whose damage is so extensive that they cannot offer or effectively trust or relate to us. Healthy adults will not form relationships with people who have major psychological issues that, at least for now, show no prospect of being managed. We release them from candidacy for a relationship while feeling compassion. This is our way of maintaining a caring connection while taking care of our own boundaries.

We may already be in a relationship with someone who is intimacy-phobic/intimacy-craving and find ourselves making continual compromises that may manage stress but usually do not lead to serenity. We rub each other the right way sometimes and the wrong way more times. That goes with the territory. If we are to remain together, ongoing therapy will be an important assisting force.

5

Healthy Sexuality

It is precisely in the spirit of celebration, gratitude, and joy
that true purity is found.

—THOMAS MERTON

OUR PSYCHE COMPRISES VARIOUS FACETS or dimensions. Some
examples from this configuration of elements are personal power, intimacy, feelings, sexuality, intellect, and spirituality. All of these happen
in embodied ways, and they interact with each other—they are not
parts or categories. If they were and did not interact, we would not be
whole people. Thus, for example, our sexuality is a whole-person experience, not simply a genital sensation. Our spirituality is a whole-
person commitment, not just candles and incense.

Each of our facets, however, requires three forms of assistance if it is
to activate itself to its full potential. The first comes from full use of our
bodymind powers to gather information and build wholesome habits.
For instance, we need to learn how to use our minds to make good
judgments and how to eat properly to build healthy bodies.

The second kind of assistance comes from being socialized. Initial
socialization happens mainly at home and at school. There, we learn

that each area opens best within healthy boundaries that take others into account. So, for instance, we learn in kindergarten that anger is legitimate at times but that showing it by hitting someone is inappropriate.

The first two kinds of assistance are in our own hands—with help from others. The third kind is in the hands of our original caregivers: it's the assistance that comes from being held. We require attunement to our feelings and to all the dimensions of our developing selves. That is what happens in a holding environment. As mentioned in the last chapter, a holding environment is any containing place or group that accepts us as we are and tunes in to our feelings. For instance, when we show anger at home, our parents might make room for it and surround it with the five A's. They might understand our feelings as legitimate and show us ways to express them so they can remain safe for us and others.

Thus, we are born with capacities that blossom in the world of caring connections. It is ultimately love that releases our full human powers and shows us how to use them to our best advantage. The following analogy may be helpful. Our capacities are like software programs for a computer. We own the disks, but they need to be properly installed in order to work. Personal work, socializing, and attunement are the ways a program such as sexuality is properly installed.

This would have meant that is was always legitimate, even encouraged, to ask about sex in our home when we were young. We would also have been taught that it was not wrong to have sexual needs. Sexual abuse was not the style at home or elsewhere. These three are the equivalent of a holding environment for the sexuality dimension of ourselves. It can only emerge as healthy when it is intelligently discussed, safe, secure, unrepressed, and considered normal and wonderful.

A family, school, society, or religion can misinstall our sexuality. Then that dimension of our personality does not work for us in healthy ways. We know it is not on track when we fear sex, can't get enough of it, are not enjoying it, engage in sexual behavior that does not help us mature sexually, or still imagine that sexual performance or appeal dictate our value as people. In healthy sexuality, it is the power to show intimacy that matters.

For most of us brought up in the fifties and sixties, our sexuality was rarely installed in a healthy way. If it is a damaged dimension of our psyche, it will be difficult to use it for our own legitimate pleasure, for mutual support in a relationship, or for healthy psychological or spiritual development. If sex could not be mentioned or talked about at home, if we were influenced by a repressive religion, if we were in a family or society that was prejudiced against any sexual activity that was not heterosexual-marriage-oriented, if our views about sex were strongly influenced by Hollywood, we almost always have work to do in the area of sex.

We can now, as adults, visit and explore this and any part of ourselves that was off-limits, damaged, neglected, or misdirected when we were children. We can look for ways to create safety and boundaries in our relationships, making it possible to experiment with our sexual edges. We have no problem doing all this in the realm of intellect, but feelings and sex are scary for all of us. We don't have to be discouraged. We can find our way in a territory that is right here within us. As Shakespeare says in *Hamlet*, "The readiness is all."

We may have noticed that one feature of our bodyminds is easy to work on, while others are difficult. For instance, we may have come from a home that did not foster good eating habits or offer us a healthy diet. As adults, it is possible for us to reconfigure our eating habits in accord with what is good for us. We find information on this topic everywhere, so it is easy to visit this part of our life and explore new options, though it is still a challenge to upgrade our diet. We can be supported in that quest by society, family, and the medical establishment. There is no shame or stigma attached to upgrading our eating habits.

Sexuality, on the other hand, isn't so easy. We are not readily supported if we choose to explore and upgrade in the realm of sex. It is still a taboo topic in many places. For all its bluster, our society still fears and distrusts full sexual emergence, especially in women. In addition, we do not have access to information about sex that is as clear and precise as what we can find about proper nutrients. Much of the information about sex is still biased by what is considered moral. Our developmental adult task is to look deeply into our sexual history to find a way to design our sexual experience so it works for pleasure, support, health, and love.

Healthy and loving sexuality is a celebration of ourselves and our caring connections. In a relationship, it is not one-sided but reciprocal. It is always a choice, not an obligation or a compulsion. It is passionate but not restless, compulsive, or insatiably needy.

In good sex, we feel a connection. In fulfilling sex, we feel a caring connection that is deeply personal and interpersonal all at once.

In sex motivated by love, our focus is on intimate closeness and on both the giving and receiving of pleasure. In a truly loving bond, our emphasis in sexual activity is primarily on giving pleasure to the other person. Our own pleasure is certainly important, not so much as something we seek but as something we receive. That configuration of ourselves in the sexual experience, receiving pleasure rather than grabbing it, is a wonderful example of how love works. It is about giving as our priority and openness to receiving as equally valuable. In a truly intimate sexual experience, both partners make the other the priority, so it all comes out even in any case, though that is not the motivation. Only the joy of giving and receiving is.

Pleasure without Guilt

Love and sexuality can happen together or separately. For instance, we can be sexual in showing our love. We can be sexual in order to run from love. We can be sexual for pleasure without feeling love. The number of possibilities makes the topic of sex confusing for many of us. It is certainly in the realm of mystery.

It helps to distinguish sexual behavior and sexuality. *Sexual behavior* refers to actions that can happen within relationships or apart from them. *Sexuality* refers to the expression of a dimension of ourselves that can be private or mutual. It includes not only sensations, as in sexual behavior, but feelings too. Exploring our sexuality is a direct path to expanding our personal limits, finding out more about who we are and what we—and love—can be.

A loving person in a relationship is on the lookout for ways to manifest his sexuality so that his body, heart, mind, and spirit show the love that is within him. He also chooses to act responsibly toward others in all his sexual interactions.

Since sexuality is so closely related to creativity, it is also a way to express our reverence for life. The fact that sexual behavior can produce new life gives us a clue to its evolutionary direction. Though it does not have to be procreative, it relates to honoring and nurturing liveliness, the threshold to creativity.

Many of us have emerged from religious traditions that instilled a fear of sexuality. We may associate sex with guilt or shame. This is not only because we may have been taught to believe that seeking pleasure is selfish. Our sexual guilt may be about our belief that we do not deserve power or that it is dangerous. The real fear about sex in patriarchal religions is that we will have an experience of personal power, the right to transcend the restraints it imposes on us, and emerge into our full autonomy.

We may have been programmed to believe that personal choices for sexual pleasure will lead to punishment. Our religion may have instilled fear about how far we can go in sex, which is the same as how far we can go in being ourselves, how much of ourselves we can know or express. An ability to let go of control or being controlled is the essence of sexual fulfillment. The only fear is of our full emergence.

How ironic that sex is about connection but can lead to guilt, to feeling disconnected from others. How antithetical guilt about sex is to our criterion for love: what includes and extends positive connection. When sex becomes a negative form of connection, it is no wonder that it is separate from love. This is the direct link between antisex attitudes and the split between love and sexuality.

At the same time, movies and advertising have capitalized on sex and sometimes made it an idol. The commercial world attempts to manipulate us by promising us power through fulfillment of our sexual desires. In reality, we are in its power when we fall for its superficial version of love.

Good sex is about excitement and soothing all at once. It includes the safety and security that come from self-soothing and represents the opposite of neediness-driven drama: managing feelings, regulating our bodily reactions, gaining a sense of mastery, accessing an abiding comfort within ourselves. When all this is in place, our core is stable and we feel integrated. Then we do not look for the one who gives us safety and security but the one who holds, reflects, awakens, and endorses it in us. Indeed, it is our lifelong project to seek positive connections that can evoke our original story and give it a happier ending.

Adults, however, don't look for safety only in the arms of others, because they have learned how to find it in themselves. In like regard, we look for sexual pleasure in others and in ourselves while noticing distinctions and limitations. For instance, we can trust that we will say yes to sex when we ask it of ourselves. We cannot always trust that others will say yes when we ask it of them. We may have a much better time with ourselves than with others or vice versa. On the other hand, feeling safe and secure can derive more powerfully from others than from ourselves, depending on the circumstances and players.

Sex can run away with us when we cling to it or desert us when we ignore it. It is up to us to tend and cultivate it so it can develop in healthy ways. That means vigilance about choices in a realm that has so much impulsiveness in it. It means caretaking our erotic inclinations so they become more and more creative. It means attention to where, how, and with whom we act on our sexual desires. This is how our sexuality can increase both our self-esteem and our opportunities for love—useful criteria for a satisfying sexual experience.

Lust and Longing

It's a funny thing to experience one's passion—sexual desire—no longer a sort of wandering thing, but steady and calm. I think, when one loves, one's very sexual passion becomes calm, a steady sort of force instead of a storm. *Passion that nearly drives me mad is far from love.* [Italics are mine.]

—Frieda Lawrence to her husband, D. H. Lawrence

Lust is strong sexual desire that does not require relatedness to be satisfied. It is different from love, even from a physical standpoint. We now understand, for instance, that in our brain chemistry, love responses are located in the tegumental nucleus and caudate nucleus, which release dopamine, a pleasure mediator. Lust, however, resides in the hypothalamus, where more primal needs, such as hunger and thirst, reside. Thus, the fulfillment of our sexual desire can feel like a survival issue. This may be why love feels good all over and leads to repose, while lust will keep us wanting more.

Lust is also associated with an increase in the release of testosterone and estrogen. The in-love state of high romance is characterized by a release of pheromones, norepinephrine, serotonin, and dopamine. This release can be sustained only temporarily, so it cannot be the basis for long-term commitment. Once "the thrill is gone," we have nothing going for us unless we mature into a deeper kind of love. Full mature bonding provides a release of vasopressin and oxytocin, the chemicals we discussed earlier, which are associated with comforting and nurturant attachment.

Love happens between two subjects. Lust is from possessing subject to possessed object, even when both participants feel the lust. Love makes our security grow, while possessiveness increases uncertainty. Real love leads to grief when the loved one is gone. Lustful possessiveness leads to anxiety and aggression when its object is not available to fulfill the subject's needs.

The less driven we are by adrenaline, the more able we are to love authentically. A bond of serene love appeals to the part of us that wants serenity, an oxytocin and serotonin response. It is not that lust is wrong, only that it has to be watched lest it obsess and possess us, as in addiction.

In the addictive state, we are caught in the illusion that there is someone, real or virtual, with whom we can have the kind of sex that will satisfy our immense longing for connection. Our desire feels oversized, because beneath an addiction is a bottomless pit of neediness—no one is enough, and we can't get enough. The bottomless pit makes too much not enough and full satisfaction impossible. Then we crave even more. We believe that more will be better or that just the right kind of touch or fantasy fulfillment will slake our frantic thirst. Connection with others seems to be just what we need, but ironically, we lack an essential constituent of intimacy: the capacity to be fulfilled in some*one*'s arms.

Addiction in this context can include sexualizing our needs so that we imagine sexual activity to be the equivalent of fulfillment of any or all of the five A's (attention, acceptance, appreciation, affection, and allowing). The ones missing in our childhood are the ones that dug a bottomless pit inside us and now deprive us of the capacity to be fulfilled in moderate, adult ways.

It's easy to see that infatuation, fascination, addiction, and lust are exciting to our egos, because they are driven by adrenaline-rich reactions. Adrenaline thrives on keeping drama at a high pitch and has become a characteristic of contemporary society and entertainment. It used to be that a sleigh ride was thrilling and exciting, but in most of society today, people demand the arousal of adrenaline in more florid, trenchant doses. Once we may have liked movies because of their stories, whereas now we've come to prefer thrillers in which the world is threatened with or undergoes destruction.

PRACTICE: HONORING OUR SEXUALITY

Our sexuality is a major but delicate part of our psychic life. Like our bodies, it requires tending. We have to take care of it or it will deteriorate or lose its capacity to serve our health, happiness, and personal growth.

Our work as adults is to look at our childhood and adolescence and ask what helped us evolve sexually and what harmed us. Then it is up to us to reconfigure our sexual style in accord with appropriate behavior and goals. We are adjusting the settings so that our psyche can accommodate our sexuality in the best interests of ourselves and others.

Consider these qualities in auditing your sexuality to see if it is providing what is optimal for you:

- Does my sexuality welcome and extend positive connection?
- How do I feel about sex without relationship?
- Is my sexual life respectful of others, or does it exploit them in any way?
- Do I use sex as a weapon or a way to manipulate others?
- If there is an absence of affection, a lack of touch, in my life, it is natural to feel tension in my body. Do I turn to sex for relief?
- Am I ashamed of sex by myself?
- Can I engage in satisfactory sex without the use of drugs, pornography, or other artificial stimuli?
- Am I comfortable with my sexual orientation?
- Has my sexual style become compulsive or addictive?
- Am I still holding on to puritanical beliefs?
- Can I be intimate without having to be sexual?
- Do I act responsibly with regard to health concerns?
- Does my sexual behavior honor the limits and agreements in my primary relationship?
- Can I express love through sex?
- How does my sexuality and my sexual behavior help me love with all that I have in me?
- Is sex a source of both pleasure and joy?
- Are my sexual choices based on religious teaching?

> If I see anything but the Beloved
> That is not love at all, only passion.
>
> —RUMI

Our Fantasy Life

We sometimes wonder about the usefulness of a particular feature of our computer's operating system. What purpose does it serve? We ask the question, but we may not have enough interest to follow it up or do the work it takes to find out. We simply trust that it is there for a reason, and we know enough not to tinker with it.

The psyche also has many programs and features in its operating system that the ordinary user does not understand. Some she never notices; others she notices but does not have knowledge of. Some she inquires into, and others she disregards.

We can trust that our sexual fantasies serve our full emergence in some way, as we trust that what is in our computer helps it work to its full capacity. Our psyche is labyrinthine, and a lifetime is not sufficient to understand it. We can, however, make an attempt at understanding by pondering questions like these, without expecting answers: "What do my particular sexual fantasies tell me about myself? What is their purpose in my life? How can they help me toward wholeness? What and how do they serve my growth? How do they reveal my real needs?"

An enduring, recurrent sexual fantasy may represent a profound, mysterious, and unexpected pathway into territory that has remained unexplored and uncharted because of our socially inherited secrecy or taboos about our sexual desires. If we allow ourselves to look directly at our fantasy life, we may find fascinating, sometimes challenging, treasures that are long-buried in the past.

"What does it serve?" was the question a medieval knight had to ask in order to begin his search for the Holy Grail. The Grail is a symbol of human wholeness. The knight does not ask the question to receive an answer; it is not an inquiry. It is his *password* over the threshold that leads to wholeness. All he has to do to show that he is the right knight for the task is to ask the right question. The higher Self, the inner Grail, will answer when the time is right.

Our main sexual fantasy is the correct password for entry into our mysterious inner world. This is not an intellectual project, problem, and solution, but a mystery to enter and keep entering. It is the mystery of being born into the full version of who we are. That will be a frightening prospect if our whole life has been one big evasion of our full emergence, a sad but not irreversible fate.

Sexual fantasies have a definiteness to them. We imagine exactly the scene and characters we desire. To stop there in our understanding of our authentic needs is a form of fundamentalism, since it takes the fantasy story as literal. We believe that only this scenario, played out in exact detail, can give us pleasure. Sometimes, seeking what we *believe* we need prevents us from *knowing* what we really need. We delve more deeply into our fantasies, feelings, and needs when we look for their connotation rather than their denotation.

A particular fantasy that is long-standing in our imagination gives us important clues about ourselves. There is usually a frozen need behind it, a need from the past that became a fixation because it was not fulfilled. It remains in its childhood state of neediness, though it can take on an adult look in our fantasy life. Such a fantasy has little hope for fulfillment and actually limits our capacity for intimacy, because intimacy requires a freewheeling openness to another person's way of loving. A rigid, definite fantasy makes for too exact an expectation. Our work in this section is to explore what arouses our sexual imagination so we can locate and assuage the ache it may be hiding.

Thus, our sexual fantasies represent deeper longings than they depict. When we explore how they may point to what we missed out on in childhood, we are on track. This is not about incest, since the original fantasy is to be treated as a metaphor, a code word for one of our early needs. How often have we thought we needed sex when our real need was for the safety and security that comes from being held. This need is much more powerful than the sexual pleasure we mistake it for. Literal fulfillment of a sexual fantasy is easier to accomplish, so we may go to that as a default. But beneath the literal, fundamentalist interpretation of a long-standing fantasy and the gross fulfillment of it is a much more difficult challenge. We can try to identify the real longing in our heart that the fantasy in our head only points to but can't fulfill. The practice that follows may help.

PRACTICE: HOW OUR FANTASIES CAN REVEAL US TO OURSELVES

You can find out a lot about your sexuality by working with one of your ongoing sexual fantasies. This is the fantasy that keeps coming back to you and is rarely fulfilled perfectly. In fact, the need to have it fulfilled perfectly is a clue to the fact that it has a deeper meaning than is indicated when it is taken literally.

To work with fixated sexual fantasies, a couple or friends can use the technique of role reversal. The person with the fantasy plays the part of his own fantasy object, while the partner or friend represents him. The person with the fantasy speaks aloud, over and over, about the sexual activity that he (now in the role of object) is going to do to for "him," using his own name.

Gradually, he will hear himself uncover unfulfilled needs from childhood and from former or present relationships. In the words of what he needs to fulfill the fantasy, he meets up with the hurts and disappointments in his life associated with people from the past, either family or former relationships. This will most likely take him to a grief that has never been addressed.

He may encounter one of the five A's—attention, acceptance, appreciation, affection, or allowing—he was hoping to receive in how he imagined fulfilling his fantasy. The literal sexual aspect of the fantasy is on the surface. Under it is an insight into a deep, too-long-repressed longing for love.

Here are the steps. Remove the grossly erotic and specifically sexual elements so that nothing remains but the human connection behind it all. Use the 4A technique to explore the real need beneath your fantasy:

1. *Acknowledge* the bare bones reality of connection, holding, or any of the five A's that you are actually seeking and how it was or was not missing in your childhood.
2. *Allow* yourself to want that aspect of love fully, freely, and uninhibitedly, with full permission to have it and full declaration that you deserve it.
3. *Act* in ways that welcome or open to that rather than seeking ways to fulfill the sexual fantasy it represents or covers up.
4. *Affirm* compassion for yourself and endorse your power to use your fantasies to find your true self. You can design an affirma-

tion along those lines, such as, "My sexual desires are helping me know my longings for love."

It is important to honor your vulnerability and personal timing in this use of the 4A technique. Take all the time you need to move from step to step.

We inevitably find out that our fixated sexual fantasies are not ultimately for the activity we are imagining but for one or more of the five A's, especially those we did not receive from our parents. We may discover a need to be held by Dad or accepted by Mom. This is a treasure map to understanding ourselves. *Our fantasy may be a metaphor we have been taking literally.* Our desire may be a pointer to our need to grieve what we missed out on long ago rather than to what we want so intensely now from another adult.

What we most wanted in childhood, such as being held by Dad, may also be what we have never learned to ask for directly or to give ourselves. Dad may have withheld from us in the past. That withholding was a loss. But how are we now withholding from ourselves? Men particularly are taught from an early age to substitute sexual behavior for grieving. Slowing down in this practice is a way to reconnect with those feelings. It may be a shock for us to realize that a long-term fantasy was not really about sexual behavior but about intimacy that can be shown sexually and in other ways.

Here is a way of slowing down and entering the mysterious realm of our feelings. Our personal grief about which needs were not fulfilled centers around questions like those that follow. Our partner in the exercise asks these questions, repeating each one five times:

What did I really need from Mom?

What did she actually give me?

What did I really need from Dad?

What did he actually give me?

What do I really need from myself?

What do I actually give myself?

Repeated responses to the same question take us deeply into our own attitudes, beliefs, and feelings. Hearing a question repeated may take us back to childhood. Our mother may have repeated her question when she thought our first answer was a lie or did not match what she believed was true. We were kept on the griddle to get the real truth out of us. As adults, we do not have to feel judged when a question is repeated, as though our original answer was not satisfactory. Our answers are insufficient only because they are not yet plumbing the depth of which we are capable. Our off-hand answers can be slowed down, and in repetition, we can go deeper into the reality of who we are and what we are really up to when it comes to sexual desire.

As knowing ourselves becomes more valuable than defending our ego, we welcome inquiry as a path to finding and being ourselves, the best preparation for good sex.

As a final word, in addition to fixated sexual fantasies about what we want, we have also had experiences of great sexual pleasure. These are also metaphors for the needs of the past. Perhaps, we were experiencing a revival of the emotional fulfillments we did receive. Hopefully, such gift moments will continue.

6

Showing Love to Others

Our job is to love others without stopping to inquire whether or not they are worthy. That is not our business, and, in fact, it is nobody's business. What we are asked to do is to love; and this love itself will render both ourselves and our neighbors worthy if anything can.

—Thomas Merton

We learn from models whom we imitate. Everyone who ever loved us, or is loving us now, has shown us how to love. We all have love in us; being loved shows us how to manifest it.

Early on, we learned to love ourselves based on how our parents loved us. Modeling by others is a main source of everything that imprints on us, and love is no exception. Only the best model of loving yields the best version of self-love. When our parents loved us but simultaneously micromanaged us, what chance did we who were so easily imprintable have? We wind up now imagining that love means caretaking by controlling.

We were born with a full range of emotions but not with the capability of regulating them. We had to learn this skill by watching our parents regulate their emotions and seeing how they helped us regulate ours. Thus, positive connection from others is a mirror in which we see how we can take care of ourselves.

Since we learn by modeling, we were also sitting ducks for being influenced by our parents' negative behavior and attitudes. I recall working in therapy with a drug addict whose fundamentalist religious parents told her she would go to hell for being gay. She did go there in her dismal, dangerous and hellish life of drugs. She found a way to make her parents right. But thanks to her recovery program, she came out into the light and could be happy with her sexual orientation after all.

Social referencing is a technical term that means getting a clue about how to design our own behavior by observing others. For instance, in childhood, a mother becomes the model for her son's way of assessing and loving his father. If Mom puts Dad down constantly, Junior does not respect him. If her love comes across as mothering, Junior comes to believe that his father is inadequate. Only later will the boy be capable of coming up with his own way of relating to his dad. We might say, we do not get a chance to know and love a parent until we are away from the influence of the other parent. Many of us do not make that transition. We still assess and feel about one parent as we were imprinted by the attitudes of our other parent. Another sector of our personal work is liberation from that influence, a way of finally leaving home.

Parents are, at first, totally responsible for an infant in all areas. Gradually, they learn to respect the growth that moves even a toddler and certainly an adolescent and a young adult beyond their early role as protectors and teachers. This is the growing boundary of love. Parent and child eventually accept each other as peers. Healthy parents work with the child's flow of growth and change the way they show the five A's. For instance, we show an infant or child a constant attention by overseeing all she does. That does not work in adolescence when our teenager needs privacy as well as limits. Then in adulthood, she needs our support as a peer who makes her own choices, irrespective of what we consider better or worse.

Many young children today are being raised with invasive scrutiny rather than respectful attentiveness. Some are being given everything they need as well as everything they want. Parents swiftly respond to their desires or even whims. The children may then not find the opportunity to grasp three basic principles of effective relating: appreciating, longing, and sharing:

- *Appreciating* is one of the five A's, the components of love. When we keep giving to our children, they may feel entitled rather than appreciative.
- Love thrives on an ongoing sequence of *longing* and having. When we respond to children's wants promptly, they may not know what it means to long for something, an important component of sensitivity and patience.
- *Sharing* is another way of describing the caring connection that is love. When we do not teach the importance of sharing with others, our children may not appreciate the virtue of generosity.

PRACTICE: EXPANDING THE WAYS WE CAN LOVE

> They do not love that do not show their love.
> —WILLIAM SHAKESPEARE, *Two Gentlemen from Verona*

We are challenged to live out a radical alternative to society's usual style in which life is about gathering all the love we can so we can feel safe and secure, a kind of "love materialism." Instead, we can learn to feel good about ourselves by showing our love everywhere. Appendix 1 of this book offers specific practices to help us get there.

We can practice showing love by imitating those who have shown us love. Our whole life has been, however hit or miss, a tutoring session in love. Every moment of love from someone is a recommendation to us to go and do likewise. Here are three examples of how this can happen:

1. We are going through a painful crisis because someone has hurt us. A friend says, "I'm sorry this happened to you." This simple statement means a lot to us. We remember her words, and when other friends have

something similarly painful happen to them, we repeat those words exactly. They help us find love in ourselves for the other person. This is the compassion element of our loving-kindness practice.

2. We tell a friend some good news about ourselves and he immediately says, "I'm really happy for you!" We can see that he is genuinely delighted about our success, and that feels to us like supportive love. We say the same words to others when they have good news. This is joy at another's success, another feature of loving-kindness practice.

3. We ask a friend to help us with a critical problem in our house, and he can tell that we are limiting our request so as not to inconvenience him too much. He suddenly interrupts us and says, "Tell me what you really would like me to help with, if you had your druthers." We realize he is willing to help us totally, not just to make a minimal commitment to our project. That feels like genuine helping, like he wants to be there for us in a supportive way. This is loving-kindness we can imitate.

In these examples, each of our three friends became a teacher, a model of how to show love. We can recall and, in our minds, thank our many splendid models when we hear ourselves quoting them. We are thankful that they loved us so palpably and showed us how to love: everything we receive becomes something we can give.

On the shadow side, people have also spoken to us in mean, uncaring ways, and we can recall them as what not to say to anyone.

Sometimes a caring connection is shown silently. In seventh grade, I had a newspaper route. Each morning, in the early light of summer or the cold dark of winter, the newspaper truck would toss a bundle of papers tied with twine on the sidewalk in front of my house. I would search for a shard of glass—in those days, the streets were littered with them—and use it to cut the twine before putting the papers into my shoulder bag.

In the afternoons, on my way home from school, I would often stop to say hello to Jenny through her first-floor window across the street from my house. She was a kindhearted neighbor who had cancer and was unable to walk. One day, she reached into a pocket of her flowered dress and handed me an aluminum ring with a sharp hook on it. She explained that it was meant to be worn on one's finger to cut through a piece of twine or rope. I realized then that she had been watching me and had found a way to help me.

Jenny had watched me scout around each morning for broken glass and had found someone to get me a tool that could make my task easier. I remember being so surprised, so grateful. I have never forgotten that gift of caring connection.

Jenny's loving awareness toward me is a model of love, and it is up to me to follow it. I want to make it my way too. This makes special sense, since the story of Jenny is full of synchronicity: Just the right person lived near me who cared about me in a way that was meaningful to me. So also by synchronicity, her way of loving must be just the ingredient I needed to add to my personal repertory of loving. She gave me a grace, one that it has helped me to recall in times when I feel more broken than whole. As William Wordsworth says in *Preludes XII*, special moments of love "retain a renovating virtue" so that

> . . . our minds
> Are nourished and invisibly repaired.

In Buddhism, teachings are said to be *transmitted,* not simply presented. Practitioners do not simply learn; they receive a transmission of the dharma, the enlightened teachings. The teachings are not words but a way of living. The modeling of love by others in the course of our life, as in the example of Jenny, is just such a transmission. We learn most about how to love by imitating the ways others have shown us love. As in spiritual practice, however, transmission still requires ongoing practice if we are to express our love in our daily choices.

Ask yourself about silent forms of love that have come your way, and write out your commitment to imitate them.

Our own love for others can be silent too. We can hold someone in our hearts in an ongoing, caring way when we are not showing or declaring our love actively. For instance, we certainly still love our children or partner or friends when they are not physically with us or when we are not thinking of them. We always hold them in our heart in a caring way. Likewise, there were people we loved in the past and have now lost track of. The old flame may have died out long ago, but we still have a kindly, caring feeling for that first love. This also applies to friends who have moved away and with whom we have no contact. We know we hold them all in our hearts with love, because we still smile tenderly when we remember any of them. Real love never ends; it just goes into inactive status.

Just about every movie has at least one example of love or the need for it. We can make a point of looking for both examples and even making note of them. We can imitate, in our own life and relationships, the examples of healthy love we see depicted on the screen. We can even ask ourselves if our need is like the one that touched us in the film. As with fixated sexual fantasies, we do not take what we see literally but seek out the deeper feelings and needs the film inspired. This is using entertainment as another way to learn how to love and how to know our specific needs for love. The actors are our models; the story is our story.

Here is one example of how this practice can work. In the touching comedy *Lars and the Real Girl,* Lars needs love but is initially afraid to find it in a real person, so he turns to a female mannequin. The townsfolk realize Lars has a problem, and they do not ridicule or humiliate him. Instead, they go along with his "relationship" to the mannequin as a way of helping him move through it—an example of how love is patient, compassionate, and respectful of someone's timing.

Later, when his "girl" is "dying" in the hospital, a small group of concerned ladies from the town come to Lars's house and keep him company during the "death watch." One of them specifically says, "We came over to sit."

In seeing this film, we might ask ourselves if we too, like Lars, have fears of intimacy. We can learn that one beautiful way to express our love is to show up, not to advise, but simply to stay with someone who is going through a hard time, as the townsfolk and ladies did for Lars.

All the characters in the film give us information about ourselves, our fears, and our opportunities to show love.

Here is one more example. In the now-famous diner scene in the film *Five Easy Pieces,* the Jack Nicholson character demeans a stressed-out waitress. This is meant to be humorous, but where did our laughter come from? We laughed at someone's pain. A careful sensitivity about love would lead us to *compassion* for the waitress, both for her rigidity and for how she was being treated. Our sense of what is humorous can be balanced by our appreciation of what constitutes loving-kindness. Our own use of humor, when we are committed to loving speech, is directed at human foibles without wounding others through sarcasm or ridicule. Our audience response to that scene helps us evaluate our relationship to compassion and humor.

We are aware that the characters on the screen are acting, so the "waitress" is not really being humiliated. But here we are exploring how we can learn from films and from our response to them, so the point remains useful.

We can begin a list of films we've seen, making note of the specific forms of loving we learned from them, as well as what they helped us understand about our own needs and fears. We want everything and everyone to become our coaches in the art of love.

Finally, we may want to *audit* our love of others. Here is a checklist that may help examine to what extent we are showing our love selflessly, as *agape:*

- Approaching others, taking the initiative to reach out to them in gentle, nonintrusive ways
- Going out of our way to be there for people, especially in a crisis
- Apologizing if we hurt them
- Showing loyalty and being trustworthy
- Supporting the full spectrum of lifestyles people choose
- Giving helpful and kindly expressed feedback when necessary (the opposite of "Your best friends won't tell you . . .")

- Escaping the chain gang of hurt and revenge
- Making the welfare of others as important as our own
- Sacrificing our own needs at times for the sake of the bond
- Maintaining both selfless, giving generosity and self-protective boundaries

The best way to be sure we are really committed to a life of love is to keep showing all the love we can in all that we say or do in every circumstance day by day, with no one excluded, banned, discarded, or ignored, and regardless of whether anyone loves us back.

Three Ways of Connecting

Now we can look at how we can show love to others in three specific and graduated forms: positive connection, caring connection, and universal caring connection.

At the most basic level, since any *positive connection* is a form of love, common courtesy is a way of showing love. We show this style of loving simply by being kind, polite, pleasant, and respectful toward others. In this regard, our work on using effective communication techniques is a practice for loving, since it helps us connect with others *and* protect our own boundaries, which is a way of loving ourselves. Common courtesy happens on a daily basis, usually briefly. It is a lifelong style with no interruption and is based on goodwill toward all: "The interests of others matter, and I respect that fact; only in critical or serious occasions do I subordinate my interests to theirs." This is societal connection, love of neighbor. This first way of loving is shown to anyone we meet, whether a stranger or an acquaintance.

We may also show love as *caring connection* within our more intimate relationships. This way of loving is usually reserved for our family members, friends, partners, and anyone close to us. This love can take the form of the five A's—attention, acceptance, appreciation, affection, and allowing—directed earnestly to those we care about: "The interests of others matter as my own, so I often subordinate mine to theirs." This is a familial and relational connection and is shown toward those we know.

We may also show our love as a *universal caring connection.* This humanitarian love can take the form of caring about and feeling compassion for people everywhere in the world, mostly those whom we do not see directly: "The interests of others matter as my own, so I subordinate mine to theirs when it is appropriate to do so. I am not, however, jeopardizing the necessities I am responsible for providing to those entrusted to me in order to offer services to the world at large." This is spiritual connection and is directed toward everyone—some known, some unknown—and to all of nature as well.

Reciprocity is important in intimate love, but it is irrelevant in common courtesy and universal caring. We can imagine a spectrum of loving from positive connection to personal caring connection to universal caring connection. Between these are a myriad of other forms of love according to the people and circumstances involved. We can look at each of the three styles in detail.

COURTEOUS LOVE: ANY POSITIVE CONNECTION

We are courteous, respectful, helpful, considerate, honest, and humane in all our dealings. It is usually easy to show this kind of love. We use rituals such as a handshake or a smile to help foster it. This is social civility, consideration, and affability. It is love in its most rudimentary form, since the motivation for it can be habit and sociability rather than intense caring. We can, however, call it a form of love, because it welcomes and extends positive connection, a minimum criterion for love.

Courteous (neighborly) love focuses on how to behave kindly in a world of others. It describes part of the social contract, what is required if society is to run smoothly. This form of connection has no bias and is unlimited in its application. It can take some patience on our part but is generally easy to practice toward people we see often or those we have just met and may see only once.

Ironically, this basic way of loving may prove daunting when it comes to people we know well! For instance, sometimes family members can be more difficult to deal with than strangers would be. We have all seen the depth of alienation, anger, and attack that can arise when there has been an injury, real or imagined, in a family. Feuds may result and remain unresolved, even clung to, despite catastrophic consequences to everyone involved. Some unresolved issues sleep and wait to be awakened. Some crouch and wait to pounce. Either way, we lose, because it is a cycle of hurt and revenge, choices that are unacceptable to an adult whose focus in life is love.

Courteous love is sometimes all a parent or siblings offer or permit. People can be close to us but not lovey-dovey, and being with them may not be comfy-cozy. We take that as a given about them and respect their boundaries. We maintain our caring connection, remain heart-centered, stay open to more closeness, but do not expect or demand more than they are willing to give.

After writing this section, a synchronicity occurred. I happened to hear Louie Armstrong singing "What a Wonderful World," and I smiled as I heard these particular lyrics by George David Weiss and George Douglas that so perfectly refer to courteous love: "I see friends shaking hands saying, 'How do you do?' / They're really saying 'I love you.'"

INTIMATE LOVE: PERSONAL CARING CONNECTION

Courteous love is directed to the faces that we meet. Intimate love is directed to the faces that we know and have chosen to include in our circle of special relationships. Intimate love, in addition to showing the five A's, includes caring about others' well-being; showing compassion for their pain; willingly forgiving their wrongs rather than retaliating; being generous toward them; remaining trustworthy toward and loyal to them; and going out of our way to help, support, or rally around them when they are most in need.

UNIVERSAL LOVE: CARING FOR ALL BEINGS

Humanitarian love resides in our evolving human brain and is motivated by concern for how the whole world, rather than simply we or our group, can survive and thrive. It is directed to the people we have seen on television or heard about in the world at large.

Humanitarian love is sometimes shown by some form of self-sacrifice in a crisis or any time of need. It can become the mission from which we design a commitment. In this way of loving, our focus is on forming a society of justice, peace, and love in simple or heroic ways. Such love *transcends* our connections to individuals, partners, and groups. By definition, it is therefore spiritual. It is likewise unconditional (not based on reciprocity) and universal (without boundary or restriction). It is courageous, altruistically motivated, and self-subordinating.

Truly humane love contravenes our natural instinct to divide ourselves into in-groups and out-groups. That division makes us likely to support and idealize "our side" and denigrate and demonize "their side." These biases kick in even when the group divisions happen arbitrarily. To love will always take both battle and welcome: We fight our natural tendency toward aggression and open to our natural tendency toward affiliation. The "fight" is, of course, more of a taming than a trouncing.

Before aspiring to the heroically humanitarian way of loving, we can ask, "How much compassion can I hold, and how willing am I to sacrifice my own comfort for others?" We take care of ourselves best when we respect our own limits and timing in our commitment to compassionate outreach. Having limits is not a sign of lack of love. We commit to what we are ready for. We can, however, also choose to stretch ourselves by aspiring to what we *want* to become ready for. The good news is that we can always become more ready and able by practice.

There are many styles of love that fall between the three listed here, especially between the second and third. Love can be demonstrated in as many ways as there are people to do so.

If we were to line up our love responsibilities, we might say that our first responsibility of caring is toward ourselves; our next concern is for our loved ones; and the full extension of our love is for the world and all its people. This may also be the order in which we share our resources or take action: I put on my own oxygen mask first, my children's second, and that of the person across the aisle third. The sequence of ourselves and our children reverses, of course, when the issue is more critical: I go without a new coat so my children can have their winter clothes.

Paul MacLean, in his book *The Triune Brain in Evolution*, proposed that our brain has three operative layers: the reptilian brain, the mammalian brain, and the human brain. We can paraphrase his ideas using this distinction. Our brain stem regulates our heart rate, temperature, and reflexes, as in fight-flight-or-freeze. It is mainly driven by genetics, so it is not easily influenced by learning. This *reptilian* part of our brain makes us apt to take care of our own survival and make our own interests primary, but we still show courteous love to maintain our connection to society.

The *mammalian* part of our brain gives us the ability to love others and make their interests primary, as in intimate love.

Our evolved *human* brain makes us capable of affection beyond our nearest and dearest, as in universal love.

Today, before I sat down to edit this page, I was listening to a call-in interview show on the radio. The guest was Lyle Lovett. None of the callers had ever met him, but I could hear in their voices and words that they deeply appreciated and cherished him and his talent. Some people said he had made a big difference in their lives. As I continued to listen to the callers, I suddenly realized that they sounded like they *loved* him, not just enjoyed what he produced. "So there it is," I thought to myself. "We don't have to know someone personally to have loving feelings for him."

This opens us to an insight: *We don't have to know someone to love him, but we only know someone when we do love him.* Moreover, when we love someone, we know ourselves as well, because the love in the other and in ourselves turns out to be the same. Only the ways we read, show, and seek love are different.

PRACTICE: THE THREE-TIERED PATH

The goal we set for ourselves in this book is to keep expanding our love so that it moves from ourselves to others to everyone. We can then see the three types of love as *steps*. We move from simple kindliness toward anyone to caring respect for our family and friends. This equips us to expand our caring toward all beings. The first two ways of loving can then be the practices that move us to activate the third possibility, our full potential for loving. Here are the three forms of love we have discussed and some ways to put them into practice:

- Positive connection: We make a commitment to offer everyone *kindness, courtesy,* and *respect.* Simply being pleasant and kindhearted is a beginning. In this practice, we behave as we ultimately want to become. Pleasantness and kindheartedness are not phony when they are practices. Acting nicely is only phony when it is used to ingratiate ourselves to others, to appease those who intimidate us, or to manipulate or cozen others. Our motivation is the key: sincere intention to become as loving as we can be versus playacting to protect or advance ourselves.

- Caring connection: We are committed to a special love for selected individuals. This shows up as *closeness, caring,* and *intimacy*—all in the context of sincere, ongoing expression of the five A's. Our commitment will include working through our fears of intimacy so we can show and allow closeness, being willing to work out problems, and keeping agreements.

- Universal caring connection: Our *worldwide, compassionate caring* can begin with including a universal aspiration in all our prayers or spiritual practices. If we affirm happiness for ourselves, we aspire to it for others too, in the style of the Buddhist loving-kindness practice. If we pray for help in our illness, we pray that all people with this same illness may find help as well. Our consciousness then increases, and soon we find more active ways to show our love—for example, volunteering for a compassionate service; contributing money to alleviate poverty; or joining in a political action aimed at bringing about a more just, verdant, and peaceful world.

How Loving and Being Loved Release Us from Fear

A legend says that the enemies of Buddha sent a mad elephant to charge and trample him. Buddha saw fear in the elephant's eyes and was stirred to compassion. He raised his right palm outward to the elephant to symbolize "No to fear." He cupped his left hand in his lap to symbolize "Yes to love." This first mudra (meditative hand gesture) soothed the elephant, which then bowed to Buddha. So love frees us from fear, because it automatically turns fear into connection; fear thrives on exclusion and division. When love comes along and includes, it rescinds the necessity for fear.

Fear sends blood to our leg muscles so we can run. This harkens back to primitive times when we had to be ready to run from predatory animals. Those who could run survived. In other words, those who felt fear and acted on it by running away survived and became our ancestors. Our genes do not favor facing fear, but our practices can. The choice is between primitive survival behavior and enlightened behavior, the evolved way to survive.

Our fears may represent our doubt that we can protect ourselves from threats or danger. Our unswerving dedication to showing all the love we can becomes a source of personal security, because our love includes setting and maintaining our boundaries so others can learn to respect our limits. Then we do not have to fear being taken advantage of.

Our fears also decrease when we are loved by others. We are reminded of what Romeo said in Shakespeare's *Romeo and Juliet.* He tells Juliet that he is not in danger from those who are feuding with him:

Look thou but sweet
And I am proof against their enmity.

This is a comment on the enduring human sense that being loved affords us a *protection.* This is not superstition unless we take it literally. It is a way of seeing the connection between being loved and finding our own sense of safety and security. As we saw earlier, when we love or feel loved, we can trust ourselves. We feel stronger and more sure of ourselves in the face of any peril or foe.

The following chart may help summarize the differences between love and fear:

Love	*Fear*
Includes	Excludes
Moves toward; connects	Moves away; disconnects
Is always our natural state	Is our temporary situational stance
Sees many options	Is caught in one catastrophic view
Trusts fearlessly	Is suspicious of trusting
Risks	Holds back
Reveals the true self	Hides the true self
Opens to feelings	Inhibits feelings
Responds	Reacts
Is generous	Withholds
Liberates	Imprisons
Forgives	Holds grudges
Casts out fear	Casts out love

The happiness that comes from making a life commitment to fearless and loving openness is enduring, but it does not guarantee constant euphoria. Indeed, happiness is not a feeling that stands alone. It is the *product* of an engagement in what is meaningful and pleasing to us. For one person, engaging in a daredevil sport results in happiness. For another, fishing does the trick. For most of us, safety and security bring happiness, but this feeling will never be assured as long as it is based outside ourselves. When our life purpose is to love ourselves and others and to be open to love from others, we feel truly safe and secure, because the basis of our happiness is within.

PRACTICE: LOVING OTHERS WHEN THEY DON'T LIKE US

When seeking opportunities to love becomes our central focus in life, we experience serenity in our happiness. With such contentment, we no longer become upset or vengeful when others do not like us. We interpret their attitude toward us as information about how they need our love more than ever. We look at why they dislike us and critique ourselves. We make changes in our behavior if that seems truly appropriate. Our self-improvement is now geared to making ourselves—our manner, our choices, our behavior, and our feelings—the best instruments for the clear expression of our love.

We may realize that others dislike us for reasons that are unknown to us or for what is not our fault. We accept that as a given of human interaction. We are not required to adjust or dispute their choice, only to witness it. We are not indignant about others' dislike of us. We see their dislike as code for the invitation to hold them more lovingly in our hearts without forcing contact. We simply keep them and everyone in our circle of love, the circle that has no circumference. Love is wooing us to itself through every reaction anyone has to us. *I surrender, dear.*

When others hurt our feelings or act unlovingly toward us, it is natural to feel pain. This is a healthy sign. It means that others matter to us, that love matters to us. Our pain becomes unhealthy when being hurt lowers our self-esteem or leads us to retaliate. We can, instead, take the experience of hurt or rejection as a spur to love more, to act more lovingly toward everyone, and to practice loving-kindness yet again. Now our hurt, and perhaps every feeling and reaction prompted by others, has become an opportunity for practicing what matters most, the love we really are. Thus, hurt can lead to our epiphany.

> When you get down to it, that's the only purpose grand enough for a human life. Not just to love—but to *persist* in love.
>
> —SUE MONK KIDD

7

Showing Love in a Relationship

Only in relationship do you see the face of what is.
—JIDDU KRISHNAMURTI

WE EMBARK ON THIS TOPIC with a summary and reminder of how childhood forces can impact our adult relationships. We began our life with two longings. We longed for approval (that is, *mirroring* of our worthiness) from our parents, and we longed for *connection* to them as people of power and effectiveness in the world. We wanted to merge with them so we could partake of those skills.

Mirroring worthiness in a healthy childhood grants self-esteem. Merging becomes our sense of power-with-responsibility. Both of these instill an inner safety and security. Thus, we trust ourselves because we were loved and empowered.

When mirroring and merging do not happen in childhood, we lack those two resources in ourselves. Yet, in adult life, there is still an opportunity to find them. We can grieve the past for what it lacked and learn to mirror and nurture ourselves in the process. This builds the inner resources we did not acquire earlier.

Establishing a healthy relationship will be difficult if we have not resolved our past damages and deficits. To have a truly healthy relationship requires having inner resources already in place. Only then can we come to a partner with something wonderful to share rather than with a gigantic need to be filled. Our learning to love makes us more likely to embrace the work it takes to move from childhood to adulthood, both personally and relationally. The practices in this book help us make that transition.

An adult partnership is meant to be a containing vessel in which the disparate experiences and traits of each partner are held caringly by mutually holding, addressing, and processing them. It is like the womb, in which growth and then release happen.

Some prospective or present partners don't want to gestate and be born as adults in a relationship. They may be afraid of the kind of love that can help them grow. We then have to release them with love and move out on our own. Our commitment to *agape,* however, means not cutting off anyone permanently. Even if we break off contact with certain people who were once close to us, we always maintain a connection in our hearts. How? Our connection is our ongoing wish for the best for them. The practice of loving-kindness helps us get there.

We may believe we know how to love others based on what feels like love to us. Yet we can love others only as *they* can receive it. Some people can only feel loved when we remain close to them; some feel more loved when we give them space. If we think certain actions are loving but the other person finds them intrusive, they are intrusive. In interactions, the meaning is based on the receiver's perception.

We can learn about how others will feel loved by noticing their reactions to our overtures and behavior. The best way is to ask them directly. In effect, being assertive in this way is a loving act, because we find out what others need by their own report rather than giving them with what we imagine they need.

Problems hearing one another can be about failing to grasp information or implication. Here is an example:

Lila phones her partner at work and asks, "What time will you be home? I want to make dinner for us."

Tyler replies, "I'll be free at seven, but I've been cooped up here all day, and I'm in the mood to go out."

"Well, what I'm cooking will be ready at six," returns Lila.

Lila is not letting in information. Tyler explicitly says that he will not be free until seven; He also implies that he does not want to eat at home tonight. Lila does not have to go along with Tyler's desire, but her loving response would certainly include her paying closer attention to it.

Tyler may now be angry and feel unheard, believing that Lila has discounted his wishes or that they do not matter to her. He does not like having to repeat that he will not be free until seven. Lila will now hear a sharp tone in his voice. It was up to Tyler, however, to be clearer and say directly that he prefers not to eat at home tonight.

This problem in Lila's hearing and the lack in Tyler's assertiveness may represent a pattern of behavior in the relationship. Such a pattern interferes with intimate bonding.

PRACTICES: HOW PARTNERS CAN BREAK UNSKILLFUL PATTERNS

FINDING OUT WHERE WE ARE • Partners may be at different stages of commitment. Checking in with one another is a helpful way of knowing whether or how our stages do or do not match up. We may also find ourselves between stages. As you read the following descriptions of the stages at which a commitment to working on things may stand, ask yourself which one or part of one fits you—or if you find yourself between two of them.

The *reaching out* stage of commitment means that you are very willing to work things out. You are optimistic and enthusiastic about the future of the relationship and trust sincerely that any wrinkles can be smoothed. When both partners are at this stage, you have the best odds for success in repairing disruptions or resolving conflicts. In fact, in this phase, a disruption will automatically generate attempts to repair the damage. All is reparable (so we feel loved), and we are part of how that happens (so we grow in self-esteem).

The *protest* stage refers to being so angry and frustrated by how things have been going between you that you want to get your rage out, directly or indirectly. At this stage, there is very little energy or care to work things out. Emotion may be flooding through you. This stage shows that the relationship has some hope, because the angry energy can be redirected in a healthy way. Yet it is close to despondency because of the frustration about all the time that has elapsed without having anything resolved. In this stage, there is no true we, only I against you and you against me. Resentments, demands, and complaints are often the three most common communications in this stage. The fuse is short, and the explosions long.

The *despair* stage has kicked in when there is no hope; no commitment; nothing left to be aroused or upset by; no interest in working things out; no belief in, interest in, or energy for change. In such gloom, nothing that happens in the relationship really matters anymore or has any impact. At this stage, things have flatlined between the two of you, and there are fewer and shorter arguments. You tiptoe around, if you are present at all. "Whatever" or "yeah, OK" is the usual reply to a comment or question by either partner.

The first stage has energy ready to use. The second has energy ready to be harnessed, so the relationship can upgrade to stage one, even though it will be a hard climb. The third stage has no energy in it for change.

Which stage are you in? Which stage do you believe your partner is in? Which stage does she say she is in? Which stage(s) did you see your parents in?

We may move from the reaching out stage to the protest stage because we have lost hope in working things out. We may move from protest to despair because we lost hope altogether. Thus, each new stage includes grief about a disappointment. Have you let yourself experience your grief if you are in stage two or three?

These three stages, by the way, reflect those discovered by psychoanalyst John Bowlby in his study of orphans and refugee children. Those words—*orphan* and *refugee*—are so chillingly antithetical to connection; they certainly ring with an ominous toll to beings like us who want so much to be held lovingly.

WHAT A RELATIONSHIP ASKS OF US • A wholesome, serious bond rests on six foundations. These are the vital signs of a relationship, and a regular, careful checkup does a lot to show us the state of health of our union:

- Trust: We can trust the other, and we can be trusted.
- Intimacy: We maintain a caring connection by giving and receiving the five A's of intimate love: attention, acceptance, appreciation, affection, and allowing.
- Commitment: We have made an enduring commitment to one another. This means we do all we can to work out our problems together, to keep our agreements to one another, and to observe the ground rules of our relationship. We are committed to staying with each other through the various phases of life together—unless there is abuse.
- Ego-surrender: We continually let go of the part of our ego that becomes caught up in control, entitlement, competitiveness, insistence on being right, refusal to forgive, and retaliation. Our goal in healthy relating is not to gratify a self-centered ego but to build a healthy ego to gratify the relationship.
- Physicality: We maintain our erotic connection. This is not the "chemistry" of infatuation, which is temporary. It is the chemistry of ongoing liveliness shown in physical, sexual, and emotional ways as appropriate to the nature of the bond and agreements.
- Spiritual practice: Each of us is dedicated to integrity and loving-kindness as a personal spiritual practice that applies to how we behave toward everyone. This practice is outlined in Appendix 1.

These six components are the criteria for successful relating. Each is a gift we can give a partner. Each may evoke fear, because we are being challenged to transcend our ego and give ourselves to another person. We know that means putting our often-wounded, still-vulnerable hearts at risk.

Ask yourself how well or poorly each of these six challenges is being met in your relationship now. How has the level of intensity of each changed since you first met? Are you fully convinced of the importance of each element? How does each one evoke fear in you? Are you satisfied with how they are coming through from you to your partner and from your partner to you?

Ask your partner to answer the same questions, then compare your replies. This is the hardest part of the practice, but it can be very useful in showing you the state of your union and whether your relationship is thriving or expiring. It is never too late to install or repair these six crucial components of a loving adult partnership. A commitment on both your parts to all the practices in this book can help you get on track, if necessary.

If you do not have a partner, the criteria for a healthy relationship can be your checklist for what to look for in a prospective partner. The checklist can also help you know how ready you are for a relationship. Can you and do you want to step up to the plate in each of the six ballparks?

SAFE CONVERSATIONS • Love brings out all the facts about who we are and who our partner is. It is said that love is blind, but real love is an eye-opener. We really see into ourselves and our partner, into our past and present.

Built into any commitment to a relationship is the requirement that we strive to understand how our partner came to be who he is. We want to understand exactly where his attitudes, beliefs, and reflexes came from so we can hold them supportively or help him work on upgrading them.

In any relationship, we are liable to experience the original distress and terror of our past. It can only be healed if we do not take that out on a partner. A relationship is meant to be the new holding environment in which old wounds can be examined and sutured—by both of us. This is why our work on ourselves is aided so much by a partner who understands us.

Indeed, since so much of our present behavior is based on our past experience, partners can benefit greatly by understanding each other's backgrounds. Intimacy in a relationship grows when partners share certain facts and experiences about their childhood—a self-conducted background check. Some of us do not recall much of our childhood. But everyone can engage in this kind of sharing in some way. To open the discussion and explore it, even superficially, starts the internal realizations that will in time bring depth to our self-knowledge and to our partner's understanding of us.

Partners need to understand how each other's needs were addressed in childhood, how feelings were expressed, and whether and how abuse or addiction happened. They take turns sharing information on the first of these issues in great detail and only then move on to the next one. While one partner shares, it is best for the other to listen without interrupting. This is a time to listen and learn without comments, judgments, or comparisons. Simple questions are appropriate, however, when they serve to clear up any confusion.

The practice ends with each partner sharing about what he or she gained from listening and being listened to. This rounds off the conversation and contributes to the sense of intimacy.

To tell our story to one another and have it received with the five A's builds mutual trust. Intimacy increases as we share our past and ourselves. Is fear of that intimacy why we avoid sharing?

Partners can disclose to each other in turn about any or all of the following topics. It is best to limit ourselves to one topic per sitting, with each partner taking a turn on the same topic.

The conversation works best when we do not editorialize but simply share the facts and our feelings about them, without blame or judgment of anyone. The listener listens without comment. Then a dialogue opens. There is no judgment, defensiveness, or evasiveness, only attempts to understand with interest and compassion. This is what makes it a safe conversation.

When the word *parents* is used, respond first about one parent and then about the other.

How my early needs were handled in childhood

1. How did my parents show me attention?
2. How did my parents show that they accepted me as I am?
3. How did my parents show they valued me?
4. How did my parents show me affection, especially in physical ways?
5. Did my parents allow me to make my own choices, or were they controlling and demanding?
6. In each of these cases, was it safe to ask my parents for what I needed?

How my needs can be met in this relationship

Tell your partner about your unique ways of receiving each of the five A's.

1. This is the kind of attention I need, and this is what helps me feel I'm getting it. . . .
2. This is the kind of acceptance I need, and this is what helps me feel I'm getting it. . . .
3. This is the kind of appreciation I need, and this is what helps me feel I'm getting it. . . .
4. This is the kind of affection I need, and this is what helps me feel I'm getting it. . . .
5. This is the kind of respect for my boundaries and freedom I need, and this is what helps me feel I'm getting it. . . .

How feelings were handled in my childhood

Respond to these questions with reference to your father, mother, siblings, and yourself in turn.

1. How was sadness expressed in my childhood home?
2. How was anger expressed in my childhood home?
3. How was fear expressed in my childhood home?
4. How was exuberance expressed in my childhood home?

In talking about these four main feelings, discuss whether it was safe to express them and whether you felt safe when your parents expressed them. Notice they spell out the acronym SAFE, so it is easy to remember which feelings to check in about: sadness, anger, fear, and exuberance.

How feelings can be expressed safely now

1. Are there any feelings you do not see as appropriate for a man or woman to show?
2. What is our plan and agreement about our expression of feelings?
3. How can I feel safe in my sadness, and what do I need from you when I am sad? How can I help you feel safe too?
4. How can I feel safe in my anger, and what do I need from you when I am angry? How can I help you feel safe too?
5. How can I feel safe when I show you my fear, and what do I need from you when I am afraid? How can I help you feel safe too?
6. How can I feel safe showing exuberance, and what do I need from you when I am really happy? How can I help you feel safe too?

Other conversations

1. How were conflicts handled between my parents and between my parents and me?
2. How do I want to handle conflicts in this relationship?
3. Was free speech encouraged in my household so that I felt safe bringing up my needs, speaking my truth, commenting on what people said or did, and stating my opinion?
4. How can I and my partner guarantee free speech between us?
5. What is my family history concerning the use of alcohol and drugs?
6. What is my history and present use of alcohol and drugs?

7. What is the history of abuse between my parents, toward me, or to or from my siblings?

8. Do we feel abused in any way by one another?

Here is a way of continuing the process:

List your parents' dysfunctional or hurtful reactions to you, such as shaming or put-downs. Show this to your partner. This builds trust because you are making yourself vulnerable. You are trusting that your partner won't take advantage of your self-disclosed Achilles' heel.

Then work toward agreeing not to act in those dysfunctional and hurtful ways toward one another. Notice any resistance to that commitment. Hold the commitment with the five A's, not with judgment, shame, or blame.

Examine how you responded to your parents when they did not act in nurturing ways toward you. When your partner acts the same way, commit yourself not to respond in your old, habitual way but to use the style of direct communication ("Ouch!") and then work toward making an agreement for change.

Some of us have learned only primitive ways to rebalance ourselves after a hurt, such as retaliation. It is wise to combine a healthy "Ouch!" with a commitment to working things out in dialogue and a practice of loving-kindness. (If necessary, review the explanation of a healthy "Ouch!" in Chapter 3.)

We can express resentments so they can be aired and resolved. Although this makes sense and is helpful, we may want to keep in mind that resentment can become a maneuver, a form of manipulation: "I won't do this for you because you did that to me." It is therefore important not only to express our resentments but to call ourselves to task if we are using them in a retaliatory or pouting way. (We will continue to address ways to work with resentments in another practice in this section.)

Ask your partner questions like these to initiate a discussion:

1. How can you and I become vigilant about our family triggers so they do not go off in our relationship?

2. Can we commit to protecting our relationship in that way?
3. Can we be careful not to insert our past into this present moment?

Since to love is to be vulnerable, what we are really saying when we love is, "My relationship to you is so valuable to me that I am giving you the power to wound my heart, but my trust in you balances that, so I also believe you won't use your power that way." Can you say that to your partner without reserve? Can your partner say it to you?

Self-awareness can arouse anxiety. Most of us do not feel relaxed enough about our self-knowledge to do this practice without prior work on ourselves. We can find some of that work in the preceding practices in this book.

One important requisite skill in understanding ourselves is being able to handle the fears that may be caused by meeting up with our own truth. It happens best when we learn to trust ourselves, build our equanimity, let go of ego defensiveness, and remain enormously curious about this reality called "me" and that reality called "we."

Our tone of voice in all our conversations is crucial to creating safety for the person with whom we are communicating. Work with your tone of voice. In your assertiveness, speak firmly but in a kind, even tone that does not sound intimidating or come across as aggressive. Beware of unconsciously reverting to your street voice or the tough-guy voice that may reflect your national origin. I was visiting a friend once and was on the phone telling my teenage son at home to do a chore. Unknowingly, I took on an aggressive tone toward him because he was refusing to cooperate. My friend walked into the room and looked around. I asked her about it later, and she said the voice she heard was not like mine, so she thought someone else was in the room! I was using my Italian gangster voice, little guessing that such a voice was in me. I have not heard it since, but I don't have the slightest doubt it is sitting in me like a gargoyle on a cathedral, immovable, ever on the lookout. It is waiting for the someone who may dare resist my controlling ego. All the work I have done on myself—we do on ourselves—whether psychological and spiritual, does not arrest my inner Al Capone.

CLEARING THE PAST • Here is an example of how to work on changing a pattern in a relationship that goes back to childhood or is a leftover from a former relationship. This can only work if both partners are open to it.

Scenario: Your partner's pattern is to cause upset, and then when you withdraw from him, he has a reason to blame you and permission to withhold. He saw his father do this often.

You may change the pattern by calling his bluff. When he is being difficult, you do not withdraw or withhold. Rather you simply stay put, focusing not on being right but only on lightening the atmosphere, such as injecting a note of humor. To exit a cycle is to intervene in it by changing one spoke of the wheel. In this instance, the cycle continues if you withdraw. When you do not withdraw, you interrupt the cycle. This surprises your partner, because he expects the response he is used to, the one that keeps him in the pattern. By getting close and creating a new scenario, you break the pattern. That is often all it takes to tame the unquiet, scared child who resides in all of us.

Finally—and this is crucial to success—you need to ask him to perform a similar favor for you to unseat one of your patterns. Then the practice is not patronizing but reciprocal, another example of a loving connection. Intimate bonding is about mutual acknowledgment of patterns and mutual offering of help. This can only happen when both partners feel safe because they trust that they both want to break patterns. This is *not* about achieving a triumph of ego; it is about gaining a victory for intimacy. Having that motivation is a way of showing a loving commitment to a relationship.

It is wise to recall the sobering statement by the attachment theorist Mary Main that we need five years of consistent responses from a partner that are different from our parents' responses to us before our fear, attitudes, and habits can change.* So this practice may take five years of compassionately staying with his resistance or entrenched ego. This gives new emphasis to the role of patience in true intimacy. As we pon-

---

* Mary Main, "Attachment: From Early Childhood Through the Lifespan" (conference at University of California–Los Angeles, 2002).

der Mary Main's five-year prediction, we wonder if, for us slow learners, even that timetable may be optimistic. Can we wait? Do we have a partner who is willing to wait?

UPGRADING OUR EMOTIONAL RESPONSES, ESPECIALLY ANGER • Emotions are visceral. William James pointed out that without a bodily reaction, an emotion would be a thought. Our emotions usually arise in a primitive form. It takes practice to align our feelings to reality and express them with loving-kindness, toward both ourselves and others. This alignment of feelings is not a rejection of them, but a taming of them, a rewiring, an upgrade from primal to civil. It is a befriending and integrating of an experience so that it stays in tune with love while using its full range of sharps and flats, the only way a tune can be fully melodic.

A word about *upgrading* in this context. To upgrade is to update, refashion, rehabilitate, revitalize, and renew our attitudes, thoughts, feelings, and habits. For instance, we update our religion when we let go of fear, guilt about our impulses, superstition, and blind obedience. Likewise with patriotism: if we have the grammar school concept of "My country right or wrong," we upgrade to the adult version of patriotism we learned in the sixties of "We speak truth to power to influence policies in the direction of sanity and peace." To upgrade ourselves automatically includes loving ourselves because we are stepping into our fully emergent self, the lovable and loving self.

The following chart may help distinguish primitive and upgraded styles of expressing emotions. We can ask ourselves where we fit.

Primitively Expressed Emotions	*Tamed, Regulated, and Managed Emotions*
Are automatic, sudden, and out of control	Are spontaneous and have awareness of what we are up to
Are so caught up in the heat of the moment that they lose touch with reality, because our prefrontal cortex goes offline	Arise from a lively energy that does not lose its contact with reality, because our prefrontal cortex remains online to manage our limbic reactions

Burst out directly from the amygdala without assessment	Are assessed in the prefrontal cortex
Are reactive	Are responsive
Perceive only a narrow repertory of reactions	Notice a wider range of possible responses
Tend to look for someone to blame (the other is the cause of our feeling)	Take personal responsibility (the other is the catalyst of our feeling)
Arise from our survival instinct	Arise from a healthy ego that is free of undue defenses or the need to attack
Disregard the importance of staying connected (if we are avoidant) or of craving undue attachment (if we are ambivalent)	Focus on maintaining a loving bond that is secure, flexible, and stable, because we have and maintain a secure attachment
Continue to cause us stress as they remain unresolved	Are processed and resolved so they can end in serenity

Anger is an example of an automatically aroused emotion that can show up in an adaptive or a primitive way. Healthy anger is displeasure at injustice that makes us want to respond by engaging our power. This power is nonharming and does not get out of control.

When our commitment is to a life of love, we choose to cultivate healthy anger responses to people and situations. We practice showing our anger by beginning with the "Ouch!" that reports our pain. Our anger immediately follows, but it is not in the embroidered style described in the left-hand column of the table. In that primitive mode, we might be cruel and intimidating to others. Our untamed anger can also distort the reality of what is happening, so we assess a situation inaccurately.

When someone angers or upsets us, we can tame our emotional response by changing our question from "Why does her behavior trigger me?" to "What are my triggers, and how can I work on them?" Mostly, they harken back to childhood and are aroused when similar things happen to us now with a partner. We can work with triggers in a relationship by distinguishing two parts of the interaction.

In part one, what she said or did that was insulting or upsetting calls for an "Ouch!" so she can know the painful impact of her words or behaviors. That happens in the house—it is between us, interactive, always respectful and nonviolent.

But part two, our ongoing or overblown reaction, is entirely ours; it is not interactive but the responsibility of our own bodymind. So that part we "take outside." I use that expression humorously, recalling the many Westerns I have seen in which, at the start of a barroom brawl, the saloon keeper wisely says, "Take it outside, boys."

The two-part distinction—What's ours?/What's mine?—applies to major resentments within a relationship. A resentment is ongoing anger. The anger part is to be expressed by one partner to the other. The other partner can show he understands it and can make amends in whatever way is appropriate. But it may not end there, because a serious breach in a relationship has a tail of pain attached to it, so the angry partner may not be satisfied. The person with the resentment takes care of that part on her own by grieving or exploring the further implications it has for her, such as how it is recalling past experiences. To be able to identify the time sequence helps a lot: "Oh, this is my past showing up again."

Part one, the resentment, is interpersonal, so it is worked on by the couple. They address, process, and resolve their issue together, at home.

Part two, the leftover pain, is personal, so it is worked on individually, outside the house. The work is usually grieving what happened in the past, especially in childhood. "Outside the house" may mean in the therapist's office.

WORKING THINGS OUT • Here is a practice model for working out problems in a relationship:

PHYSICAL PREPARATION: SCAN AND REPORT

We begin with a physical check-in. We tune into our body to scan where we are comfortable/uncomfortable, flexible/constricted, calm/anxious, and lively/depressed. We notice if we are fidgeting, if our heart is racing, if we can't catch our breath, if we are stammering, if our palms are sweaty, if we have butterflies in our stomach, or if we have a tight neck. All of these are signs of anxiety about addressing concerns. They tell us this is not the time for us to deal with issues. We may need more time to calm down so we can come from a position of strength and clarity.

We may also feel fine physically but know intuitively that we need time to ponder and incubate our concerns before addressing them.

When the other person insists that now is the time, self-caring may require that we speak up and say, "Not yet." That insistence may become the first issue to address. When the situation is reversed and our partner is not ready, we have to be patient enough to let go of dealing with things until he is ready. It takes practice to deal with our bodily issues and hesitations. It is an act of love for others to work on handling what can be handled in as timely a manner as possible. It is an act of love for ourselves to take all the time we need. Somewhere between those two is the middle path of mutuality in relationships.

Breathing and relaxation techniques may help. We then use our body as a resource, not only as an indicator. We can use it to regulate our feelings so we are gradually able to experience them in whatever range they require while maintaining our equanimity.

To deal with issues in a relationship is to address, process, resolve, and integrate our concerns. We are ready to do this only when our bodily reactions do not get in the way of our being fully present, both to speak and to listen. We are ready only when we are not afraid of speaking freely. We are ready only when we are sure we can recover if things get scary, high-pitched, or too close for comfort. We are certainly not ready if we have not worked on our ego, and it still becomes indignant that someone dares to challenge us, question us, or call us to task.

The practice of addressing, processing, resolving, and integrating is not about concepts and logic. They can get in the way of working on our issues. Our intellect can keep us one step removed from our real feelings, which are physical and sensual, not logical and linear. Thus, talking can be an avoidance if it keeps us in our head without moving us forward.

This practice of working things out with one another is more about process than content. It is therefore an *embodied* practice. Our bodily feelings have to be on tap for full participation. In addition, it is useful to report in to one another about where in our body we feel reactions to what is being said or what is happening.

To do any of this, we have to be open to challenging truths and not just comforting truths. We have to be able to ask direct questions and give direct answers. We will soon find out if we are with the kind of person who is open to that kind of discourse. If we perceive that there is no openness or chink of an opening, our best bet is to pause and return another day or get help from a therapist. A partner who refuses to address concerns with us at all is not really with—connected to—us. We can meet the challenges of resistance and reluctance from a partner, but not refusal.

Here are some hints on how we can address, process, and resolve our problems and concerns in an embodied way, once we feel ready. Each of the steps in the work of handling conflicts is itself a form of love, using our criterion for love as a welcoming and extending of connection. The steps can happen in any order or more than one at a time. This practice has to be mutual in order to work.

Step One: Addressing

This only works if we can be open and forthcoming about ourselves, our feelings, and our behavior. There is nothing to fear if there is nothing to hide.

To address an issue in our relationship means the following:

- We check in on which of the three stages we are at—still trying, protesting, despair—in our relationship as of now. (See the earlier section in this chapter.)
- We talk about what is going on with us internally and externally and ask the same about our partner.
- We state the problem in words as each of us sees it. We use non-threatening facial expressions and gestures that further describe it.

- We ask ourselves whom are we talking to when we argue. Are we talking to one another as adults or as stand-ins for our parents, former partners, or anyone other than our current partner?
- We assess our present situation candidly and directly and are open to the other's assessment without arguing our point or having to be right.

When we become mindful in daily life, we begin to see others and their behavior in a neutral way. We are witnesses, not juries. We may assess, but we do not make anyone wrong. Nor do we take what happens personally. It becomes information. We can ask others for accountability. In some instances, all we can do is accept the givens about others. This may call for grief on our part, but not blame. Grief keeps us in our own feelings. Blame hijacks grief in favor of rage, resentment, or retaliation.

Step Two: Processing

To process our conflict with someone in an embodied way means the following:

- We express our emotions nonviolently and hold them as our own without blame.
- We keep reporting about where we are in our body.
- We identify which of our reactions or actions come from ego.
- We acknowledge that our own shadow may be lurking behind our projections onto our partner.
- We make the connection between this issue and our past relationships or childhood.
- In working with a fear, we use the 4A technique: We *admit* or acknowledge that we are afraid, noting where the fear is in our body. We *allow* ourselves to feel our fear bodily. We *act* in such a way that fear can no longer stop or drive us in our decisions and choices. We *affirm* our newfound power.

When we feel neediness, haunted by a need that cannot be satisfied, we apply the same 4A approach. We *admit* or acknowledge that our need is a relic from the past, and we seek to identify it. We recall and *allow* ourselves to feel the pain associated with its nonfulfillment. We are careful not to be overwhelmed by how much pain we let ourselves feel, but we allow more in than we usually do. As adults with power, we *act* in a way that does not pander to our neediness; for example, we endure not having what we crave or seek healthy outlets for our frustrations. We use an *affirmation* that helps us remain aware of the practice and continues it.

STEP THREE: RESOLVING

To *resolve* our relationship concern means the following:

- We apologize and make amends if necessary.
- We forgive if appropriate.
- We do not harbor rancor or resentment.
- We have no plan to retaliate.
- We make an agreement to do things differently in the future. Agreements are meetings of minds, and that is love according to our definition of positive connection.

Finally, here is a helpful check-in that encapsulates the preceding practices. We ask four questions about the unfinished business of our past. Each of them strongly impacts our adult relationships. Each can be worked with using the practices presented so far. These questions depict the elements of childhood or of relationship that are most difficult for the majority of us to deal with, but we are now gaining tools to work with them.

1. What needs were unfulfilled?
2. What feelings were unexpressed?
3. What conflicts were unresolved?
4. What events were unclear? (This refers to events and behaviors whose meaning was never clear to us, such as family secrets.)

Why We Hurt the One We Love

> Look at how I was wounded in the house of those who
> loved me!
>
> —ZECHARIAH 13:6

We hurt those we love by:

- Judging or inhibiting them for who they are
- Choosing to control them
- Disregarding or minimizing their needs, boundaries, and feelings
- Insisting that our desires are the only ones that matter
- Withholding appreciation
- Being physically, emotionally, sexually, or spiritually abusive
- Taking out on them the rage that comes from our childhood
- Retaliating when they cross us

We can explore ten possible explanations of the phenomenon of hurting those we love.

1. IT GOES WITH THE TERRITORY.

All of us cause disappointment, so pain is inevitable in any relationship. In addition, the givens of life, such as endings and changes, certainly leave a wake of pain. In a love connection, each person becomes important to the other. It is therefore natural that each takes what happens in the relationship seriously. This increases the pain that may result from any betrayal or disappointment between the two people. The stronger the bond, the harder we are hit by what happens between us. We also can't be happy when the one we love is in pain. Thus, to love anyone is to open ourselves up to feeling hurt in some way. To choose to love is to be vulnerable. But it is not victimization. It is accessibility to the given of pain in human relating. As we say yes to the givens of love, our pain shows itself to be a feature of adulthood, of building inner strength, of cultivating compassion.

2. WE ARE TOO CLOSE FOR COMFORT.

The one we love often lives in close quarters with us, or we see her often. Because she is close by when we feel bad, she is in the line of fire. Close quarters lead to stress and can make us impatient with one another. We may irritate one another and become angry at each other. As she pokes at us, she can wound us. We automatically hit back in defensive aggression. The closer we are to the one we love, the more cautious and patient we have to be if our love is to survive and flourish. How sadly ironic that we do the opposite—keep taking chances on the survival of our relationship by running roughshod over our partner, the one who deserves our special care.

3. WE TRY TO MAKE SOMEONE OVER.

A phrase we often hear in love songs is "You are mine." It is natural to become possessive of those we love; it goes back to our cave ancestry. In addition, we want to make over anything we possess, upgrade and redesign it to fit our changing needs. This need to make people over takes the form of control and inappropriate jealousy. Our confining behavior causes pain to the other, who resists that interference with who he is. There is still too much neediness in our way of loving. The other person knows we love him in our own somewhat dysfunctional way and wants to please us. Yet he wants to be himself, so he contests our attempts to control. This ambivalence is itself a form of pain in those we love.

4. THERE ARE TABOO FEELINGS.

It is normal to have erotic feelings toward those we love. It is not appropriate to act on them within a family, in a teacher-student relationship, or with someone who is in a monogamous relationship with someone else. We may not want to admit to ourselves that we have such feelings. We may then act contrary to the way we feel, usually in exaggerated ways. We may become aggressive as a way of creating distance, even though distance is the opposite of what we actually desire. This form of hurting the other is meant to protect us from admitting what we feel, from acting in a way that is unacceptable to us or crossing a line we do not want to cross. We hurt those we love when we do not employ appropriate ways to handle our feelings. These ways include noticing our feelings, realizing that they are inappropriate, and not acting on them. We do all this while maintaining kindly attitudes and loving behavior toward the other person.

5. THERE'S THE RUB.

To rub something causes friction. To squeeze tightly can lead to chafing. Touching can lead to poking. In relationships, it is the same: nearness can lead to abrasiveness. We can love someone so intensely that we want constant contact. We get so close that she feels trapped. We do not realize that what we are doing causes pressure and pain. Our love is stronger than our sensitivity to limits. We dismiss her "Ouch!" or do not even hear it. If she does not say it, she may be in on continuing the pain, letting it happen and passively welcoming it. Love has respect for boundaries and caution about the hazards in too much closeness. How many "Ouches" go unnoticed or unannounced? How many are stored inside each of us?

6. WE PREFER THE COMFORT OF OBLIVION.

True love takes vigilance over how we speak and act. We become so comfortable with the people we love that we tend to forget that. Our trust in the durability of their love can override our caution about their feelings. Love gives us free rein to be ourselves, and we forget that our freedom has to be responsible. We forget that we have to stay on the alert for that cruel ego reaction that can sometimes arise in any of us. We may say something without pausing to ask if it may hurt someone's feelings. We may act in haste and disregard someone's boundaries. We may take the one we love for granted and not show gratitude for all he does for us.

7. WE HAVE LEFTOVER ANGER FROM CHILDHOOD.

Most of us have not done the work of clearing the pain and resentments we carry from our experience with our parents in early life.

This work involves grieving the past and letting go of it, the only guarantee that we will not repeat it in an adult relationship. We may still be enraged at how our parents disappointed us, even when there was no abuse. Our survival may have been at stake if we spoke up in childhood. In a relationship of trust, we are not in that danger. Thus, we may displace our original anger onto our partner. We may be trying to get back at our parents by our hurtful actions toward the person we love now. Our anger was never resolved, so it festers inside us and lashes out at the one on whom it is now safe to inflict it. We may also displace our anger about our daily frustrations, such as work problems, onto our partner. She is not as threatening as our boss and is certainly more forgiving.

8. WE HURT THE WAY WE WERE HURT.

Some of us carry a history of abuse from our childhood. This history is not just an intellectual memory. Indeed, the harsh events of childhood do not resound in us like the clap of a hand that begins and ends in an instant. They are like strikes on a gong that reverberate for a lifetime. The gong is our body.

As long as it is still unresolved, it remains in us as a model of behavior and can exhibit itself to others when they displease us. Our automatic reactions to others, no matter how close they are to our heart, may be a replay of what happened to us. Then the past hurt makes for present hurting. We do not do this deliberately; it is unconscious. Our conscious intentions are pure, but our unconscious may be mean. This is why part of loving is staying on guard lest we react in ways that hurt those we love the way we were hurt.

9. OUR SHADOW SIDE EMERGES.

A shadow side of intimacy is excessive dependency. We usually resent the person we need. The more we depend on her, the more anger we may have toward her. We may then deliberately though unconsciously cause her pain. Another shadow dimension of intimacy is entitlement. We may also be angry that she does not love us with the same intensity we show toward her. We are, unbeknownst to ourselves, retaliating against the one who does not come through for us as we expect or believe we deserve. No matter how close we are to someone, moments of anger arise in any relationship. When that anger is not expressed and resolved, it is likely to come out in passive ways. Then we hurt the one we love without having to admit to ourselves that so much aggression is in us.

10. TRUST CAN ATTRACT BETRAYAL.

Trust is safety and security. In a relationship, we may be sure the other loves us and will not retaliate if we offend him. Ironically, there is something about that perfect love that may make it safe to stray. We most easily betray the person we can most securely trust. This is a self-defeating tendency, a sly mystery about us humans. Something in us chooses to hurt the other and upset what is working so well for us. Perhaps we can't believe happiness can last, so we preempt it. Perhaps we have an impulse to damage beauty rather than cherish and protect it. Perhaps we can't give peace a chance but have to upset and violate our serenity. Perhaps, strange as it sounds, we are testing the one we love: "Will you love me, shadow and all?" There is no final answer. To call this the power of the dark side or our tragic flaw is to beg the question. All we know is that betrayal can happen when there is no reason for it. It is as if trust hired the assassin of love to attack and destroy itself. Enigmatic and poignant indeed are the tears in our human story.

> O Rose, thou art sick!
> The invisible worm
> That flies in the night,
> In the howling storm,
>
> Has found out thy bed
> Of crimson joy:
> And his dark secret love
> Does thy life destroy.
>
> —WILLIAM BLAKE

PRACTICE: BEING ON THE LOOKOUT

In each of the preceding sections, our best practices were mindfulness and loving-kindness. Mindfulness helps us remain aware of what we do. Loving-kindness helps us do what is kind. We can also benefit from these commitments:

- We keep engaging in the grief work that can help resolve the childhood issues we carry over into adult relationships.
- We watch for the surfacing of a mean streak, even if we think we don't have one.
- We admit to those we love that we have a shadow side and that no matter how much we care about them, it may rear its head—though we are committed to staying on the lookout.
- We ask others to call us on being hurtful in any way. We welcome feedback and are open to hearing and honoring an "Ouch!"
- We declare our commitment to be as direct as we can be about our feelings, especially anger.
- We express appreciation regularly to those we love so as not to take them for granted.
- We remain aware of the boundaries of others and respect them.
- We do not hurt the one we love by deliberately wanting to cause pain, or wishing the downfall of the other. That is not love at all. But we accept the given that we may hurt those we love, and we are always ready to show our compunction for what we have done, acknowledge the pain we triggered in the other, make whatever amends are appropriate, and commit to change. (This practice is appropriate whenever we have offended or hurt someone in any relationship.)

A friendly eye could never see such faults.
—SHAKESPEARE, *Julius Caesar*

8

Showing Our Love Everywhere

> The mind of love . . . increases immeasurably and eventually can embrace the whole world.
>
> —MADHYAMA AGAMA

SPIRITUAL PRACTICES, such as *agape* in Christianity or loving-kindness in Buddhism, are intended to help us expand the scope of our love from ourselves and those close to us to people everywhere: "First I love me, then I love some others, then one other, then all others." We reach from our self-caring into every corner of our life and world with limitless love.

Traditionally, psychological health has focused on how each person successfully separates and individuates. This certainly reflects the themes of the heroic journey archetype: we leave where we are, go through painful struggles, surmount obstacles, find the prize of higher consciousness, and bring it home (that is, share it with those we love and everyone).

However, separation and individuation honor only the journey element of our development. They leave out the *affiliation* element of life. Self-fulfillment means evolving into our full stature physically, psychologically, and spiritually. Our complete stature is reached when we express our full capacity for caring connections. This leads us to transcend our traditional definition of growing up as separating and individuating.

Instead of configuring separating as breaking away from others, we see it as a path to relating to the world outside our home while maintaining our original bonds. Instead of imagining that individuating requires ruggedly striking out on our own, we see it happening in the holding environment that supports our unique gifts, needs, and goals.

Psychological maturity then focuses on establishing, tending, and maintaining intimate bonds with others. We separate only to expand; we individuate only because we have bonded. Otherwise, separating and individuating are misunderstood by the ego as permission to focus on itself and thereby miss its chance for the joy of self-giving love.

Our focus on the heroic journey theme in the self-help movement has helped us understand our life and purpose more richly. It is time for us to open the journey motif so that it is not limited to us as individuals. We are individual pilgrims but within a pilgrim humanity. The heroic journey is not only for individuals; the whole world is on a journey of evolution toward consciousness and love. Our journey is a collective one, accent on the "one." We have a collective identity, so our love is necessarily both personal and cosmic-collective, accent on the "we."

We can trust that our life purpose is appropriate when it aligns with nature. Since the whole cosmos participates in evolution, our life purpose is to align with the direction of evolution toward convergence in synergy. Since synergy is connection, all that is left for us to be whole is to join in caring at a universal level. The transition from "me first" to "all together" is the synergy of love. I recall being taught in Catholic high school that Jesus promised anyone who received communion on nine consecutive first Fridays that he or she would not die without the opportunity to receive the last rites. My thought was, "Oh, I have to be sure to do that so I can be preserved from hell." It occurred to me only in recent years that true devotion does not mean comfort in the fact that "I'm all set" but in having a heart as big as that of the God who made the promise. Then my response would have been, "I offer all my devotion and merit so that everyone can be saved, not just me." That is the Sacred Heart in all its glory, *agape*.

Universal and unconditional love is *radical* because it is so unlike our often narrow way of loving. It is not based on attraction, selection, comparison, deservedness, or how others treat us. It is utterly without discrimination.

Here is a chart that helps us distinguish between selective love and universal love.

Loving Someone	*Loving Everyone*
Exclusive	Inclusive
Reciprocity seen as important	Reciprocity seen as unnecessary
Conditional	Unconditional
Connected to our childhood needs and issues	Not limited or designed by our personal issues
A response to being pleased by someone	Arising from spiritual consciousness
Based on how appealing someone is to us	Based on a giving of ourselves, no matter how unappealing others are
Based on what we need from others	Based on how others need us
Shown in face-to-face contact	Shown also to those we do not see
Nurtured by daily interactions and often unconscious psychological motivations	Nurtured by daily caring and compassion, often with a spiritual motivation
Possibly temporary	Enduring
Ordinary	Radical

Here are some more reasons that universally extended love is radical:

- Rugged independence is not an acceptable lifestyle for us, because our primary focus is on interdependence.

- Our compassion and caring are impartial.
- We never give up on others.
- No one is ever exiled from our hearts permanently. Even when we break off contact with people, we still wish the best for them.
- We act in ways that attempt to include others and maintain a connection.
- We do not hurt back, no matter how others treat us. We hope for transformation and not retribution, for reconciliation and not division, reconnection and not estrangement.

Here are three wise comments on the universal love that does not give up on anyone:

> Self-love but serves the virtuous mind to wake
> As the small pebble stirs the peaceful lake;
> The center moved, a circle strait succeeds,
> Another still, and still another spreads;
> Friend, parent, neighbor, first it will embrace;
> His country next; and next all human race;
> Wide and more wide, the o'erflowings of the mind
> Take every creature in, of every kind;
> Earth smiles around, with boundless bounty blest,
> And heaven beholds its image in his breast.
>
> —ALEXANDER POPE

> As man advances in civilization, and small tribes are united into larger communities, the simplest reason would tell each individual that he ought to extend his social instincts and sympathies to all members of the same nation, though personally unknown to him. This point being once reached, there is only an artificial barrier to prevent his sympathies extending to the men of all nations and races.
>
> —CHARLES DARWIN

During the Vietnam War, I meditated on the Vietnamese soldiers, praying they would not be killed in battle. But I also meditated on the American soldiers and felt a very deep sympathy for them. I knew that they had been sent far away from home to kill or be killed, and I prayed for their safety. That led to a deep aspiration that the war would end and allow all Vietnamese and all enemies to live in peace. Once that aspiration was clear, there was only one path to take—to work for the end of the war. When you practice love meditation, you have to take that path. As soon as you see that the person you call your enemy is also suffering, you will be ready to love and accept him. The idea of "enemy" vanishes and is replaced by the reality of someone who is suffering and needs our love and compassion.

—THICH NAHT HANH

Over-the-Top Ways of Loving

Even if bandits were to sever you savagely limb from limb with a two-handled saw . . . you should train thus: "Our minds will remain unaffected, and we shall utter no evil words. We shall abide, compassionate for their welfare, with a mind of loving-kindness, and without inner hate."

—BHIKKHU NANAMOLI AND BHIKKHU BODHI

Over-the-top means supererogatory, or more than what is required, expected, or usually considered necessary. Over-the-top ways of loving can include going the extra mile, turning the other cheek, even giving our lives and fortunes for others. This is *heroic agape*.

There have always been teachers who recommend such self-sacrificing love. They ask for dedication and courage in a way that certainly seems foolish and foolhardy to the ordinary person. What such teachers recommend as spiritual practice is counterintuitive to fairness, let alone self-survival.

Any form of love includes inconveniencing ourselves for the sake of those we care about. But unconditional altruism means sacrificing ourselves for enemies too. Engaging in this over-the-top way of loving represents a powerful faith in our potential as humans, since it contradicts our natural instinct to look out for number one. Is this a foolish misunderstanding of love, or is it what love can be in its highest, wisest form?

Altruism and self-sacrifice can come across as top-down and seem disqualified as authentic love, since they do not include a sense of equality. Love seems to happen in a context in which self and others are equal. The only exception happens in special, critical moments when we sacrifice our own safety, such as to rescue a drowning man. Perhaps self-sacrifice is reserved for those occasions.

In modern times, we can consider the counterintuitive recommendations of Gandhi and Martin Luther King, Jr., as examples of a call to show a self-sacrificing love not only in a crisis but for a cause. The cause *is* love, because it is invariably about establishing connection, such as equality among various sectors of society or reconciliation through nonviolent resolution of conflicts.

Gandhi wrote, "Examining human life, we see much violence. Yet life goes on, so there must be a higher law than that of violence, the love that does not burn others but burns itself." It is a challenge to commit to a love like that, a trust that it is our true nature to dedicate ourselves so courageously to nonviolent action against oppression that we put our life at risk. Martin Luther King, Jr., made this suggestion in his acceptance speech for the 1964 Nobel Peace Prize: "We will take direct action against injustice without waiting for other agencies to act.... We will always be willing to talk and seek fair compromise, but we are ready to suffer when necessary and even to risk our lives to become witnesses to the truth as we see it."

In the paragraphs that follow, we will encounter some suggestions along these rather agitating lines. The teachers speaking in this section are indeed disturbing, because they propose that we make choices that do not ensure our safety and security. Their teaching requires putting everything on the line in a bold and self-forgetting way. By their own experience and example, they promise us that this love is self-fulfilling.

Such love is radical—to some, foolhardy—because it is based on commitment rather than on reason, on hope in humans' kindly response to goodness. Yet even if we are confronted with an aggressive reaction from others, our love endures. Where love is missing, we trust that we can reinstate it. Where love has died, we trust that we can bring it back to life.

Preserving the value of our ego-dignity and of life itself becomes secondary to this unconditional and universal love, the essence of heroism. We see how a reckless love can stretch us beyond our usual limits, as if we were already saints or buddhas—just what we are.

We will look into the recommendations of three teachers: Jesus; Shantideva, an eighth-century Indian Buddhist teacher; and Saint Isaac of Syria, a seventh-century Eastern Orthodox bishop and monk. They propose self-sacrificing love *even without a crisis or cause,* simply as the full measure of love we are all capable of with practice. This is a way of saying that over-the-top, or heroic *agape,* is possible for everyone, not a special calling. Gandhi commented, "The religion of nonviolence is not meant merely for the rishis and saints. It is meant for the common people as well." By working on a program of love, such as in the practices in this book, a special calling becomes simply the gift and result of the perseverance possible in any of us. Heroic love can be cultivated.

We find this challenge easier to accept when we take our stand with others who earnestly and supportively join us in this new way of being in the world. Standing alone is scary, but marching with a thousand like-minded people is doable for most of us. At the same time, we still do all we can to ensure respect for our bodies, avoid abuse of ourselves and others, and intervene in malevolent behavior—all without violence.

We are not forgetting our shadow side. It is ironic that the three main ways we poison love and wisdom are also supererogatory: greed is over-the-top acquisitiveness; hate is over-the-top hostility; and the illusion of separateness is an over-the-top attachment to ego.

In the Sermon on the Mount, Jesus advised us to love our enemies, to give more than they demand to those who want to take from us unfairly, to let others take unfair advantage of us. Here is a passage from Matthew 5:

> You have heard that it was said, "Eye for eye, and tooth for tooth." But I tell you, Do not resist an evil person. If someone strikes you

on the right cheek, turn to him the other also. . . . If someone forces you to go one mile, go with him two miles. . . . You have heard that it was said, "Love your neighbor and hate your enemy." But I tell you: Love your enemies and pray for those who persecute you.

Along these lines, B. Alan Wallace, in *Buddhism with an Attitude,* wrote, "'Love your enemy' doesn't mean love the person you hate. You can't do that. Love those who hate you." In other words, our love makes us love those who hate us rather than hate them back.

The story Jesus told of the good Samaritan illustrates neighborly love beyond the call of duty. According to Luke 10:30–35, a man helps a stranger in physical distress by attending to his wounds, bringing him to an inn, and paying for his keep. He says to the innkeeper, "Look after him and when I return, I will reimburse you for any extra expense you may have." The phrase "over and above" is what is meant by supererogatory love that goes way beyond what is expected and transcends the ordinary limitations we usually place on giving and caring.

If we were to join the journey of the good Samaritan, we would be *impartial* in our way of showing our concern; we would be willing to give in equal measure to strangers and to our nearest and dearest. To be impartial is to love everyone, but impartiality does not mean loving everyone in the same way. We love our children differently from the way we love strangers. But the good Samaritan crosses that line and shows love to a stranger as he would show love to his own family. In the over-the-top style of love, our generosity is based on responsiveness to need alone. Our love flows from our solidarity with the human family, even if it has to be unilateral.

The bigness of "God is love" as our animating motivation in how we assess others is visible in this reflection on a story, told in Luke 23: 39–43, that took place at the crucifixion:

One of the criminals who hung there hurled insults at him: "Aren't you the Christ? Save yourself and us!"

But the other criminal rebuked him. "Don't you fear God," he said, "since you are under the same sentence? We are punished justly, for we are getting what our deeds deserve. But this man has done nothing wrong."

Then he said, "Jesus, remember me when you come into your kingdom."

Jesus answered, "I tell you the truth, today you will be with me in paradise."

This story illustrates the caring generosity of Christ toward someone who approached him humbly. But we can consider other possibilities when the story blossoms into a more expansive—and challenging—style of loving: The repentant criminal might have said, "Jesus, remember *us* (instead of *me*) when you come into your kingdom." Jesus might have replied, "I tell you the truth, today *both of you* will be with me in paradise, one of you because of my compassion and the other because of your faith."

The first speaker (who, we notice, asked that both criminals be saved and not just himself) would be welcome in the kingdom because he spoke in ignorance, so Christ had compassion for him. Christ's unbounded love became his passport to heaven. The second criminal spoke humbly, so Christ appreciated his faith and kindness. His acceptance of grace was his passport to heaven.

The first version of the story is based on the reward-punishment model—the style we often meet up with in so much traditional religious teaching. The second version is based on the loving-kindness model. This is the all-inclusive love that does not depend on virtuous action or is still caught in the reward-punishment model. It cancels limits on who is deserving, because it has the largesse of love, the wide-ranging embrace of mercy and compassion in which we are all deserving just by being and not because of doing. We hear this more generous message in some religious and spiritual settings today.

The narrow ego's response is, "Why should the man who reviled Jesus be given the same reward as the one who honored him?" The opened ego recognizes unconditional bounteousness as true love. The Jesus in the revised story could have reached out to the scornful criminal and possibly converted him by his bigheartedness. Instead, Luke's

Jesus only repeats the same old style of rewarding the good and ignoring the wicked. It is hard to find a new kingdom in that version.

In any case, the story does not include punishment for the first criminal, only silence. Perhaps we can imagine that Jesus was praying for his conversion.

The story has a dualistic style. We cannot love fully and heroically when we are caught in us versus them, insider versus outsider, good people versus evil people, good thief versus bad thief. Then love is impossible, since it has to be all-inclusive to be real. When we act from prejudice or any form of exclusivism, we disable our natural ability to love.

When we reconfigure what it means to be human by acting in accord with our true nature (love), our xenophobia vanishes. What becomes valuable is not maintaining our status as insiders but including everyone in our circle of unconditional love. The ego's version of connection is safety in being an insider and in keeping outsiders out. The true self's version of connection is inclusion so there is no longer an inside or an outside. Others may place us outside, as they did Jesus, but we don't do that to them.

In our own day, Martin Luther King, Jr., showed how to apply Jesus's teaching on unilateral love. In his sermon "Loving Your Enemies," he said,

> To our most bitter opponents we say, "We shall match your capacity to inflict suffering by our capacity to endure suffering. We shall meet your physical force with soul force. Do to us what you will, and we shall continue to love you. We cannot in all good conscience obey your unjust laws because noncooperation with evil is as much a moral obligation as is cooperation with good. Throw us in jail and we shall still love you. Bomb our homes and threaten our children, and we shall still love you. Send your hooded perpetrators of violence into our community at the midnight hour and beat us and leave us half dead, and we shall still love you. But be ye assured that we will wear you down by our

capacity to suffer. One day we shall win freedom but not only for ourselves. We shall so appeal to your heart and conscience that we shall win you in the process and our victory will be a double victory."

Shantideva, in *The Way of the Bodhisattva,* affirms a willingness to suffer injustice and abuse at the hands of others. This includes not choosing to get back at those who harm him:

> For the sake of accomplishing the welfare of all sentient beings, I freely give up my body, enjoyments, and all my virtues. . . . For the sake of all beings, I have made this body pleasureless. Let them continually beat it, revile it, and cover it with filth. Let them play with my body. Let them laugh at it and ridicule it. What does it matter to me? . . . May those who falsely accuse me, who harm me, and who ridicule me, all partake of awakening! . . . For as long as space endures and for as long as the world lasts, may I live dispelling the miseries of the world.
>
> Directly, then, or indirectly, do nothing that is not for others' sake. And solely for their welfare dedicate your every action to the gaining of enlightenment.
>
> May beings everywhere who suffer torment in their minds and bodies have, by virtue of my merit, joy and happiness in boundless measure.

For Shantideva, people who act in evil ways toward us lead us not to revenge but to an aspiration for their transformation: "All those who slight me . . . or do me any other evil, may they attain the fortune of enlightenment."

> He has freed himself from the retaliatory instinct:
> Throughout the spheres and reaches of the world,
> In hellish states as many as there are,
> May beings who abide there taste
> The bliss and peace of Sukhavati [bodhisattva of perfect joy].

And may the very pits of hell be sweet
With fragrant pools all perfumed with the scent
of lotuses,
And lovely with the cries of swan and goose
And waterfowl so pleasing to the ear.
May all those languishing in hell now come to perfect bliss.

—SHANTIDEVA

Saint Isaac of Syria was greatly respected by the author Fyodor Dostoyevsky, who kept a copy of the *Homilies of Saint Isaac of Syria* by his bed. In *The Brothers Karamazov,* Father Zossima speaks of Saint Isaac as his teacher, and his own teachings are a paraphrase of the saint's theology. Referring to Saint Isaac, Father Zossima declares, "Love animals, love plants, love each thing. If you love each thing, you will perceive the mystery of God in things. Once you have perceived it, you will begin tirelessly to perceive more and more of it every day. And you will come at last to love the whole world with an entire, universal love."

In his *Homilies,* Saint Isaac proposes this lofty form of love. We notice its similarity to the teachings of Shantideva:

> Let yourself be persecuted, but do not persecute others. Be crucified, but do not crucify others. Be slandered, but do not slander others. . . . The person who is genuinely charitable not only gives charity out of his own possessions, but gladly tolerates injustice from others and forgives them.
>
> Do not distinguish the worthy from the unworthy. Let everyone be equal to you for good deeds, so that you may be able to also attract the unworthy toward goodness. Rebuke no one, revile no one, not even those who live very wickedly.
>
> Love is not loath to accept the hardest of deaths for those it loves.
>
> God is not One who requites evil, but who sets evil right. It is absurd to assume that the sinners in hell are deprived of God's love. Love is offered impartially. God's recompense to sinners is that, instead of a just punishment, God rewards them with

resurrection. In the fire of love, our compassion extends even to the demons.*

Love May Make Us Outsiders

In every recommendation of unconditional and universal love described in the preceding section, we are called to transcend the ordinary style of "sensible" social behavior. Since spirituality refers to that which goes beyond the usual, this transcendence shows us that we have ventured into the realm of mature spiritual consciousness. Our ego won't be at home there until it bows to the heart's purposes. Ultimately, though ego fears the vulnerability that happens in openness, it wants to surrender, because that is its most wonderful destiny.

Letting go of ego, our spiritual awakening, means a full and joyous partnership with the higher self, with that place in us where love, wisdom, and healing preside. In that realm, there is no more fear. If we notice we are not quite like everybody else, that does not mean we are separated from everyone, only that we are marching to a different drummer. Our connection to humanity is actually more solid than we might think. We seem to be apart only because our commitment to over-the-top loving is reckless, foolish-looking, not the "prudent" way of operating in the mainstream world.

Indeed, a commitment to heroic, or self-sacrificing, love has often made exiles of those who practiced it. Their love led to ridicule and disconnection. How ironic when love is connection! Exile can happen by choice or because of expulsion or rejection by others. Nonetheless, it can lead to finding something meaningful and paradoxical about our destiny. Thus, we read in the Epistle to the Hebrews: "Jesus also suffered outside the city gate. . . . Let us, then, go to him outside the camp, bearing the disgrace he bore. For here we do not have a lasting city but are looking for the city that is to come."†

---

* Adapted from Bishop Hilarion Alfeyev, *The Spiritual World of Isaac the Syrian*, Cistercian Studies 175 (Kalamazoo, MI: Cistercian Publications, 2000).

† Heb. 13: 12–13.

This passage points so clearly to three prerequisites for self-sacrificing love:

1. We are *willing to be outsiders*. Being immersed in the values of the conventional world no longer matters as much as our commitment to what we see as important for love to flourish. In the spiritual world, everything is reversed. In that realm, we do not cling to connection but are willing to be marginalized because of our beliefs and choices. We are not afraid of life outside the safe, conventional center, since we are secure in our sense of personal mission. Our love is not a strategy to gain success or to convince others we are right. It stands for itself. We love only because we love. We love because we are love.

2. Once we do not espouse mainstream values, we may be excluded or persecuted. We seem irrational because we are *willing to endure ridicule or ignominy*. Being honored, successful, and established no longer matters as much as our commitment to our values. To reject the world of greed, division, rank, and "me-first" can make us look misguided to the outside world. A person with spiritual values does not fear that judgment. What everyone else calls foolish is, to her, the supreme wisdom.

3. We find comfort and spiritual support in our trust that *we have something going for us that is beyond this reality*. This does not have to refer to heaven or the hereafter. It can be anything that transcends our individual needs, such as the common good, the betterment of our community, or the spiritual evolution of world. Thus, we are shored up by a faith in a higher power rather than what conventional values offer. That power can be God, the dharma, or anything that transcends ego. It is a power that can carry our ego to its full destiny of service.

In many religious traditions, we see the theme of people leaving home, surrendering safety and security, and finding themselves in an outland where they are disenfranchised deportees:

- Buddha leaves his palatial home to live as a lowly, poor ascetic. His enlightenment happens when he has nothing left and is no longer recognized in the world of luxury and fame.

- In the Hebrew bible, Jacob leaves home and, at Luz (later Bethel), dreams of a ladder of angels joining heaven to earth. When he awakens, he says, "How awesome is this place! This is none other than the house of God and the gate of heaven."*
- In his Night Journey, the prophet Mohammed was mystically transported to the Temple Mount in Jerusalem, from which he ascended into heaven, transcending the limits of time and place.

These are examples of the archetypal theme of exile. The people on that path are consciously choosing something that leads to their becoming refugees and outcasts. Over-the-top commitment to caring connection is a daunting challenge to all of us. Yet supreme blessings are promised to lovers who leap.

> Becoming a refugee is acknowledging that we are homeless and groundless, and that there is really no need for home or ground. Taking refuge is an expression of freedom because as refugees we are no longer bounded by the need for security. We are suspended in a no-man's land in which the only thing to do is to relate to the teachings and to ourselves. . . . You then experience a sense of loneliness, aloneness—a sense that there is no savior, no help. But at the same time there is a sense of belonging: You belong to a tradition of loneliness where people work together.
> —CHÖGYAM TRUNGPA RINPOCHE, *The Heart of the Buddha*

PRACTICE: PATHS TO LOVE

Here are some ways of living that can ready us for the over-the-top love that may challenge us someday (or today):

- Become aware of the hideouts and refuges meant to help you escape discomfort of any kind. They remain in place by habit and

---

* Gen. 28:17.

by the illusion that they are the only game in town. The healthy alternative is the courage to believe, or behave as if you believe, that everything can be faced and worked on directly. Safety and security are then no longer founded on external sources. As you reconfigure obstacles as opportunities, you are more likely to trust what life brings your way. This grants a sense of safety and security that makes you more willing to sacrifice for others, since you have nothing left to lose. When you work on your issues in that brave way, with trust in their workability, you find it easier to give up your standardized shelters. They were never more than lean-to shacks in any case.

- Reject and protest against any familial, religious, or patriotic belief that endorses separatism or exclusivism or legitimates violence or retaliation, all the opponents of caring connection. Do this without blaming or discrediting anyone but with an aspiration that others will come to trust the power of love.

- If your God is one who punishes with eternal hell (meaning eternal torture), then revenge is still prominent in your psyche. Ask if you have a higher power who is free of hateful plans, one who gives you the five A's: the transcendent source of support *attends* to you rather than scrutinizes you, *accepts* you rather than judges you, *appreciates* or values you unconditionally, holds you *affectionately* no matter what you do, and *allows* you the freedom to live in accord with your fully emergent powers. The only higher power that can help us love is the one who is love. When you see love, rather than merit or avoidance of punishment, as your motivation for acting or not acting, you automatically love more. Thomas Merton said in *Seasons of Celebration*, "The mercy of God is gratuitous mercy that considers no fitness, no worthiness, and no return."

- Recall that you are not alone on this challenging path of love. Your choice to keep engaging with this book and its practices, your intention to love more and more, has attracted many saints, angels, and bodhisattvas to your side, and they are helping you. A trust in the power of such grace, the assisting force always and everywhere at work in our daily lives, makes loving easier than ever. Something, we know not what, we know not how, is always with us to make us more loving than we have been.

Loving Our World

> He prayeth well, who loveth well
> Both man and bird and beast.
> He prayeth best, who loveth best
> All things both great and small.
>
> —SAMUEL TAYLOR COLERIDGE,
> *The Rime of the Ancient Mariner*

Love was conceived at the big bang, when all connections began. Love was born when, for the first time, one being formed a caring connection with another being.

As we saw earlier, love is, by its very nature, about moving into a deeper union and a wider circle of caring. The way the world works in evolution is how love works in our lives, continually going beyond and transcending itself. We can say that our highest goal in evolution is more connection, more caring, and more love. It is also the only way this planet can survive. A commitment to love is how evolution becomes personal in the here and now of our lifetime. We are not in the world learning to love but acting in accordance with who we really are by loving the world.

The possibility of transcending our ordinary life and limits relates to the concept of *emergence* in science. This means that something new comes into being that is more complex than, but continuous with, what existed previously. Yet it is transcendent, more than the sum of its parts.

Love has many other features in common with what science describes the universe to be like: Love is *free,* not determined.

Love is *evolving*. It is continuously and gradually developing innovations that are better equipped to handle changes in the environment. The fact that our human origins can be traced back to earlier species shows continuity, another indicator of connection.

Love *survives* disruption. In chaos theory, systems transform expeditiously when there is a breakdown or disequilibrium. Love endures through crises, conflicts, and distance. It begins, can go into hiding, and can resume. It can pass through moments of entropy but can restore itself.

Love is a *system* of relationships. It is not solid, discrete, or linear but contextual. Each experience of it affects the whole.

Love is *holographic,* since each part contains the whole. Love is immediate and total in each moment. Thus, each of the five A's—attention, acceptance, appreciation, affection, and allowing—is included if it is real. In addition, to be a loving person is to love everyone.

Love is *fractal* in that the same patterns repeat at each level of complexity. Loving in little ways resembles and expands how we love in big ways. This is reminiscent of how Pythagoras saw the essence of life as pattern.

Unity in diversity is the natural state of the universe. Love produces *union while maintaining individuality.*

From Einstein's work on *relativity,* we know that what we imagine to be mass (palpable and real) is actually energy that does not exist separately but is connected to the vast web of life, the matter-energy that comprises the rest of the universe. All work together for the good of the whole. We love when, by cooperation, we show universal compassionate connection. We do this when we feed the hungry, shelter the homeless, and work for peace instead of war or equality instead of division. This means reducing our self-centeredness, letting go of a separatist, sectarian ego, so we can subordinate our individual needs to the greater good of all.

In a quantum leap, electrons jump into the next available level with no need to travel a distance from A to B; they simply appear elsewhere with no definable path in between. For Isaac Newton, a cause-and-effect relationship required two things to hit one another, as in billiard balls. Pioneer quantum physicist Niels Bohr suggested that subatomic particles can be responsive to influence from afar without any physical touching, essentially a "nonlocal" type of influence. In physics this is called *entanglement,* a nonlocal interconnectedness that is constant in all reality, irrespective of time and place. In love, we are like electrons that influence one another by such nonlocal connectivity and do not require proximity of place. This also means that we have power, even if we are only one voice in the wilderness.

Entanglement can also be seen psychologically in shared experience. For instance, shared pain leads to shared empathy. That is exactly what happens to our psyches in the love experience.

We know that a photon, a quantum of visible light, demonstrates both wave and particle properties in accordance with how we choose to measure or interact with it. There is no single character—no either-or—of light. When light behaves like a wave, it presents its wavelike aspect. When it behaves like a particle, it presents its particle aspect. Bohr referred to this dual dimension of reality as *complementarity*. Things are not globally determined in any one configuration. We participate in how things happen and in what they mean in the moment. There is no sharp distinction between subject and object. This is also what love can achieve and is about. When we choose not to divide and punish but to reconcile and forgive, our love has the character of complementarity.

We can contrast complementarity and opposition. For instance, we ponder the question, "How can someone who hates a particular group truly love anyone? Can a torturer truly love his family?" The question is not whether he can love or not. Of course he can. The question is, what impact does this level of hate, prejudice, and violence have on how he loves? Now we are handling our question in an inclusive, rather than a prohibitive, style while still noticing causes and effects. This is the nondualist style of complementarity in physics that works in how we compassionately hold human conundrums.

A scientific definition of the mind helps us understand love: The mind is an embodied and relational process (that is, not an entity but an action) that regulates a flow of energy and information. Love is an embodied experience of positive connection, a flow of relational energy. We may block the energy flow that connects us to others, but it is still in all of us, ready to be activated at any time.

Love is a *field;* like a magnetic field, it influences and draws things to itself. It surrounds us and stabilizes us, on the planet and in relationships, at multiple levels. People are drawn to love us more as we become more loving. We form a field of love by our loving connections.

Scientist David Bohm showed how nothing is fundamentally separate or autonomous, but all things simultaneously exist in a *holomovement.* He wrote, "The new form of insight can perhaps best be called Undivided Wholeness in Flowing Movement."* Love is just such an undivided wholeness flowing through us, to us, and from us in ever-widening circles until all beings are included.

Along these lines, poetry is always reflective of and way ahead of science in discovering mystical truths. Thus, Ralph Waldo Emerson stated in his poem "Celestial Love":

> Substances at base divided,
> In their summits are united;
> There the holy essence rolls,
> One through separated souls.

The last line of that quatrain refers to the universe as a relationship. Personal transformation happens when we join in that relationship. It is committing ourselves to solidarity with others and with the planet in a caring way. This means that when we see a wounded world, our moral sense makes us want to do whatever it takes to make it hurt less. Otherwise, we become demoralized, and our only goal is our own satisfaction.

We Are Important Here

Our full realization as humans, the enlightened state, the expression of our wholeness, is sustained by a long series of choices for generosity rather than greed, for love rather than hate, and for reality rather than illusion. We keep letting go of obstructions—the topic of our next chapter—and our natural, positive inclinations are then activated. Such

---

* From David Bohm, *Wholeness and the Implicate Order* (New York: Routledge, 1980).

a shining presence in the world is how our commitment to love makes us glow with and become bearers of light.

Evolutionary spirituality incarnates our own signature expression of love in the world. There are, indeed, innumerable ways of showing love. Each person has a unique style, like fingerprints or kisses. Perhaps each and every unique type of love, *yours,* is required to create just the medley that tunes the world to evolve in its full range of rhythms.

Many diverse flowers are required to make a meadow; many individual characters are necessary to stage *Othello;* many different faces in our family album are necessary for our life story to be complete. In the same way, the human enterprise requires each and every brand of love that humans can contribute for its evolution. Indeed, if everyone on earth, this outpost of heaven, loved everyone else in the style uniquely their own, then the full spectacular pageant of love would play out before our eyes. Instead of inequality, war, and hate, the real life that we are coded for would bloom, a life of justice, peace, and love. Then we would know, incontrovertibly and assuredly, why we were born.

Lorenzo, speaking to Jessica, in Shakespeare's *The Merchant of Venice,* points to the night sky and attunes to the harmony of the stars and spheres. He then says, "Such harmony is in immortal souls." The attunement that we now know is so important in human relating is also crucial in our connection to nature. We love others when we attune to them in a communion of understanding and caring. We are enlightened when we attune to the oneness of our world and ourselves in the same way.

In the dualistic world of Descartes, meaning and purpose are believed to exist only in humans, because only we have souls. The world is only matter in motion. The human self is separate from all else and above it all, since humans have consciousness and nothing else does.

The primitive view was actually much more inclusive. Ancient peoples believed that all of nature was alive and in motion, all forms of life full of divinity. Human inner life was seen to be continuous with it all. In this more naturalist-spiritual view, the self is participatory, not proprietary. There is soul and sense in all beings. We recall Buddha's words upon enlightenment, as related by Eihei Dogen Zenji: "When the morning star appeared, I and the great earth with all its beings simultaneously become buddhas."

In the new cosmology, the universe has a passion all its own and unfolds in us and all natural things. We are the hands and feet of the universe. Our purpose is to align ourselves to its futurist, or evolutionary, momentum.

As we let go of a linear perspective, we realize that we are not moving toward an absolute apex-ending of evolution. An endpoint would be an interruption. We are journeying in an expanding, ever-opening universe. A reverent "nothing is final" is a commitment to join in the opening. Thus, the evolution of the universe has a direction (diversity and complexity) but not an end target. The heroic journey archetype built into our psyche is animated by our inner urge toward renewal instead of destination. It takes the direction of ever-more integration rather than arriving at a final New Jerusalem or a cataclysmic Armageddon.

Love is the driving force of evolution. It is not a stretch to say that love is the sacred heart of the universe. Our love for the earth and all its people is how we join the evolutionary thrust toward relatedness that is built into nature. Such devotion means acting in ways that acknowledge how everything is interconnected. Indeed, if our origin is from a big bang, then diversity arose and keeps arising from an original oneness. The world is a holistic model for how we can live together in love: honoring one another's differences while remaining in continuous and caring connection. All it takes is wholehearted surrender—and some practice.

> I yielded myself to the perfect whole.
> —RALPH WALDO EMERSON

PRACTICE: COSMIC CONSCIOUSNESS

How do you contribute to a planetary shift away from the three poisons to our environment (greed, hate, and ignorance) to the three drivers of our evolution (justice, peace, and love)?

A zeal for the transformation of society and the world is how we personally evolve in love. This means that when we fight against the domination systems of aggression and inequality, we are showing our love for the world.

Once earth is no longer the ground we walk on but our living mother, we are called to protect and nurture her as she does us. Only when we love earth and its people do we love fully. Then we pray *with* Mother Earth, not just for our personal satisfaction or gain, which means conscious respect for the feminine principle on everyone's part. When we love, we go into labor with the earth-feminine birthing principle to co-create and coheal the world so it can evolve. Connection is implicit in cocreation, since we all join to help the world evolve by conscious intention and specific actions that foster justice, peace, and love.

This is how we become planetary citizens. Our individual consciousness and our earth consciousness become one, with no division, no dualism, no ranking. Once love and connection are accepted as our authentic identity, war and hate have no place in our heart or our world. Care for the ecology of the environment and cooperation with others become our intensely cherished commitments.

We work in whatever way we can to stop any further denuding of the earth's natural resources, and we do what it takes to renew the powers of the earth. That is love for the world shown in action. Love is then our primary principle, value, and law.

The narcissistic prejudice is the idea that we have dominion over the earth because we are at the top of the chain of life. With that attitude, the fullness of love cannot penetrate and beam through us as it is meant to do. But we can still believe that the noises around us are death throes and birth pangs all at once. More and more of us are becoming aware of and responsive to the needs of our planet by participating in conscious evolution.

We can audit our earth-and-its-people love by checking into our attitudes and contributions to the following social sins:

The unjust distribution of goods that is based on the vast differential between rich and poor

Destruction of the environment and its ecology

Violence, war, and nuclear arms

Oppression and prejudice based on race, gender, sexual orientation, religion, and political affiliation

The political and religious oppression of women in patriarchal societies

A common element in all five of these forms of social injustice is domination, which happens when egalitarian relations are denied. Love can't survive with domination, violence, and repression. It thrives with equality, peace, and freedom. Love, like our psyche, is not only personal but collective.

Politics and the life of the spirit are inseparable.

—MAHATMA GANDHI

Politics is the supreme expression of charity.

—POPE PIUS XI

9

What to Watch Out For

Love is the drama of completion, of unification. Personal and boundless, it leads to deliverance from the tyranny of ego.
—HENRY MILLER

IN THE THERAVADA TRADITION of Buddhism, *buddha nature* refers to our potential for enlightenment. This potential is activated through study and practice. It reflects the psychological understanding that infants show a tendency toward aggression and have to learn to be social.

In the Mahayana tradition, buddha nature is seen as inherent and primary within us, a quality rather than a potential. Thus, we do not attain buddha nature, because we have it in us all the time. In fact, all beings do. Our practice does not cause enlightenment but only manifests it. It uncovers rather than achieves. The *Platform Sutra of the Sixth Patriarch* (written by Hui Neng in the seventh century) uses the analogy of the moon covered with clouds. When the clouds evaporate, the moon is revealed. The clouds are not constructing the moon, only uncovering it. Likewise, with respect to love, we have it in us all the time, but our task is to clear away obstructions so it can be visible. The major obstruction is the dysfunctional and sometimes inflated ego.

What Is Ego?

Ego is the Latin word for "I." It refers to the conscious self, our personality, located in the parietal cortex of the brain. This center of thinking and acting is what we call our identity, or self.

We have one ego, and it can shape itself in many ways. It can be functional or dysfunctional. It is functional when we act in ways that fulfill our three basic goals in life—health, happiness, and personal growth. It is dysfunctional when we do what harms our health, makes us unhappy, and does not help us grow psychologically or spiritually. It operates on the basis of what Buddhism calls the three poisons: greed, hatred, and delusion. It operates on the basis of vices rather than the virtues of functional ego choices.

Like Goldilocks, the ego is faced with three choices. It can assume three sizes: too big, too little, or just right. When the ego is functional, it does not take itself too seriously and has reasonable self-esteem. We might say it is just right, an appropriate size. This ego respects its place in the lineups we all encounter. It does not place itself first, nor does it believe it should be last; it takes its place in whatever position works best in its interactions at the moment. It is sometimes first, sometimes last, and a lot of the time in between.

When the ego is dysfunctional, its size—its view of itself and of the way it can impact others—is inappropriately inflated or deflated. The inflated ego is self-centered, arrogant, vain, and entitled. It has a me-first attitude and makes its choices accordingly. The deflated, impoverished ego has a low opinion of itself. It engages in self-loathing, believing itself inadequate. It takes a me-last, or victim, position in the world.

Our evolutionary task in life is to build a functional ego of appropriate size. This is the ego that acts for health, happiness, and personal growth. It is the one that can achieve intimacy in a relationship and makes us good citizens. This is the ego that is meant to last a lifetime. It is to be built, not let go of. No one acts from this ego all the time, but we can all strive to give it priority in as many ways and as much as possible.

The dysfunctional ego, active in every one of us on a daily basis, is meant to be tamed so that more and more of it can become functional.

This is a constant battle, since there is more adrenaline associated with dysfunction than with functionality. We usually find more entertainment value in being dysfunctional, especially in our youth, when we are oriented that way and have the energy for it.

In later life, we have less adrenaline, so it is easier to let go of our dysfunctional and inflated ego. An older person who still has the ego of a ninth grader has subverted that natural transition; he has forced his psyche to maintain what is not in the best interests of his health, happiness, and personal growth. That is the equivalent of saying no to the heroic journey, which is always about moving from too much to just right.

Our bodies may become weak, our minds demented, our memories unclear, but our ego can remain firmly arrogant and controlling throughout our life span. Ego is not susceptible to aging only to a conversion by some life-changing comeuppance or spiritual transformation.

Here is an example of the various forms of ego appearing in one person: Randy starts the day by flossing (functional ego). He then has his first cigarette (dysfunctional ego). He drinks two glasses of orange juice instead of one, leaving none for his wife (inflated ego). Randy is courteous on the highway and lets another driver have the right-of-way (appropriate ego). He does not ask for a promotion at work, since he discredits himself and has thereby lost his ambition and self-confidence (deflated ego).

Randy is not alone. We all act from each of the five forms of ego in the course of each day. We never cancel out any one form totally and permanently. It is not a matter of either functionality or dysfunctionality. The best we can do is to show more and more functionality rather than trying to be perfect. Our dysfunctional, inflated, or deflated ego keeps making its appearance in our thoughts and actions. Perhaps this is the psyche's way of keeping us humble.

Here is an example of the difference between the functional and dysfunctional ego in two people:

Violet wants to attend an art school that she knows will help her increase her skills and eventually land her a good job. She takes the courses that prepare her to enter the art school she respects; she applies in time to meet the deadline; and she saves up enough money to pay her tuition. She also applies to her second-choice school in case she is not accepted at her first choice. Violet is acting from a functional ego in this entire process.

On the other hand, Vilas has superior artistic and intellectual skill but does not apply himself to his studies, so his grades do not make him eligible for the college he would really like to attend. He does not apply to a second or third school, because his inflated ego made him cocksure that he would be accepted by his first-choice school no matter what his grades were.

There may no consistency in how the ego shows up in any of us. For example, Violet, who is so functional in the realm of her career, is an alcoholic refusing recovery and in a relationship with a man who abuses her. Vilas, who is dysfunctional in planning for the future, takes good care of his health and is in a wholesome relationship.

Our proclivity toward dysfunction explains our need for psychological work. Our inclination toward inflation shows our need for spiritual practice. Together, they help us redirect our ego from its dysfunctional habits to "the better angels" of its nature: health, happiness, and personal growth.

In psychology, we learn to build a healthy functional ego and to avoid what disrupts our relationships both in society and in intimate bonds. In spiritual teachings, we learn the importance of letting go of attachment to fears and cravings, which is so common in dysfunctional behavior.

"Letting go of ego" does not refer to the healthy functional ego. That is the ego we need if we are to make the choice to follow a spiritual path and have the discipline to engage in the practices that foster it. In relationships, we act from a healthy ego when we build our functional ego and choose a partner who is psychologically healthy too. We are with a partner who wants a serene happy life together, and we are both committed to making that happen. We work together on our problems and keep our agreements. We choose health, happiness, and personal growth.

To trust a partner is not to have a guarantee that she will never hurt, disappoint, or betray us. We trust ourselves to receive her trustworthiness with gratitude. We also trust ourselves to handle untrustworthiness by establishing our personal boundaries and not stooping to reprisals.

The inflated ego in a relationship fears that its entitlements might not be respected. For instance, we might expect our partner to give us a guarantee that he will never abandon or betray us. These crises, however, are what can happen to anyone in a relationship. But our ego believes that it is entitled to special treatment and demands assurance from a partner.

Such an attitude will not lead us to serenity, which results from accepting what we have no control over. For that, as for loving, nothing less is required than the unconditional surrender of ego. It takes saying yes to whatever happens to us as *unexempted* humans. We then automatically build trust in ourselves to face what may happen, and we gain more strength to handle it when it does. Our ego deflates itself to a healthy size, and that is the same as becoming stronger. We no longer have to rely on others to keep us safe from crisis, a promise no one can make anyway.

The depth of the surrender of our ego is expressed well by William Blake in these sobering words: "I will go down to self-annihilation . . . lest the judgment come and find me unannihilate and I be . . . given into the hands of my own Selfhood."

To let go of ego is to let go of an ultimately feeble and unreliable bodyguard. We can instead, like the psalmist, "walk through the valley of the shadow" without fear. This means staying present to our experience rather than running to drama, drugs, alcohol, sex, or any other form of avoidance. What we trust about ourselves is not our power to stop bad things from happening to us. We trust our commitment to the psychological work and spiritual practices that help us go through whatever happens with integrity and loving-kindness. Our practice then becomes a shepherding accompaniment.

How Ego Moves from Fear to Freedom

Fear in the ego is not like ordinary fear; it comes through as a panic with life-and-death implications. The ego fears it will not survive if it does not get its way or if it loses what it is so convinced it needs. Thus, the feeling of fear is utterly incompatible with how the arrogant ego sees itself. It does not have full permission to feel fear, only anger. This is what makes the inflated ego dangerous—not its fear, but its quick switch to rage or hate.

Here is an example: Jason has an inflated ego, also called machismo. He and his partner, Bernice, are waiting to be seated at a restaurant. Jason goes to the restroom. Meanwhile, Bernice begins to chat with the man behind her in line. As Jason returns, he notices this. The rest of the evening is marred by his pouting and fuming in unjustified jealousy. He finally blows up at Bernice and may even feel justified in picking a fight with the man in question. Bernice, who probably has seen versions of this reaction from Jason before, tries to explain that "it was only small talk and not a threat to you," but that cannot salve his affronted ego. It is rock hard in rage, because its possession (Bernice) has dared to cross its line. Bernice feels compassion for how upset Jason has become, but she also cuts the evening short.

Bernice later comes to the conclusion that a major overhaul of Jason's ego is necessary if their relationship is ever to work. Nothing will convince her to increase her commitment to him except the gentling and eventual surrendering of his ego.

Ironically, neither Jason nor Bernice may realize that Jason's ego looks inflated in his swaggering behavior but is actually deflated in his personality structure. He is really scared of his own feelings and the freedom of others. Since he hides from—remains unconscious of—that humbling fact, his only options are control and aggression. That sad impotence is the real reason to feel compassion for Jason.

The unhealthy ego in relationships is a Rube Goldberg machine. It goes through complex, convoluted gyrations to reach a useless goal—in this case, adrenaline-filled drama. This inflated ego uses a relationship to aggrandize and gratify itself. Its relationship is unhealthy, unhappy, and not moving toward personal growth. People with this kind of ego, by the way, usually have no problem finding a mate; their charm and apparent strength are appealing to someone who is needy.

Early in life, an alloy was mixed into our golden human nature. The inflated ego crept into the palace of the functional ego and created pandemonium. This upstart ego is constantly conniving to advance itself and maintain center stage. It will insist that it is entitled, justified, and incontrovertibly right. Such an unhealthy ego can remain mired in a lifelong campaign to protect its territory and to stay in control of whatever it has become attached to. It may be obsessed with fear, greed, hate, or delusion, the obstructions to love. All this, like any restriction of our movement toward our goals, can happen in moments or as an ongoing pattern.

Becoming a loving person takes work if we have an ego like this. We have to dismiss our charlatan ego—the great pretender, the imp of impostures—as the claimant of our rightful inheritance, which is the capacity to show unconditional and limitless love. Our unhealthy ego does not have to be destroyed, only transformed, reconditioned, and redirected toward psychological and spiritual health—what it really wanted all along. We can work with each limiting trait of ego to open it into something useful.

Arrogance is meant to be transformed into openness and humility. Jacob wrestling with the angel humbly *wants* defeat by a higher power than his ego; that is the blessing of access to a fully aware and awake self.

Control is meant to be transformed into cooperating with others so that our coordinating skills can be put to their best use. This requires allowing others to be free and letting go of the compulsion to have things be just so or come out exactly as we demand.

Entitlement is meant to be transformed into a combination of standing up for our rights and simultaneously accepting the fact that sometimes life is unfair. This means letting go of seeking revenge against those who are unfair toward us, though we can always say, "Ouch!" and open a dialogue that works toward a just resolution of our conflicts.

Insistence on being right is meant to be transformed into working things out together until reconciliation, consensus, a meeting of minds, or mutual understanding can occur.

Since love is an instinct, it can be surrounded by defense mechanisms that are meant to protect us from danger and stress. The healthy ego can be of great assistance in that enterprise; it is able to assess clearly and make the decisions that fulfill our goals of self-esteem and effective relating. There is help for this in the practices of mindfulness and loving-kindness:

Mindfulness frees our ego by focusing on the here and now rather than on the fear of what might happen or craving what we desperately need to make happen. The solidity of ego is confirmed by believing its own projections: judgment, comparison, fear, desire, and attachment to an outcome. These are the decorations we place on reality. They are imprecise, hit-or-miss, but dramatic and appealing because they thrive on fear and desire. Mindfulness brings us to bare attention, a direct view of reality that is free of the ornaments of ego. In mindfulness, we become able to hold our ego without being burned by it.

Loving-kindness practice also provides help for our unhealthy ego through our commitment to the four immeasurable qualities of enlightened living:

- *Loving-kindness* is the antidote to aggression and retaliation.
- *Joy* at others' success is the antidote to envy.
- *Compassion* means aspiring that others be happy and free of pain, so it is the antidote to hatred.
- *Equanimity* frees us from getting caught up in drama and our addiction to adrenaline, so we can love serenely and sanely. It helps our unhealthy ego face its great fear of grief. That fear vanishes when we embrace the three component feelings of grief with composure: *Sadness* helps us awaken to the reality of loss and the life-affirming disposition to let go of the clinging style of the threatened ego. *Anger* helps us awaken to injustice and the challenge to take a stand against it, without having to employ ego aggression in the process. *Fear* helps us know where dangers and threats may be lurking. The more we realize that nothing can really happen to us that is not already and always a useful part of our personal story, we find a way out of fear and no longer need our arsenal of ego defenses.

Our resultant sense of freedom shows us that life has wonders in it and that we have a capacity to enjoy them. This confidence does not happen in the braggadocio swagger of ego but in calm, centered equanimity.

Yet the swaggering ego can be important sometimes. The strong ego with all its arrogance can be useful when heroic, daredevil action is required. But in intimate relationships, it is deadly, because love is connection, while the win-lose style of the unhealthy ego is rivalry that plays out as disunion and not togetherness.

The inflated ego can certainly manifest during a breakup, as in a "messy divorce." A hostile, retaliatory breakup makes us wonder what the partnership was really about to begin with. Did we really love one another? Was what we called love a commitment to intimacy or an attachment that felt good? Was what we called connection our own neediness and expectation or true bonding? *Real love in a relationship does not turn to hate.* When the end comes, we grieve, let go, and move on. We may be angry, but we do not have rancor. When love was sincere to begin with, we maintain an ongoing caring for the other person. The love remains; the commitment to how it was shown—and of course, our address—is all that has changed.

Many years ago, I visited Paris with a friend, and our backpacks were stolen. We had left them in a locker at the train station while we went off to see the cathedral at Chartres. When we returned at the end of the day, our locker was empty. That night, I recall saying, half-jesting but nonetheless meaning it, "May the person who took our stuff rot in the ninth circle of hell!" My loss led to a spiteful wish for retribution as severe as Dante's in *The Divine Comedy*. The extent of my loving-kindness had not developed.

More recently, I visited Rome and had my pocket picked. That night in bed, before falling asleep, I recall spontaneously wishing, "I hope my money will be used to help someone needy rather than to buy drugs." I then remembered my reaction to the Paris robbery. I suddenly realized I had advanced in my humanity. My wish for retaliation had turned into compassion and concern. In my Paris days, I did not care; in my Rome days, I did. I was very happy with my transition. I know I owe it to my Buddhist practices in the interim.

The transition from the Paris reaction to the Rome response was from ego-centeredness to caring connection. That transition is possible for all of us with practice. It wants to happen, because love is what we are all about, made for, meant for, and here for. The ego that has to be center stage is only the marionette we use to protect ourselves from the vulnerability that comes with being who we are. But our loving self can make a personal appearance, and that will, of course, be the epiphany of grace that makes love the possibility of possibilities.

PRACTICE: CLEARING THE OBSTRUCTIONS OF EGO

> Our adult task is to work indefatigably with the ego's deceptions—using skillful means, not easy outs.
> —CHÖGYAM TRUNGPA RINPOCHE

Some of us fear letting go of our ego, because we imagine we will then feel totally empty. We do not trust or have forgotten that true bliss, love, and wisdom are sitting in wait under all the obstructions of ego. Our joyous, positive qualities are activated by the practice of letting go of ego. We don't lose anything but our fear.

Obstructions to universal, unconditional love arise from the shadow side of our reptilian brain. With these obstructions in your relationship repertory, love becomes impossible; for example, you can't be trusted not to retaliate if your partner crosses you.

Love can't breathe in atmospheres such as these:

- Payback is demanded.
- Unremitting grudges, a form of retaliation, are held.
- There is a controlling style in the relationship.
- One up, one down games are practiced.
- Win or lose is favored over cooperation.
- Only my way is the right way.
- Might makes right.
- People are for my use or abuse.

- Cutthroat competition in encouraged. (Mutual caring connection will not be possible in a business setting if it includes this style.)

When these concepts are excised from our vocabulary, we operate on new premises about life, those that free us from the cage of a dysfunctional ego.

The taming of the dysfunctional, inflated ego is doable. It just takes psychological work and spiritual practice. As we are released from our self-centered attachments, we notice that our ego can be redirected to healthy goals. The ego at first fights the new direction and feels threatened by it. But soon it notices the empowerment and tranquillity of its new home and loves being there, because it has found an authentic holding environment. Our ego, after all, was meant to join in an axis of power with the higher self, our true self, where love abounds.

Here are some specific practices that can help soften the inflated ego—what it always desired but was too scared to go for—so that love can flow. In each of these practices, we feel compassion for the scared ego part of ourselves, not shame, antipathy, or revulsion. We hold our unhealthy ego with the same tender but strong interventions that a caring healer would:

- We move from self-concerned to other-concerned choices and behavior.
- In a feud, we are always ready to make the first move toward reconciliation.
- We give up keeping track of all we gave others and how good we have been.
- We give up keeping track of how others have wronged us.
- We can choose not to retaliate. Making that choice over and over leads us more readily to forgiveness.
- We place no conditions on those we forgive.
- We no longer defend ourselves but admit our shortcomings and apologize when necessary.
- We are willing to change when someone speaks a critical truth.
- We can say, "I love you."

- We hear others at a feeling level.
- We stay open to what may be true in opposing opinions.
- We tolerate the freedom of others rather than having to be in control of them.
- We let go of needing to be complimented for being successful at letting go of ego.
- We are able to receive feedback without construing it as criticism and becoming defensive or aggressive.

A scoffer who is rebuked will only hate you; the wise, when rebuked, will love you.

—PROVERBS 9:8

Our work on our impoverished, deflated ego is addressed in every practice in this book, since they all help raise our self-esteem. In addition, an assertiveness training group is crucial. Here are the main features of assertiveness that are necessary to loving interactions:

- We act in accord with our own deepest needs, values, and wishes.
- We ask for what we want.
- We are clear about and show our feelings directly.
- We take responsibility for our behavior and feelings.
- We have boundaries in our relationships, so we decide to what extent we are responsible for helping others, how close we allow others to get to us, and how our privacy is to be respected.
- We can choose the lifestyle that fits us, no matter how others judge it.
- We can put ourselves first when appropriate.
- We stand up for our beliefs and choices.
- We do not let others take advantage of us, but we act with love and generosity.
- We assert our truth or need, but if it falls on deaf ears, we can let go and not keep pushing. We *want* to get through to someone, but we let go of the *compulsion* to make it happen.

When Narcissism Appears

> Last time I saw him, he was walking down lover's lane holding his own hand.
>
> —FRED ALLEN

Narcissism refers mainly to extreme self-centeredness. As a personality disorder, it refers to an enduring and pervasive pattern of dysfunction in relationships because of unremitting self-absorption.

As narcissists, we are plagued by disturbing inner contradictions. We imagine ourselves to be above others, yet we loath ourselves at the same time. We imagine ourselves to have abilities and gifts that we may not actually have. We cannot tolerate criticism and cannot apologize when we are wrong. Inside we feel empty, but we act as if the world were our oyster.

We demand that others acknowledge our importance, perhaps because our inflated grandiosity from toddler days was never cut down to size. Therefore, we imagine and believe that we are omnipotent. But our unconscious, the other side of us that is our self, can't be fooled; we have many self-doubts.

Yet, consciously, when we notice we are not all we have cracked ourselves up to be, we take that as a failure in others to acknowledge us properly. To us, others are not autonomous beings but adjuncts and annexes meant to serve our ever-more expansive entitlements. They can only relate to us if they are willing to give up their autonomy and serve ours. Our sense of self is fused with what we imagine others must be. To be there for others in a trustworthy way, as in sincere, self-giving love, is therefore impossible because we come first.

We expect that others will honor our greatness, go along with our opinions, and fulfill our needs and wishes. Usually, we are charming and easily get people to like or follow us. Our physical appearance matters greatly to us and becomes part of our appeal to others.

The narcissistic inflated ego's version of self-trust is, "I will always come out on top." Healthy self-trust sounds like this: "I have and will take care of myself somehow." Work on our ego can lead us to that healthy narcissistic style. Narcissism as healthy self-nurturance is pleasantly different from what we have been describing. The following chart shows the characteristics of each.

Narcissism as a Self-Disorder	*Healthy Narcissism*
We cannot truly care about another person, only about ourselves.	We give priority to our own needs but can care about others' needs too.
We have a grandiose sense of self-importance and believe we have a right to be taken care of by everyone.	We have an appropriate sense of self-esteem and self-nurturance.
We demand that others honor our superiority, even when it is undeserved.	We ask for respect but know it is important to earn it.
We believe ourselves to be entitled to special treatment by others and by life.	We accept the fact that people may or may not appreciate us, though we are assertive enough to ask for what we need.
We believe that we are above the ordinary person and should be ranked with people of high status.	We know we have unique gifts, and we share them without one-upmanship.
We do not think it is wrong to exploit or use others for our own gain.	We believe we have a right to receive from others, but we do not take advantage of their generosity.
We resent having to help or give to someone else.	We may become impatient with having to help, but as long as we are not being taken advantage of, we take it in stride.
We lack empathy and are incapable of sincere compassion.	We can be empathic, attuned to others' needs and feelings, and compassionate toward them.
We envy others who have more than we do and imagine that they envy us.	We admire others for what they have accomplished and believe we can do likewise.
We act in a pretentious, arrogant, or haughty manner without realizing we are doing so.	We realize that our talents are gifts, and we show them but do not show off.

We sometimes engage in competition in a cutthroat way.

We compete and want to win, but we are able to focus on cooperation.

We demand that our family or friends admire us unconditionally.

We want our family and friends to be proud of our special talents while seeing us realistically.

We imagine that the world revolves around us.

We know the world is not here to serve us, and we still want it to help us evolve.

We believe we have a right to do as we please with no obligation to explain ourselves.

We believe we can make our own choices and are willing to explain them to those we trust.

We become angry and retaliatory when crossed or criticized.

We take critiques in stride, look for the truth in them, decide what works for us, and do not retaliate.

We do not experience true remorse and cannot apologize sincerely.

We apologize and make amends if necessary.

Others have to listen to us, but we do not have to respond in kind.

We listen to others and want them to listen to us.

Physical appearance is a high priority.

Physical appearance is important but not in an exaggerated or obsessive way; we can look our age without embarrassment.

We are charming, predatory, and usually find a partner who is very taken with us without much difficulty.

We are authentic, not trying to use others and continually working on skills for more effective relationships, though we may not always be in one.

We expect that our partner will fulfill our needs perfectly.

We want our partner to be real and that satisfies us.

We doubt that people would really be interested in us unless we maintained our image of perfection.

We trust that others like us and are interested in us as long as we are genuine.

We may idealize others but are disillusioned and chagrined when our opinion of them proves unjustified.

We may admire others and are disappointed if they show themselves to be other than we imagined.

We swing from exaggerated self-importance to a sense of unworthiness.

We accept the fact that we may sometimes have an inflated or deflated sense of our positive qualities, so we pay attention to what the record shows and ask for feedback from others.

People with this personality disorder have some, but not necessarily all, of these traits. The symptoms are destabilizing and enduring. They appear to others as aggressive.

A person with these traits is assertive without being aggressive, entitled, or self-centered.

Power and Control

> O, it is excellent to have a giant's strength,
> But it is tyrannous to use it like a giant.
> —WILLIAM SHAKESPEARE, *Measure for Measure*

We mammals are social beings. Our groups are usually divided into rankings such as leaders and followers. We all realize that such distinctions are useful for the smooth running of a society. The problem is not the levels of power; the problem is in how the powers are held.

We have heard the wise axiom penned by Lord Acton in a letter to Bishop Creighton in 1887: "Power corrupts, and absolute power corrupts absolutely." When love is our purpose in life, we take that warning seriously. We don't want to be seduced into a loss of integrity by any power we may have. We don't forget that power includes an inherent inclination toward aggression if it is threatened in any way.

Thus, power is dangerous, because at times we might use it to take advantage of others or of situations for our own gain. We might manipulate others to do our will against their own or put our own needs first at the expense of the common good. We might turn to aggression or lack of integrity to "protect" ourselves or our institutions. We can easily become sociopathic, believing we have a right to take what is not ours, to run roughshod over others, to do something immoral with impunity. We might hide our misdeeds while preaching moral rectitude. We do not see this as hypocrisy, since we see ourselves as above the norms that govern ordinary people. This must be why medieval kings appointed court jesters, who had the right to call the rulers on their arrogant misuse of power.

Throughout history, there have been and are toxic, criminal, and even insane political leaders who have been tolerated and even praised, no matter how unjust or cruel their actions. This may be because they appeal to the shadow side of the populace, whose darkest desires and most hateful wishes they are willing to carry out. In exchange for silence and obedience, such misusers of power offer safety and security, irresistible seductions to those who live in fear. Such authorities are successful in every era because they offer us a specific way out of fear. They encourage anger in us, and then they tell us whom to be angry at, just as Adolf Hitler did.

Robert Kennedy—in a speech given in 1968 at the City Club of Cleveland, the day after Martin Luther King, Jr., was shot—said, "Too often we honor swagger and bluster and wielders of force; too often we excuse those who are willing to build their own lives on the shattered dreams of others." Our first developmental challenge was a sense of self, then a sense of "you," then a sense of "us." A bully—an example of an abuser of power—suffers from arrested development; he never made the transition to "us."

Some people had their trust betrayed early on, their vulnerability exploited. Thus, hypervigilance became their only defense against devastating invasion. They may have lost the self-trust that comes from resilience and stability. They live in fear of what might happen rather than in resonance with it. They use control to stave off their fear of surprise and spontaneity. Controlling people find it hard to love freely, since they cannot flow easily with what life may bring their way. Letting go of control, becoming open to the extemporaneity of life, terrifies rather than excites them.

A controlling person falls into chaos when things don't go his way. In contrast, a *person in charge* remains stable when things go wrong. He uses his power for the benefit of everyone around him. Such mindful, service-oriented power combines strong limit-setting with restorative compassion. The more there is of this positive power, the more does it accomplish. Shakespeare alludes to this phenomenon in *The Merchant of Venice,* when Portia speaks of mercy: "'Tis mightiest in the mightiest."

A healthy adult ego may want to be in charge but not to control as the dysfunctional ego does. To control is to direct someone's actions; unduly influence someone's beliefs or decisions; manipulate feelings, behavior, and choices. Control is the style of the inflated ego that thinks itself above everyone else and entitled to have its own needs take full precedence over those of others. As such, control corrupts our integrity just as power does.

When we love, we open our constricting ego. We are no longer imprisoned in our narrow need to be number one. What opens is the doors of fear that have been slammed shut up until now. When we really love, we become fearless protectors of ourselves while becoming fearlessly vulnerable at the same time. We no longer need to be in full control. We accept that at some times we have some control, and at other times we do not. We are humble enough to pay homage to the givens of life that are—and always were—the ones in full control.

When others try to control us, we can respond with love by perceiving their controlling behavior with an understanding compassion. We recognize that they are actually being controlled by their need to be in control, because they feel that need as a compulsion. We say "Ouch!" We do not allow them to control us. In any case, we don't make them wrong or bad for being who they are.

Where love is absent, power fills the void.

—CARL JUNG

PRACTICE: LETTING GO OF OUR COMPULSION TO BE CONTROLLING

We begin by exploring any power we may have in our community, at work, or in politics. When we are focused on love, we cherish our personal gifts of leadership and want to use the power we have for good. We realize that our power places a responsibility on us to serve others rather than granting us an opportunity to control or exploit them. We know there are hierarchies, but we want to use them cooperatively rather than tyrannously. Our spiritual practice of loving-kindness helps us find an alternative to top-down rankings. In that practice, our caring does not favor any one person over another. We wish for love and happiness for everyone equally. We do not rate people for levels of worthiness and then parcel out our love or respect accordingly.

However, since power does indeed corrupt, it is a given that at some point, in some way, we will somehow abuse our power. It is only a matter of when, not whether. No one is immune; we are all vulnerable to corruption. It is wise to remain ever wary of the royal-pretender ego who waits inside us for the chance to usurp the throne that is meant to be shared.

The path of love is *not* to trust ourselves unless we have some safety precautions in place. We realize that we may not know we are abusing power; hence, we will be continually probing ourselves. Here are some practices that can help us preserve integrity and accountability:

- Enlist feedback from others before making decisions rather than acting unilaterally, especially in the top-down way.
- Report in about your decisions to all those affected by them rather than operating secretly.
- Delegate some of your power to others.
- Refuse to engage in glad-handing, good-old-boy protections, selling someone down the river, or one-hand-washes-the-other machinations.
- Be wary of being seduced by the incentive of personal advancement for playing the game or covering up injustices.
- Be able to speak up to the person above you in the hierarchy of power rather than appeasing her.
- Don't be afraid to blow the whistle on someone and/or on yourself.
- Don't punish whistle-blowers; instead, welcome their feedback.

- Don't trust colleagues or supporters who want to help you increase your power unless they acknowledge your need to stay aware of your limitations and take necessary precautions.

Since the misuse of power is so subtle, cunning, and unavoidable, it is also necessary to appoint an auditor, an overseer of unimpeachable honesty, unswerving candidness, and unassailable directness. This person cannot be bought or intimidated by you and will look objectively at your use of power and call you on your misuses of it. Yes, there are people like that, but they work as volunteers, not on the payroll.

We now look at how we hold our power in our family and relationships. To believe we have to be in control means believing we have no spiritual resources. We are it, all there is. This is why control is not only a matter of fear and compulsion to be dealt with psychologically, but a spiritual issue that must be dealt with by a consciousness of the role of grace in our lives. These practices may help:

- Mindfulness meditation helps us notice and label our mind's appetite for control of outcomes.
- The loving-kindness practice helps us with its focus on equanimity, taking things in stride as they occur rather than trying to preempt them so we can control the outcome.
- These three affirmations can be helpful:

    1. I declare my gratitude for the love in me and in my life.
    2. I am thankful for the graces that keep coming my way. They are trying to convince me to trust the life that unfolds rather than trying to fold it up by controlling it at every turn.
    3. I say yes to what is and ask for the serenity to accept the things I cannot change.

- Our neurotic ego thrives on entitlement to full control. Letting go of ego therefore includes letting go of control. We can use this version of our 4A approach:

1. We *admit* we are being or trying to be controlling.
2. We *allow* ourselves to feel the tension and discomfort that naturally arises when we let things take their own course, when we allow others to do what they choose to do, and when we accept the things we cannot change.
3. We *act* in ways that show trust in what happens. This means letting events unfold in their own way and letting the chips fall where they may. Then we act with trust in our ability to handle whatever may occur. We reconcile ourselves to the fact that we may receive a lower dividend than we expected from what does finally happen. We experience our grief while aligning ourselves to reality—just the healing combination that all our controlling prevents. We thereby reduce the wallop of any disappointment we may feel.
4. We *affirm*, now and daily that we let go of control and find our real power. We now stabilize ourselves by our surrender to reality.

The Urge to Retaliate

> One act of retaliation burns down a whole forest of merit.
> —DHAMMAPADA

We have all heard the saying "Revenge is sweet." It is a curious fact that we do not quote John Milton correctly. He shows in *Paradise Lost* that retaliation is ultimately a painful event:

> Revenge, at first though sweet,
> Bitter ere long back on itself recoils.

When people offend us, we can choose retaliation or reconciliation. Retaliation is the style of retributive, or punitive, justice. Reconciliation is the style of restorative justice. When our goal is retributive justice, it is from the street, our reptilian brain, our cave-dweller origins. (It is significant that the Greek goddess of retributive justice is called Nemesis.) When our goal is restorative justice, our style is from heaven's gate, a higher power within, fully evolved love.

To choose reconciliation or forgiveness involves forgoing satisfaction from knowing that "they got theirs." That is a lot for the indignant ego to give up. But the joy of lovingly seeking the transformation and growth of others yields contentment, a deeper kind of satisfaction. The former serves our ego, the "I" at the center. The latter fulfills the core of our higher self, the enlightened buddha immovably within us.

In primitive times, humans had to come up with a swift aggressive reaction to assaults or threats. Otherwise, animals or other tribes might take advantage of their passivity and pounce on them. Retribution for any insult or attack was necessary for survival. Without retaliation, a person would become prey.

It takes a spiritual consciousness and practice not to act on our archaic, vengeful instincts. Psychology does not get us there. When we are committed to a life of love, we diligently employ a spiritual program, knowing psychology is no match for the Cro-Magnon within. With a spiritual practice such as loving-kindness, we can experience anger yet remain nonviolent regardless of how others behave. We can also genuinely hope for their transformation. This means that showing healthy anger is a spiritual practice, because it is a way of clearing the decks so love can proceed, unhindered by attachment to gaining revenge. Without retaliation as part of our repertory, we are showing love no matter what, *agape*.

Our choice is not between retaliation or passivity. We can choose the strong alternative to retaliation, assertiveness—that is, saying "Ouch!" and then setting limits and protecting boundaries. With this practice, our goal is not to endure but to keep ourselves safe and not harm anyone else. We are not getting back at others viciously or maliciously. In fact, we are placing a sincere intention for their transformation. We will then be like Ralph in *Lord of the Flies,* proud of ourselves for the rest of our lives because we maintained our humanity against savage odds, no matter what others did.

Retaliation is ultimately a defense against our full "Ouch!" We may be ashamed of saying we are hurt, ashamed of grieving a loss or insult. In fact, losing face or being shamed are the most likely triggers of revenge. People caught in embarrassment or shame are less likely to regulate their aggressive responses. The deep-seated, primal aggression in us has to be regulated if we are to live cooperatively in society or ever be able to love at all. This regulation of our impulses begins in childhood with help from adults both at home and at school.

Retaliation in Early Life

Good parenting means setting healthy limits on children while simultaneously mirroring their feelings. This combination helps them learn to organize and temper their responses to frustration, then they can employ alternatives to violence or vengeance. For instance, in kindergarten, when we hit the child next to us, our teacher said, "I know you are mad and I understand. But you can use words to show that; you don't have to hit." When children notice that adults attune to their feelings ("I know you are mad and I understand"), they feel understood. They are also finding models for how to attune to themselves and others. This is empathy, feeling the other's pain *with* him. Sympathy is seeing the other's pain and then feeling *for* it. That, too, is a loving response.

Both empathy and sympathy override the urge to retaliate. Both impact the healthy development of the orbitofrontal cortex, where we also access the ability to handle stress in nonviolent ways. Vengeful thoughts have been shown to activate the dorsal striatum in the brain, an area related to satisfaction from punishing. It is strongly stimulated by acts of retaliation: "They got what they deserved." When we weigh the consequences of our choices to see what works best for everyone, the more evolved prefrontal cortex comes into play. We use our prefrontal cortex for powers of reasoning and to distinguish right from wrong. The left region of the cortex is for moving toward a goal; the right is for planning to avoid an outcome. Planning for revenge takes place on the left side, since it is about gaining satisfaction, the poor man's version of contentment.

Hostile parenting does not foster the brain's development of abilities to regulate aggression. Bullies often come from homes that were lacking in warmth or characterized by physical abuse. Aggression and retaliation became their models of behavior; no other options were available. Hurt people are the ones who hurt others. A school bully may be a child who is being abused at home, where it is not safe for him to retaliate. He displaces his aggression onto fellow students who are weaker than he is. In all this, we see that retaliation has its origins in negative life experiences rather than positive ones. That in itself makes the case for expunging it from our repertory of responses.

The feeling of a right to retaliate was programmed into us in those hundreds of times in childhood when our misdeeds were punished. This style—at home, at school, on the street, in religious doctrine— may have been meant to teach us rather than to hurt us. But it none- theless made retaliation seem legitimate. The belief that we are justified in acts of revenge cancels the sense of guilt, so apology or forgiveness is unlikely. This is especially true when the harm to us was intentional.

By age one, children react to unfairness toward themselves. By age four, they are able to learn to be fair to others. By age nine, they distin- guish between intended and accidental harm to themselves by others. They have the capacity to modulate their retaliatory responses on that basis, as well as in accordance with the age of or their relationship to the harming person. At any age, immediate apologies will mitigate the reaction of the victim, but apologies that happen much later than the offense have less effect on the victim's aggressive reactions.

Retaliation in Relationships

It is unfortunately common for us to retaliate against those who injure us, especially people we do not like. It is certainly surprising, however, that we also use retaliation in responding to a partner we say we love!

Revenge in close relationships contradicts our heritage from our Cro-Magnon ancestors. They learned to cooperate *within* their fami- lies and tribe and to retaliate only *outside* their tribe. We retaliate in both areas. What a love-defeating riddle.

Unconditional love in a relationship sounds like this: "I behave lovingly toward you no matter what you do, but I will speak up and say, 'Ouch!' if you hurt me. I won't permit ongoing hurt, but I won't withdraw from dialogue either. My love is not based on what you do but on who I am choosing to be in the world, someone who has found alternatives to retaliation. And I always want spiritual progress for both of us."

An incomplete love sounds like this: "I will act lovingly toward you when you don't cross me; otherwise, I will be vindictive, so watch your step." In this instance, the retaliation can be conscious or an instinctive reaction from our primitive, reptilian brain. Perhaps half our acts of revenge are *unconscious*. Here, we see how fostering awareness through mindfulness contributes to intimacy. The more we accustom ourselves to pausing and looking at what we are thinking or doing, the greater chance we have to choose love over aggression.

Breaking our habit of retaliating means that what others may do to us has no bearing on how we behave toward them. It is the style of *agape*, unconditional and unilateral love. Our commitment to loving-kindness rather than revenge overrides what happens in favor of what we are.

The unconscious retaliatory instinct within us does not affect our ability to show love. Here are three options:

1. When we act vindictively without thinking (that is, unconsciously), we do not cancel our love for someone.
2. When we consciously and actively *choose* to be vindictive, we interrupt our commitment to love the other until we cease and apologize.
3. When we consciously choose and intend to keep retaliation in our armory of reactions to a partner, we don't yet fully love her.

A partner who blames will often be likely to retaliate as well, because the accent in retaliation is on wrongdoing and how it requires punishment, the opposite of reconciliation. It is a choice to inflict pain rather than to work things out. Indeed, the revenge style is based on a domination rather than an affiliation model. In that sense, there is not yet a loving bond, because equality is missing.

Letting go of the inclination toward revenge is a crucial element in an authentic commitment to resolving conflicts. In my own marriage, before finding Buddha's path, and certainly in working with couples over the years, I have become aware of how often our actions in relationships are vengeful, usually without our fully realizing it. We may be getting back at our partner for our unresolved anger toward one of our parents, a former partner, or women or men in general. We are covertly balancing the books toward people in the present because of unresolved imbalances with people in the past. Is this an insight into the mystery of why we use payback with people we say we love?

Most partners' animosity or unskillful behavior toward one another is a form of revenge for something the other partner did to him or her. This motivation is usually unconscious. For example, Cynthia puts her husband, Placid, down often, and he takes it without speaking up. Placid certainly feels angry about Cynthia's abuse, but he does not express it. Instead, he is constantly late and refuses to accompany Cynthia to her family events even though they matter so much to her. Placid does not see this as retaliation; he has definite, logical reasons for not wanting to go. The revenge element is unconscious. In any case, Placid's missing "Ouch!" could have been a tip-off to him—and to Cynthia—that revenge would soon follow.

When we love, we intend and want to see the transformation and not the punishment of the other. This is hard to imagine if we imitate a court system that mostly equates justice with punishment. We have few models for the alternative. In the practice that follows, we find some help in that direction. Also, the discussion of bodhicitta in Chapter 1 and the "Over-the-Top Ways of Loving" section in Chapter 8 provide reflections about how transformation can become a motivating factor for our behavior.

Recently, I called a friend to ask him to help me with a computer problem. He soon became impatient, as he had several times before, and suddenly said he had to get off the phone, without fully responding to my problem. As soon as I hung up, I felt cross with him, but I have come to understand his limitations and don't take them personally. Thus, I could immediately relax into a half-smile and not hold his impatience against him or plan to be vindictive. I was writing this chapter at the time, and I recall thinking to myself, "So this is what it's like to feel angry at someone but not vengeful!" Later, I thought, "I can be that way to everyone if I cultivate practices that lead to my goal of full-on loving."

I also learned from my reaction to the phone conversation that I do not demand that my friend come through for me in precisely the way I need him to. I accept his limitations and boundaries and do not hold them against him. Also, I do not tell myself that people only love me if they go all the way to be there for me. I do not impose my criteria for friendship or relationship on them. I believe they love me based on what they can, or are willing, to give. This is new for me. As I look back on my life, I see that I had a strict set of criteria for how people were supposed to love me. Now I have reconciled myself to whatever dividend comes my way—except abuse—even if it is less than what I hoped for. Isn't this reconciliation to reality what we adults are meant to do all the time?

Now all I have to do is remember this. I trust that the person who can appreciate this realization has some chance of putting it into practice.

A spiritual program includes trust in grace, not only in our own efforts. In Samuel Taylor Coleridge's poem "The Rime of the Ancient Mariner," the main character kills a creature of nature, the albatross, a bird of good omen. As a punishment, the crew tie the dead bird around his neck. Later, the Mariner suddenly feels love for the creatures of nature, thanks to an unexpected grace: "Sure my kind saint took pity on me, / And I blessed them unaware." Then "the albatross fell off, and sank / Like lead into the sea." The Mariner suffered retaliation from the crew, who represent the ego world. He finds transformation from his "kind saint," who represents the power of grace, the assisting force deep in our human psyche and in all of nature. It is always right there (or rather, right here) waiting for us—even now.

I share the response of a friend of mine when I asked him for feedback on this section of my manuscript: "The revenge thing is very difficult. I do not act on it but often want to. Sometimes I feel like a coward because I do not strike back or not a real man because I do not retaliate. But getting to the point of forgiveness and, in turn, letting go of the thoughts of revenge is the struggle. How foolish is it to allow those who have hurt us still to have their claws in us, when they have moved on but we keep the wounds open? It is odd how we know something, but getting there seems so impossible to achieve."

PRACTICE: GIVING UP GETTING EVEN

We may imagine that revenge will lead to a change, but it is only punitive, just as sending a criminal to a harsh jail punishes but does not transform him.

Revenge is impotent rage. We feel powerless to effect a change, so we find our satisfaction in punishing the one who hurt us. The missing link is dialogue, a *direct* expression of anger; retaliation thrives on being indirect. Healthy relationships operate on a new definition of power. It is about skill in nurturant love, not about the ability to conquer and control.

Our need to retaliate can be reduced by speaking up, showing nonviolent anger, and opening a dialogue about our mutual hurts and how things can change for the better. Direct confrontation of an issue and communication about it is the best way to avoid unconscious, primitive revenge tactics in a relationship. Or is our choice for personal vindication through retribution a way of avoiding the intimacy that comes from sincere communication? Are we that subtle escape artist in our flight from intimacy?

"No matter what you may do to me, I will never retaliate against you." Can you promise your partner this today? Can you let it be all right that he or she does not respond in kind? Can the joy of being this enlightened in your way of loving become more important than tit for tat?

Mindful awareness is crucial in letting go of retaliating, because the reflex to get even is often passive, unconscious, cunning, and subtle. The more awareness we have of what we are up to, the easier it becomes to shift our behavior into more gentle and humane responses.

Ironically, our ability to forgive is directly proportional to how we hold our anger. If it carries revenge in it, forgiveness (defined as letting go of the need to retaliate) becomes impossible until that impulse is gone. In any case, we have to say our "Ouch!" loudly enough to be heard, so assertiveness is necessary. This includes asking for restitution, amends, or an apology. Thus, assertiveness becomes our antidote to the aggressiveness in acts of retaliation. This is an example of how a psychological practice such as becoming more able to ask for amends assertively contributes to our spiritual advancement of letting go of vengefulness.

Here is a simple example of how we can move toward letting go of the revenge impulse. When someone speeds ahead of us on the highway and we see her weaving in and out of lanes in a dangerous way, we can change our usual thought response from, "I hope she gets a ticket," to "I hope she slows down and arrives safely." To hope someone gets a ticket is not caring and not connective, since we have ill will toward the other driver. To hope she slows down is caring and makes a connection of well-wishing from us to the other driver. In this simple and not-so-personal incident, we learn to move from divisive revenge to caring connection. At first, we may perform this practice simply by mouthing the words without really meaning them. But faking it still helps us achieve the goal of liberation from vengeful wishes and plans. Gradually, we will believe what we say. It is then reinforced as we notice that we like ourselves more for being this way.

To let go of retaliation requires the wish for transformation of the other (drive more safely), not for her downfall (get a ticket and have to pay more in insurance).

When "What goes around comes around" is a wish that "he get his," we are hoping the universe will retaliate for us! We can convert our desire to "May what goes around come around in such a way that we all become better people because of it. May what goes around turn us around." With this affirmation, we aspire to transformation and confirm our spiritual realization that transformation is always possible. This is what it means not to give up on others—or ourselves.

To let go of revenge and work toward the transformation of others rather than their punishment, some of our beliefs and attitudes have to go. Each is a justification of our right to exact vengeance:

- "Everything in my relationship has to be reciprocal." This has to yield to unilateral generosity, an essential quality of love.
- "My justifiable outrage at losing face gives me permission to strike back." "He has to pay for this insult." "I have to get satisfaction." These all express the old bantam-ego "challenge to a duel" mentality. The will to get even cancels love.
- "I have to show I am justified in my behavior, and everyone has to acknowledge it."
- "I believe there is a hell of eternal punishment or karma as a vindictive consequence to unacceptable behavior."
- "Retribution is a legitimate form of justice."
- "Apologies, admitting my error or mistake, or any such form of humility is really humiliation and is incompatible with my greatness."
- "What goes around comes around." This is asking the universe or a higher power to retaliate for us, to change its kindly attitude into police-state tactics.

Letting go of these magical beliefs is a fast track to letting go of ego, the favorite sport of which is retaliation.

> The history of vengeance committed in the name of God is not a function of any one religion but of the union of religious and political power. It is one of the great paradoxes of religious history that sacred injunctions designed to contain the worst impulses of men and women have, when wedded to secular power, so often been vehicles to express those very passions. . . . The Christianity preached by Jesus makes abandonment of vengeance a condition of personal salvation; the Christianity expounded by ecclesiastical authority has, at many points in history, made vindictiveness a condition of institutional survival.
>
> —SUSAN JACOBY

How Hate Happens

> I hold myself incapable of hating any being. By a long
> course of prayerful discipline, I have ceased for over forty
> years to hate anybody. I know this is a big claim. Neverthe-
> less, I make it in all humility.
>
> —MAHATMA GANDHI

Love is connection that can let go and forgive. It may be tough, but it is
never mean. Hate forecloses on our capacity to love; it is a disconnection. Being possessed by hate is like having an addiction: we cannot be
mean enough, hostile enough, enraged enough, malicious enough, or
get enough revenge. Hatred can lead to violent, abusive, or evil actions.
It seeks to destroy others with no desire for transformation. It is un-
moved by repentance. People who hate have had their trust in humanity so severely betrayed at some time in their lives that they cannot give
others a second chance, the chance they probably never received.

Ongoing hatred of others is like a tumor that eventually becomes
malignant. To carry something so toxic as hate in our heart is to cancel
out the best quality of our humanity, namely love. This is the tragic flaw
that makes hate the downfall of the hero each of us was meant to be.

Our spiritual response when we see someone filled with hatred is
compassion. We wonder what terrible things must have happened to
him, how horribly he must have been abused and humiliated. Then all
we can do is set an intention for his transformation, while realizing how
inadequate we are to make that happen for him.

To love universally does not overlook the problem of evil. It is a potential, an inclination in all of us, given that we all have a shadow side.
But it does not triumph as long as there are some people who still live
according to their true nature, indissolubly linked to one another in caring connection. Connection is as crucial an instinct to the psyche as
survival is to the body. Indeed, ecology applies to human connections as
well as nature. Since connection is a foundation of love, we can say that
our inner goodness is indestructible. This means that evil is real but *not*
primary or final. It is love that is primary and final in the human story.

What drives us toward malicious choices? Some possible answers are fear, hopelessness, severe betrayal of trust, and self-loathing that may have been instilled by an abusive parent or other authority figure. We all have inclinations toward aggression, but we learn how to show it through models. The way we hurt others is how we were first hurt. What impels us toward loving acts? It is the joy of connection, self-diffusive goodness, a commitment to show our best graces, and imitation of all the models of love in our life.

A loving person may feel anger and dislike, but never hate. Since we all have love in us, it is especially painful to see someone possessed by hatred. We feel sad for how scared that person is and how much she is missing from life. Our loving responses are disarming, and that's what leads to connection. We are also more likely to be loving toward others when we see our own shadow side in everyone who treats us badly. We have treated others badly; we have that potential. As we acknowledge our projections, we feel a deeper connection: "I am like that too." Thus, befriending the shadow, as we saw earlier, is a practice that equips us to love others more, because it increases both our sense of connection to them and our compassion for them and ourselves.

German has a word for "glee at the calamity of others": *schadenfreude*. This is the opposite of the joy at others' success that we learned about in our loving-kindness practice. Here are some possible explanations of the strange phenomenon of taking pleasure in others' pain:

- When we hear of troubles, we feel an adrenaline rush. This is appealing to us, pleasurable, because it is more exciting than news that all is going well. This is the equivalent of others' disasters having entertainment value for us.
- Happiness about the unhappiness of others may also be related to the sense of scarcity: "Only one of us gets to be happy. There is too little happiness to go around, so if he is unhappy, I will be happy."
- We unconsciously connect suffering with punishment, a juvenile belief. Since punishment is supposed to come as the result of badness, and we think we are bad, our elation about others' pain is relief that "she got the punishment instead of me."

- We may also think that now the other will need us, and that is our way of feeling important to him. Our ego feels triumphant and valued when others have to depend on us.

These are all primitive mind-sets that can be disarmed and disabled by our loving-kindness practice. Now we see the wisdom of that practice: it aims directly at excavating and disabling the rude Cro-Magnon weaponry buried deep within us.

The more spiritually evolved practice of returning love for hate and hurt does not mean that we give up our right to safety and security; it means that we see the pain in those who act in hating or hurting ways. They are letting us know, in a sadly convoluted manner, that they need us. They want the happiness and love that everyone wants. But they need so much to learn that *loving is how to ask for love.* When we kindly notice all this about people's behavior, we have not given up on humanity. Our practice can be like "Cezanne's doubt." The French artist would tilt his head to see a subject he was painting in a new way. We can tilt our hearts to the pain in others rather than focusing only on the hate.

Our own safety and security is primary, so it is best to avoid contact with those who hate us. Yet we benefit when we hold them in our loving-kindness practice. Their hate can move us to caring concern, not fear or resentment. Indeed, it is the absolute folly of unconditional, universal love that offers the most solid answer to the mystery of evil. When evil most seems to be triumphing, people can likely find their deepest humanity and show unusual and heroic love. We can trust that this love disarms their ferocious ego and helps their hearts open. Thanks to spiritual leaders like Gandhi and Martin Luther King, Jr., we saw how such so-called folly can even transform a nation.

Father Zossima in Fyodor Dostoyevsky's *The Brothers Karamazov* says, "At some thoughts one stands perplexed, especially at the sight of people's evil choices, and wonders whether one should use force or gentle love. Always choose gentle love. If you resolve on that once and for all, you may subdue the whole world. Gentle love is marvelously strong, the strongest of all things. There is nothing else like it."

The fact that this advice comes from a spiritually oriented person shows us that freedom from hate requires conversion more than therapy. To love those who hate or hurt us is surely a difficult task, since we do not feel much incentive to move in that direction. There is very little to motivate us. This is why it takes a spiritual practice such as *agape* or loving-kindness to habituate ourselves to loving intents and loving responses, no matter what the behavior of others. We keep seeing the perfect power of unconditional love.

In this context, we see that hell is the place built by hate, since it too can be satisfied only with unending punishment for offenders. As alluded to earlier, if we still believe in such permanent torture after death, we have a God who is not love. That God never heard the Sermon on the Mount or met Gandhi. In addition, hell as a "final solution" to evil is a denial and repudiation of the invincibly transformative power of love. To carry a belief in hell in our heart abridges our powers of love, because that belief clings to punishment, an opponent of loving-kindness.

There is an ancient belief in Christian theology called *apocatastasis.* It proposes that all people—and demons—will be saved and brought to heaven at the final consummation of history. This doctrine was taught by Saint Clement of Alexandria, Saint Gregory of Nyssa, and the theologian Origen in the early centuries of the Catholic Church. The doctrine was condemned by Saint Augustine and later by the Church Council of Constantinople in 543. It remained in some Protestant traditions as *universalism.* The challenge in supporting this doctrine is determining how much our hearts can stretch, how extensive is our wish for happiness for all beings, and whether we can believe that God is love.

> Nothing can destroy a person who refuses, no matter what
> is done to him, to hate back.
> —Martin Luther King, Jr.

Practice: Radical Affirmations

Throughout this book, we have been using the word *radical* to describe a special kind of love, one that does not require appreciation or reciprocity. It does not select certain people but is extended universally. It is not based on conditions such as attractiveness or trustworthiness; it is unconditional. It is not the effect of whether others love us or how they treat us.

Radical love has no strings attached. It does not have the motivation of commandeering others to love us in return. We love for no reason other than that love is what we are.

As a final practice, consider the seven following affirmations. They are based on what you have read so far. Copy them out longhand so you can read them in your own handwriting. Meditate on one each day, and use it throughout that day. It will take one week to do this. Then repeat the daily affirmations for two more weeks. You will find a radical change in how you appreciate the love in yourself and a radical challenge to show your love in new ways. When you do what you have too rarely dared, fear will never again defeat you.

Day One: Love is my real name, who I am, all I am, and all I do.

Day Two: I show my love without expecting anything in return.

Day Three: I let go of the need to retaliate. I look for ways to include everyone in my circle of love.

Day Four: I have all the love I need. I welcome all the love that comes my way.

Day Five: I trust that everyone has love, and I act as lovingly as I can to help release it.

Day Six: I trust and thank the many assisting forces in me and in the world that keep showing me how to love.

Day Seven: I trust the power of love to bring the world to justice, peace, and harmony.

This prayer/aspiration can be used repeatedly throughout each day:

I say Yes to everything that happens to me today
as an opportunity
to give and receive love without reserve.
I am thankful for the gift of love in me
from the Sacred Heart of the universe.
May I open my heart more and more.
May everything I think, say, feel, and do
foster justice, peace, and love for all humanity.
May love be the guiding light of my life,
my sacred trust, my destiny,
the richest grace I can receive or give.

How comes this gentle concord in the world
That hatred is so far from jealousy
To sleep by hate and fear no enemy?
—SHAKESPEARE, *A Midsummer Night's Dream*

Epilogue

There Is Hope in Our Limitations

Most gladly therefore do I glory in my infirmities.
—2 Corinthians 12:9

Submit to being called a neurotic. You belong to that splendid and pitiable family which is the salt of the earth. All the greatest things we know have come to us from neurotics. It is they and they only who have founded religions and created great works of art. Never will the world be conscious of how much it owes to them, nor above all of what they have suffered in order to bestow their gifts on it.
—Marcel Proust, *Guermantes Way, Vol. I*

In recent years we have been finding out how many agencies and institutions in our society—and how many nations—are dysfunctional in some way. So are all of us. Everyone is wounded, inadequate, and at times dysfunctional. Yet we somehow manage to live basically adequate, functional lives.

The good news is that we don't have to be psychologically healthy to love. We don't have to be spiritually adept or perfect in any way. In fact, sometimes wonderful forms of love come through us in our moments of greatest weakness and disarray. Of course, we can love fervently and creatively as healthy and happy people also. Love is unconditional even about where it resides.

Likewise, others don't have to be perfect to deserve our love. Thomas Jefferson wrote, "Were we to love only those without imperfections, this world would be a desert for our love." To love only those who match what we think is perfection eliminates our chance to show genuine love. We have love in us, so we are fully able to love anyone, no matter what his or her condition or level of acceptability.

In the earlier quotation, Marcel Proust proposes that neurotic, eccentric people are "the salt of the earth." This is a way of affirming that anxiety can become an alchemical force: something negative and apparently useless, or "pitiable," turns into something highly valuable, or "splendid" in Proust's words.

Such a transformation takes work. The practices in this book help us get there. They show us ways to locate love in ourselves and others and to find ways to express our love no matter what our hang-ups. We can then discover exciting possibilities for expanding whom and how we love, gaining wider social consciousness, experimenting with new styles of eroticism, composing impassioned love poems—whatever opens us creatively and provocatively.

Many artists were eccentric or neurotic. They knew that they were different and wanted the world around them to be different. That is the very basis of creativity, seeing things differently, expressing things differently, being different—exactly what happens in the radically universal, unconditional love we have been describing. That love is different, because we are not loving only "our own" or only on condition that others please us. Radically universal and unconditional love opens us to new ways of being with others, different ways of reading what tenderness can be, and inventive ways of showing our affection.

When all we want from life is to keep things on an even keel, then smooth sailing, safety, and security become our main goals. However, a permanent 98.6 may not release our unique creativity and passions, the lively portals into love. It is when the highly disturbing, unusually exciting, and frighteningly fierce become the landscape of our world that something altogether new is most likely to emerge from deep within us.

Saying yes to the unsettling is a password to creative innovation in any art. Our art in this book is love, and an unconditional yes to whatever life brings is the password to it.

When we are in a quandary, when what we have relied on is crumbling all around us, when we are floundering and losing our bearings, awkward and unsure, we are definitely on the threshold of the heroic journey. Then our struggle is not to restore ourselves and everything to its original stable condition. It is to pause long enough to flow with the tide. We are then most apt to find surprising alternatives.

In crisis, stress, in helplessness, and depression, an inner power may emerge. It does not arise from hope; it grants hope. It does not show us where safety and security can be found; it is a safety and security of the heart in the midst of chaos and dismay. Indeed, Chögyam Trungpa Rinpoche says, "Chaos should be regarded as extremely good news."

There is a relevant parallel we can draw from Nobel Laureate Ilya Prigogine's theory of dissipative structures. The word *dissipation* is used in physics regarding structures that use up energy in order to survive. This describes, in essence, what happens in all beings, including ourselves. As energy moves through a structure, it causes minor or major fluctuations. In some cases, the dynamic forms of the structure itself then change in ways that last either for a while or for good. These are sometimes referred to in science as "phase transitions." They can lead to innovations, or changes in how a system operates with the input that comes to it. The parts can reorganize so that a new whole emerges from the original. In other words, breakdowns can lead to upgrades. This fits with the experience of the "healing crisis" that comes so mysteriously to people suffering from physical and/or psychological maladies.

We can see a metaphor in this theory for how our psyche works. It reacts to flows of energies, coming through us from childhood forces, life crises, deficits and deficiencies, bodily and mental collapses, so many shocks to our sensitivities. But our self-restorative powers are thereby marshaled, and we form new options or inner resources. We arrive at higher levels of conscious awareness in a way that elegantly mirrors the known laws of the universe as they relate to dissipative systems.

We also create ourselves anew from the ashes of dissipation. This is why the neural plasticity of the brain, present throughout our life span, is so crucial to the fostering of our psychological health. It is never too late for our transition from breakdown to upgrade.

In our most unsettled, ungrounded state, we can draw new remedies from our wounds, new structures of strength from the rubble of our predicaments. This is the alchemy of the human condition: in the crucible of our collapses, dislocations, injuries, and miseries, there is gold to be found in the lead that weighed us down.

All it takes is our unconditional yes, and our next chapter—the chapter in which we find ourselves and our serenity—will start all by itself. This time we will be on a new path, one with encouragement because we are acting with self-support, power because we are embracing our defenselessness, and liveliness because we are not threatened by any encounter with ephemerality.

Dogen Zenji, founder of the Buddhist Soto Zen school, wrote, "Even in the muddiest puddle the entire full moon is reflected." So, after all that has happened to us, no matter how disheartening, the full moon of love within us can still shine.

Life experiences can rob us of serenity. What people do to us can hurt our hearts. Distressing events can pile up on us. Griefs can weigh us down. We can make one mistake after another, even repeat the same ones. But nothing can divest us of our capacity to love. We were designed for love, and with practice, we can display it. Daredevils like us will certainly keep chancing love's radical, reckless, and resounding leap.

> We know that we have passed from death to life because we love one another.
>
> —1 John 3:13

Appendix 1

Commitments to Loving-Kindness
*toward Ourselves and Others**

1. I do my best to keep my word, honor commitments, and follow through on the tasks I agree to do.
2. I am making every effort to abide by standards of rigorous honesty and respect in all my dealings, no matter how others act toward me.
3. I forgo taking advantage of anyone because of his or her ignorance, misfortune, or financial straits. My question is not "What can I get away with?" but "What is the right thing to do?" If I fall down in this, I can admit it, make amends, and resolve to act differently next time. Now I apologize more easily and willingly when necessary.
4. If someone is overly generous toward me or has an exaggerated sense of obligation to me, I do not want to exploit his or her lack of boundaries. Instead, I want to express appreciation and work out an equitable way of interacting.
5. I keep examining my conscience with true candor. I take searching inventories of how I may have harmed others; how I

---

* Based on David Richo, *Coming Home to Who You Are: Discovering Your Natural Capacity for Love, Integrity, and Compassion* (Boston, MA: Shambhala Publications, 2012).

may not have activated my potentials or shared my gifts; how I may still be holding on to prejudices or the will to retaliate; and how I may still not be as loving, inclusive, and open as I can be.

6. I welcome feedback that shows me where I am less caring, less tolerant, and less open about my real feelings than I can be. When I am shown up as a pretender or called on being mean or inauthentic, I am not defensive but take it as information about what I have to work on. I appreciate positive feedback also.

7. I am letting go of the need to keep up appearances or to project a false or overly impressive self-image. Now I want to appear as I am, without pretense and no matter how unflattering. I do not want to use any charms of body, word, or mind to trick or deceive others. Being loved for who I am has become more important—and more interesting—than upholding the ever-shaky status of my ego.

8. I now measure my success by how much steadfast love I have, not by how much money I have in the bank, how much I achieve in business, how much status I have attained, or how much power I have over others. The central and most exhilarating focus of my life is to show all my love in the style that is uniquely mine in every way I can—here and now, always and everywhere, no one excluded.

9. As I say yes to the reality of who I am, with pride in my gifts and unabashed awareness of my limits, I notice that I can love myself and that I become more lovable.

10. I never give up on believing that everyone has an innate goodness and that being loved can contribute to bringing it out.

11. I am learning to trust others when the record shows they can be trusted while I, nonetheless, commit myself to being trustworthy regardless of what others may do. I am always open to rebuilding trust when it has been broken if the other person is willing.

12. I remain open to reconcile with others after conflict. At the same time, I am learning to release—with love and without

blame—those who show themselves to be unwilling to relate to me respectfully. I accept the given of sudden unexplained silence or rejection by others and will never use that style myself.

13. I am learning to be assertive by asking for what I need without fear or inhibition. I ask without demand, expectation, manipulation, or a sense of entitlement. I can show respect for the timing and choices of others by being able to take no for an answer.

14. I do not knowingly hurt or intend to offend others. I act kindly toward others, not to impress or obligate them, but because I really am kind—or working on it. If others fail to thank me or return my kindness, that does not have to stop me from behaving lovingly.

15. If people hurt me, I can say, "Ouch!" and ask to open a dialogue. I may ask for amends, but I can drop the topic if they are not forthcoming. No matter what, I do not choose to get even, hold grudges, keep a record of wrongs, or hate anyone. "What goes around comes around" has become "May what goes around come around in a way that helps him or her learn and grow." I am thereby hoping for the transformation of others rather than retribution against them. This commitment also means that I do not gloat over the sufferings or defeats of those who have hurt me. "It serves them right" has changed to "May this serve to help them evolve."

16. I am practicing ways to express my anger against unfairness directly and nonviolently rather than in abusive, bullying, threatening, blaming, out-of-control, or passive ways.

17. I do not let others abuse me, but I want to interpret their harshness as coming from their own pain and as a sadly confused way of letting me know they need connection but don't know how to ask for it in healthy ways. I recognize this with concern, not with censure or scorn.

18. I have a sense of humor but not at the expense of others. I want to use humor to poke fun at human foibles, especially my own.

I do not engage in ridicule, put-downs, taunting, teasing, snide or bigoted remarks, sarcasm, or comebacks. When others use hurtful humor toward me, I want to feel the pain in both of us and look for ways to bring more mutual respect into our communication.

19. I do not laugh at people or at their mistakes and misfortunes; I look for ways to be supportive.

20. I notice how in some groups there are people who are humiliated or excluded. Rather than be comforted that I am still safely an insider, especially by gossiping about them, I want to sense the pain in being an outsider. Then I can reach out and include everyone in my circle of love, compassion, and respect.

21. I look at other people and their choices with intelligent discernment but without censure. I still notice the shortcomings of others and myself, but now I am beginning to see them as facts to deal with rather than flaws to be criticized or ashamed of. Accepting others as they are has become more important than whether they are what I want them to be.

22. I avoid Criticizing, Interfering, or giving Advice that is not specifically asked for. I take care of myself by staying away from those who use this CIA approach toward me, while still holding them in my spiritual circle of loving-kindness.

23. I am willing to participate in the harmless conventions and social rituals that make others happy.

24. I am less and less competitive in relationships at home and at work, and I find happiness in cooperation and community. I shun situations in which my winning means that others lose in a humiliating way.

25. In intimate bonds, I honor equality, keep agreements, work on problems, and act in respectful and trustworthy ways. My goal is not to use a relationship to gratify my ego but to dispossess myself of ego to gratify the relationship. Also, I respect the boundaries of others' relationships.

26. I want my sexual style to adhere to the same standards of integrity and loving-kindness that apply in all areas of my life.

More and more, my sexuality expresses love, passion, and joyful playfulness. I remain committed to a responsible adult style of relating and enjoying.

27. Confronted with the suffering in the world, I do not turn my eyes away, nor do I get stuck in blaming God or humanity but simply ask, "What then shall *I* do? What is the opportunity in this for my practice of loving-kindness?" I keep finding ways to respond, even if they have to be minimal: "It is better to light one candle than to curse the darkness."

28. I want my caring concern to extend to the world around me. I am committing myself to fighting injustice in nonviolent ways. I support restorative rather than retributive justice. I am distressed and feel myself called to action by violations of human rights, nuclear armaments, and economic and racial injustice. I tread with care on the earth with what Saint Bonaventure called "a courtesy toward natural things."

29. I appreciate that whatever love or wisdom I may have or show comes not *from* me but *through* me. I give thanks for these encouraging graces and say yes to the stirring call to live up to them.

30. I am not hard on myself when I fail to live up to these ideals. I just keep practicing earnestly. The sincerity of my intention and my ongoing efforts feel like the equivalent of success.

31. I do not think I am above other people because I honor this list. I do not demand that others follow it.

32. I am sharing this list with those who are open to it, and I keep believing that someday these commitments can become the style not only of individuals but of groups in the world community: corporate, political, religious.

Working with this list, one entry each day or each week, is helping me integrate love into my daily life.

Appendix 2

A Checklist of Well-Being
Place a check mark before each entry that fits for you.

Personal Issues

_____ Do you experience major stress or conflict in yourself, on the job, or with others?

_____ Do you generally feel sad or down on yourself and/or have low self-esteem?

_____ Do you seem to require the approval or presence of others in a needy way?

_____ Is your lifestyle one predictable routine with no goal or apparent purpose?

_____ Are you depressed most of the time?

_____ Are you angry most of the time?

_____ Are you overly concerned with your appearance, financial status, or reputation?

_____ Are you continually guilt-ridden, or ashamed?

_____ Do you usually focus on the negative side of things?

_____ Is your life one crisis after another?

_____ Do you believe the purpose of your life is to endure pain?

_____ Do you mostly feel victimized by others?

_____ Do you often feel painfully lonely?

_____ Even when you have enough of what you want, do you feel you still need more?

_____ Do you give a lot to others but then feel you have not given enough?

_____ Do you have sharp mood swings?

_____ Do you sometimes feel that you have more than one personality?

_____ Do you have frequent, unwanted, disturbing thoughts?

_____ Do you hear voices or believe you are being controlled by outside forces?

_____ Do you have physical symptoms with no medical explanation?

_____ Do you believe others are out to get you?

_____ Do you hold in your tears in either joy or sorrow?

_____ Do you feel unloved or even unlovable?

Relationships

_____ Do you become resentful or punitive toward others when they fail to admire, love, or honor you as you believe you deserve?

_____ Would you say you are controlling toward others?

_____ Do other people tell you that you take advantage of them?

_____ Are you unable to feel empathy toward others or identify with their pain?

_____ Do you trust everyone, believe everyone has good motives, and deny there is a dark side to others?

_____ Do you let others take advantage of you?

_____ Do you blame others for the path your life has taken?

_____ Do you usually think you are better than others?

_____ Do you usually think you are less than others?

_____ Do you believe you are always right and others are always wrong, or vice versa?

_____ Do you feel you are not OK unless you have a partner?

_____ Are you unable to tolerate abandonment?

_____ Do you shy away from physical closeness or fear it as engulfing?

_____ In a relationship, do you keep going back for more when there is only less?

_____ Are you in a relationship that is abusive, full of discontent, or not really working?

_____ Are you resentful or punitive toward a partner?

_____ Are you sometimes violent or abusive toward others?

_____ Do you sometimes idealize and sometimes demonize the same person?

_____ Do you believe you can remain independent all through life and never need others?

_____ Do you hate or are you estranged from one or both of your parents or other family members?

_____ Do others accuse you of being self-centered?

_____ Does your life revolve around your job or other people or things to the neglect of yourself?

_____ Do you feel so afraid of being alone that you choose relationships that do not nurture you?

_____ Do you feel that it is impossible for you to show love, or impossible for others to show you love?

Fears

_____ Do you suffer from panic attacks?

_____ Are your fears so strong that they stop you from doing what you want or drive you to do what you don't want to do?

_____ Do you fear making commitments?

_____ Do you fear being alone?

_____ Do you have phobias?

_____ Are you usually passive rather than assertive?

_____ Arc you afraid to speak up?

_____ Do you hide, squelch, or deny your feelings?

_____ Are you uncomfortable expressing joy, anger, fear, and sadness?

_____ Do you feel uncomfortable when someone expresses those feelings toward you?

_____ Do you act more out of obligation than choice?

_____ Do you fear being loved or being loving?

Compulsions

_____ Are you constantly worried about something?

_____ Do you overeat or undereat in an out-of-control or overly controlled way?

_____ Do you engage in compulsive rituals or behavior?

_____ Do you find yourself habitually or automatically lying?

_____ Regarding money, do you have a problem with spending, earning, saving, or enjoying?

_____ Do you have a problem with loaning, borrowing, giving, or receiving?

_____ Do you gamble compulsively?

_____ Do you cheat or steal?

_____ Do you act impulsively in ways that hurt others?

_____ Do you often engage in risky behavior?

_____ Do you have a secret life?

Alcohol and Drugs

_____ Are you drunk at least once a month?

_____ Do you sometimes drink with the intention of getting drunk?

_____ Do you turn to alcohol when things do not go well?

_____ Do you continue to include drinking in your lifestyle even after it has had negative consequences?

_____ Have you ever decided to drink a certain number of drinks at a party and then totally lost control? (impaired control)

_____ Are you proud of being able to drink a lot (such as five or six beers) without getting drunk? (high tolerance)

_____ Do you occasionally have blackouts after drinking?

_____ Have your friends told you that you have an alcohol problem, and do you resent them for it?

_____ Do you smoke cigarettes or marijuana and either cannot or do not want to stop?

_____ Do you drink so much coffee that going without it is a problem?

_____ Do you use painkillers or tranquilizers on a regular basis?

_____ Do you use illegal drugs either regularly or recreationally?

_____ Do you self-medicate?

Sex

_____ Are you afraid to know, explore, or act on your sexual orientation?

_____ Do you have unsettling questions about your gender?

_____ Do you seek closeness primarily through sex?

_____ Do you engage in risky sex?

_____ Do you feel shame or guilt regarding sex?

_____ Do you engage in sex in a compulsive way?

_____ Have you ever experienced sexual trauma or abuse?

_____ Do you have sexual feelings toward children?

_____ Have you lost interest in sex?

_____ Do you remain unsatisfied even after having sexual experiences?

_____ Are you afraid to say no to unwanted sexual advances?

_____ Are you unconcerned with the pleasure of your partner when making love?

_____ Do you seek mostly sexual experiences or love relationships?

_____ Can you show intimacy without it having to lead to sex every time?

_____ Are you secretly breaking the agreements in your intimate relationship, such as by having an affair?

_____ Do you believe that you confuse sex with love?

_____ Do you seek sexual gratification on the Internet in an obsessive or compulsive way?

_____ Do you notice that love and sex do not come together for you?

Religion

_____ Do you belong to a cult?

_____ Are you blindly obedient to any person or belief system?

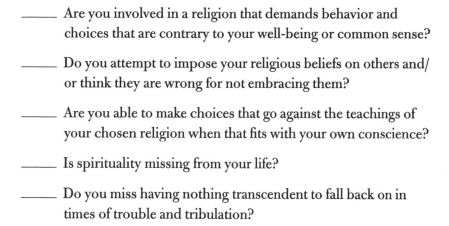

_____ Are you involved in a religion that demands behavior and choices that are contrary to your well-being or common sense?

_____ Do you attempt to impose your religious beliefs on others and/or think they are wrong for not embracing them?

_____ Are you able to make choices that go against the teachings of your chosen religion when that fits with your own conscience?

_____ Is spirituality missing from your life?

_____ Do you miss having nothing transcendent to fall back on in times of trouble and tribulation?

Each of these listings represents a possible obstacle to well-being. No one has to remain unhappy or stressed out. If you checked one or more of these questions, consider trying psychotherapy to help you address, process, and resolve whatever your issue may be. Your commitment to repairing what distresses you so that you can be happier is a way of loving yourself. It also helps those you love, because your way of relating to them will be smoother and less conflicted.

About the Author

David Richo, PhD, MFT, is a psychotherapist and workshop leader who lives in Santa Barbara and San Francisco, California. He combines Jungian, Buddhist, and mythic perspectives in his work. He is the author of the following books:

*How to Be An Adult: A Handbook on Psychological
and Spiritual Integration* (Paulist Press, 1991)

Happy, mature people have somehow picked up the knack of being generous with their sympathies while still taking care of themselves. We can all evolve from the neurotic ego through a healthy ego to the spiritual Self. We can deal with fear, anger, and guilt; be assertive; have boundaries; and build intimacy.

When Love Meets Fear: How to Become Defense-less and Resource-full
(Paulist Press, 1997)

Our lively energy is inhibited by fear, and we are often needlessly on the defensive. By considering the origins and healing of our fears of closeness, commitment, aloneness, assertiveness, and panic attacks, we can free ourselves from the grip of fear so that it no longer stops or drives us.

Shadow Dance: Liberating the Power and Creativity of Your Dark Side
(Shambhala Publications, 1999)

The shadow is all that we abhor about ourselves and all the dazzling potential that we doubt or deny we have. We project these qualities onto others as dislike or admiration. We can acknowledge our limitations and our gifts. Then both our light and dark sides become sources of creativity and awaken our untapped potential.

How to Be An Adult in Relationships: The Five Keys to Mindful Loving (Shambhala Publications, 2002)

Love is not so much a feeling as a way of being present, and it is present with the five A's: unconditional attention, acceptance, appreciation, affection, and allowing others to be as they are. Love is being present without the five conditioned overlays of ego: judgment, fear, control, attachment, and illusion.

CDs of the author reading the book will be available September 2012 online at Shambhala.com and in hard copy January 2013.

The Five Things We Cannot Change and the Happiness
We Find by Embracing Them (Shambhala Publications, 2005)

There are unavoidable givens in life and relationships. By our unconditional yes to these givens of existence, we learn to open, accept, and even embrace our predicaments without trying to control the outcomes. We begin to trust what happens as gifts of grace that help us grow in character, depth, and compassion.

The Power of Coincidence: How Life Shows Us What We Need to Know (Shambhala Publications, 2007)

Meaningful coincidences of events, dreams, or relationships happen that are beyond our control. These synchronicities influence the course of our lives in mysterious ways. They often reveal assisting forces that are pointing us to our unguessed, unexpected, and unimagined destiny.

The Sacred Heart of the World: Restoring Mystical Devotion
to Our Spiritual Life (Paulist Press, 2007)

This book explores the symbolism of the heart in world religious traditions and then traces the historical thread of Christian devotion to the

Sacred Heart of Jesus into modern times. It focuses on the philosophy and theology of Teilhard de Chardin and Karl Rahner to design a new sense of what devotion can be.

Mary Within Us: A Jungian Contemplation of Her Titles and Powers
(Human Development Books, 2007)

The Jungian archetype of the feminine aspect of God as personified by Mary is built into the design of every human psyche. The ancient titles given to Mary are a summary of the qualities of our essential Self. In fact, every religious truth and image is a metaphor for all the potential within us and in the universe.

Wisdom's Way: Quotations for Contemplation
(Human Development Books, 2008)

This is a book of quotations from a variety of sources, especially Buddhist, Christian, Jungian, and transpersonal ones. The quotations are brief and can be used as springboards for meditation. They are divided into three sections: psychological insight, spiritual awareness, and mystical realization.

Making Love Last: How to Sustain Intimacy
and Nurture Genuine Connection
(set of three CDs, Shambhala Publications, 2008)

Here is a lively workshop on relationship issues given by David Richo at Spirit Rock Retreat Center in California. Some of the topics are how love can endure, fears of intimacy and commitment, trust and fidelity, resolution of conflicts, the phases of a relationship, and how early life affects adult relationships.

When the Past Is Present: Healing the Emotional Wounds
That Sabotage Our Relationships (Shambhala Publications, 2008)

Transference is a tendency to see our parents or other significant people in our life story in others. This book explores how our past impacts our present relationships. It shows ways to make transference a valuable opportunity to learn about ourselves, deepen our relationships, and heal our ancient wounds.

Being True to Life: Poetic Paths to Personal Growth
(Shambhala Publications, 2009)

Poetry may have seemed daunting in school, but here is a chance for it to become wonderfully personal and spiritually enriching. This book offers an opportunity to use our hearts and pens to release the full range of our imagination to discover ourselves through reading and writing poetry.

Daring to Trust: Opening Ourselves to Real Love and Intimacy
(Shambhala Publications, 2010)

This book teaches us how to build trust, recognize a trustworthy person, work with our fears about trusting, and rebuild trust after a breach or an infidelity. It helps us find ways to trust others, ourselves, reality, what happens to us, and a higher power than ourselves.

How to Be an Adult in Faith and Spirituality (Paulist Press, 2011)

Here, the text explores and compares religion and spirituality with an emphasis on how they can both become rich resources for personal growth. It increases our understanding of God, faith, and life's plaguing questions in the light of mysticism, depth psychology, and our new appreciation of evolutionary cosmology.

Coming Home to Who You Are: Discovering Your Natural Capacity for Love, Integrity, and Compassion (Shambhala Publications, 2012)

Here are practices that can usher us into a new way of being alive—as cheerful agents of the goodness that is in us all. Our choices for integrity and loving-kindness reflect that goodness and help us cocreate a world of justice, peace, and love. This is an owner's guide to being an upright and loving human.

How to Be an Adult in Faith and Spirituality
(set of four CDs, Paulist Press, 2012)

These live recordings of a workshop given at Spirit Rock Buddhist Retreat Center in California explain how to design and practice an adult spirituality. We also learn to discover the archetypal riches in religion and cherish them. We let go of what is not in keeping with our adult growth, both psychologically and spiritually

Embracing the Shadow: Discovering the Hidden Riches
in Our Relationships (set of four CDs, Shambhala Publications, 2012)

In this live presentation, David Richo teaches us to work with our unskillful tendencies in relationships so that we can tame them and grow because of them. We notice our projections onto one another and find the gifts we might not yet have dared to recognize or show. Working *with* the dark rather than *in* it lets the light of intimacy through.

The Power of Grace: Recognizing Unexpected Gifts on Our Path
(Shambhala Publications, 2014)

Perhaps you've had one of those moments when everything simply falls into place; or, when you've been puzzling over an impossible question and—*pow!*—the answer suddenly arises. These and other such experiences arc moments of *grace*, the gift dimension of life. David Richo shows us how to open our eyes to the sources of grace everywhere and in everyone.

For more information, including upcoming events and a catalog of audio/video programs, visit davericho.com.